AMERICAN POEMS

American Poems

(1793)

EDITED BY

ELIHU HUBBARD SMITH

A FACSIMILE REPRODUCTION

WITH AN INTRODUCTION, NOTES, AND INDEX

BY

WILLIAM K. BOTTORFF

GAINESVILLE, FLORIDA

SCHOLARS' FACSIMILES & REPRINTS

1966

SCHOLARS' FACSIMILES & REPRINTS
1605 N.W. 14TH AVENUE
GAINESVILLE, FLORIDA, U.S.A.
HARRY R. WARFEL, GENERAL EDITOR

REPRODUCED FROM A COPY OWNED BY

WILLIAM K. BOTTORFF

L. C. CATALOG CARD NUMBER: 66-60007

MANUFACTURED IN THE U.S.A.

TYPESETTING BY J. N. ANZEL, INC.
PHOTOLITHOGRAPHY BY EDWARDS BROTHERS
BINDING BY UNIVERSAL-DIXIE BINDERY

INTRODUCTION

The year 1793 is not now remembered as an especially important one in the history of American civilization. There were no wars, no revolutions, no elections to shake the newly founded nation. Yet the states of the young country, composed of something over four million souls, saw a procession of events that were certainly considered noteworthy then; some of them, as we can now see, did affect the future of the United States more or less profoundly. It was the year, for example, in which Eli Whitney produced his cotton gin. It was the year in which Thomas Jefferson resigned as Secretary of State (and in which he invented the moldboard plow). The Supreme Court handed down its first major decision in Chisholm v. Georgia. President Washington proclaimed American neutrality as Britain and France made war. Alexander Hamilton was under severe attack over his fiscal policies. And Citizen Genêt came to inflame American feelings.

It was also the year of the great yellow fever epidemic in Philadelphia; when Philip Freneau discontinued his *National Gazette* there; when the cornerstone was laid to the U. S. Capitol in the new District of Columbia; when

Oliver Holden published *The Union Harmony,* containing the famous hymn, "Coronation" ("All hail the power of Jesus' name"). And it was the year in which a young man of letters named Dr. Elihu Hubbard Smith edited and published the first general anthology of American poetry, *American Poems, Selected and Original,* at Litchfield, Connecticut.

The book went on sale July 17, 1793, at the price of one dollar a copy ("Those who subscribe for six books, will be entitled to a seventh-gratis"). The anthology saw one printing, of one edition, in one volume (though it is called "Vol. I" on its title page, and a series was proposed). Since *American Poems* is the first general anthology of American poetry ever to appear, its historic importance as a literary landmark is beyond question. Its contents include representative works by all the leading poets of the time, several of whom were E. H. Smith's close friends. All sixty-five of the book's poems were written by Americans, most of them still living in 1793. Among the major poets are Joel Barlow, Timothy Dwight, David Humphreys, and John Trumbull — the Connecticut Wits. Some of the minor Wits are represented too, such as Lemuel Hopkins and Smith himself. Included also are several pieces by the leading woman poet of the day, Sarah Wentworth Morton; poems by figures famous in other fields, such as Francis Hopkinson and William Livingston; and one poem by Philip Freneau. *American Poems* is a rich source-book for the student of late eighteenth-century American life and letters, something of a documentary, poetic summary of its era.

It might also be a source for the literary critic, for there has been — from then until now — almost no literary criticism concerning American neo-classical poetry. It has often been noted that such verse was required to be both elegant and useful (following Horace's *dulce* and *utile*), and that our poets too often mis-matched the prosaic image with high-flown, unharmonious rhetoric. The poets worked entirely without any American theoretical statements on prosody, entirely without any American critical tools or standards. Our poets read, admired, and imitated British poets, but had little access to British poetic theory beyond the example of the poetry itself. *American Poems* clearly documents the fact that, to 1793, we had produced no important poets, and it shows us some of the reasons for this.

The chief reason is that the American poets were not primarily poets at all. They were preoccupied. They were soldiers, sailors, statesmen, teachers, theologians, traders, journalists, doctors. This, coupled with the severely limited amount of talent most of them displayed (which smallness of talent forms the second chief reason, of course, why we were poor in poetry), gave us such results as we find in *American Poems*.

If we briefly list the most notable features of the poetry in our first anthology, we find a dominance of rhyme (as opposed to blank verse), often forced rhyme; over-frequent elisions; numerous allusions (biblical, classical, historical, mythological); time-honored phrases and figures of speech; great concern for antithesis and balance of syntactical elements. (Several of these points are summarized by Alexander Cowie in *John Trumbull, Connecticut Wit.*) Parenthesis, apostrophe, and repetition are also very common motifs (as pointed out by Bruce I. Granger in *Political Satire in the American Revolution, 1763-1783).* The relationships between rhetoric (oratory) and verse are clear, especially in the college commencement poems of Barlow, producing a highly didactic poetry (see Gordon E. Bigelow's *Rhetoric and American Poetry of the Early National Period).*

Structurally, the most popular meter proves to be iambic, often in heroic couplets, but frequently in four- or five-foot alternating rhymed lines as well. This meter is usually quite regular, almost unrelieved by variation, and thus often forced by inversion and elision. The imagery of the poems is too often flat, lacking sharpness and vividness, due to the tendency toward the general or collective image rather than toward the particular and concrete. All this is to say, merely, that most of the poetry is neo-classical and conservative, quite closely modeled after the British masters (primarily Pope), and, unfortunately, after some of the lesser British poets as well.

Many reasons for this imitation have been advanced through the years. An especially penetrating one is suggested by the words of William Dunlap, as late as 1832. His topic is drama, but his words reveal an attitude shared by most of the more conservative and hesitant poets in America's first anthology: "It may here be a fit subject of inquiry how far we ought to wish for a national drama [or poetry], distinct from that of our English forefathers .... The plays of Shakespeare, and Jonson, and Ford, and Marlowe ... and all the old poets of the drama, are ours, as much ours, being the descendants of Englishmen, as if our fathers had never left the country in which they were written. We say the same of the philosophy of Milton, and Locke and Newton. Old English literature, as well as that of remote antiquity on which it is founded, is the basis on which we build, and is an integral part of our mental existence" (*History of the American Theatre*, I, 162). That is, a deliberate striving for difference or "Americanness" was anathema to the majority of our poets. They delighted in working within the tradition of literature in English, of recognized practices. Their abundant use of classical allusions is thus partly explained also; they felt a kinship with all Western literature, and they were, furthermore, learned men who wrote allusions as naturally as they wrote couplets. There was neither need nor reason, impulse nor desire to break from tradition.

A few of the late eighteenth century poets represented in *American Poems* were more individualistic. There are poems heralding romanticism, however weakly. One of these is Freneau's "Verses Written at Sea." Others are the poems of Richard Alsop. His Scandinavian poems, for example, have exotic settings, Gothic scenes, a freshness of subject matter. They celebrate their heroes, heroes of nonclassical myth, in a way not found in the neo-classical poems alluding either to Greek and Roman mythological figures or to the heroes of the Revolution. The boldness and fierceness of Alsop's Scandinavian heroes are out of step with the staid pictures of Washington, Franklin, Greene, or Warren in so many of the other poems in the anthology.

This documentation of attitudes toward American heroes is interesting. Washington was, of course, "first in the hearts of his countrymen." He is alluded to several times, and directly celebrated in Mrs. Morton's "Ode to the President." But also recognized are a great many lesser heroes, some of whom are now little known. We have lost sight of the Indian fighter Lewis, in Barlow's "The Prospect of Peace," and of Bushnell, the inventor of the submarine, who is alluded to by Dwight. The same is true of the allusions to villains of the day, and of the historical incidents mentioned also. In Trumbull's "Elegy on the Times," for example, we may know of Franklin's being attacked in Parliament, but not the name of his assailant (not even, perhaps, the name of the prime minister derided in the poem). Again, we may know the circumstances of the closing of the port of Boston, but not of Greene's southern campaigns (Richards' "Ode to General Greene"). And it seems strange to us that Ethan Allen would be the the subject of invective for his religious views (Hopkins' "Verses on General Ethan Allen"), for we have little knowledge of the controversy engendered by his *Reason the Only Oracle of Man.* One measure of how far we have moved from the America of 1793 is in these allusions. Yet such allusions were undoubtedly easily understood by the reader of the broadside, the magazine, the book of poetry in that day.

American Poems tends to document for us more than the literary and historical points just outlined. Such areas as humor, education, religion, science, medicine, and politics are parts of the American culture at least sketchily documented by *American Poems*. The humorous poems, for example, are quite representative of such efforts in eighteenth-century American verse (aside from major works such as Trumbull's *M'Fingal*). We may select "The Country School" from which to draw some conclusions. Many of the aspects of American humor outlined by Walter Blair in his illuminating *Native American Humor* are found in it: the native quality of its subject matter; exaggeration; the comic portraiture of the particularized schoolmaster, quite unlike the generalized figures of the English humorous pieces so often imitated in America; and dialect. *American Poems*, then, gives more than a glimpse at the developing techniques of native humor in our early national period.

In the area of education (apart from the college commencement poems that were obviously a vogue in eighteenth-century America, and the satirical view of medical school wranglings in Hopkinson's poem) the only light shed by *American Poems* comes again from "The Country School," though precious little light it may seem. We know that certain new, non-European modes of education developed in America before 1800, that by the time of the poem (1787) rural schools were almost entirely under local (as opposed to state) control, and that standards were often exceedingly poor (as in the poem; for these points see Bernard Bailyn's *Education in the Forming of American Society*). Furthermore, the picture of the school in the poem tends clearly to support the generalizations outlined in such a source as Ellwood P. Cubberley's *Readings in Public Education in the United States*:

the short school session; the frequently incompetent instructors; the very mechanical teaching methods; the simple physical plant, with its open fireplace or stove. Thus "The Country School" apparently gives an accurate picture of a typical frontier or semi-frontier school house and its occupants and practices around 1787.

In the area of religion a little more can be said. The most notable religious figure in the book is, of course, Timothy Dwight. We find in his poems explicit claims for the need of Christian belief in the new America. (Just as we find a similar implicit assertion in Hopkins' "Verses on General Ethan Allen." Livingston's long "Philosophic Solitude," written much earlier, seems to fluctuate between a Calvinist, Presbyterian persuasion and an Enlightenment or nearly Deistic view.) Furthermore, Dwight's very lack of poetic emotionalism, in the *American Poems* selections, complements his religious bias. His is a rather cool, perhaps rigid, yet essentially optimistic attitude. Dwight's poems seem to shed no light, however, on the question of the strain of his Congregationalist orthodoxy. There is no reason, based on the pieces in *American Poems,* to challenge Dwight's biographer's assertion (Charles E. Cuningham, *Timothy Dwight*) that Dwight adhered to the Old Calvinist faction within his sect, rather than to the Hopkinsian faction. (The biographer dates the controversy during Dwight's lifetime as having taken place largely in the years following the appearance of *American Poems.*) At least Dwight's unemotionalism adds credence to the contention that Dwight could support only a "quiet," comparatively unemotional revivalism during that second Great Awakening, which began in the 1790's.

Lemuel Hopkins' "The Hypocrite's Hope" sheds still a little more light on religious matters, assuming that Hopkins' views were Calvinist, and admitting we are unable further to characterize them accurately. First of all, Hopkins is disturbed at the acceptance of the Half-Way Covenant because it had produced the hypocrisy attacked in the poem. The man in the poem has practiced the public confession in the church aisle ("Broad Church-alley"), which had become essentially meaningless, or hypocritical, since it was a formula merely, involving no true repentance. And this hypocrite gained church membership solely through the opportunity offered by the Half-Way Covenant (he had quite obviously undergone no "experience" of personal religious conversion). Religious practice has become for the hypocrite a formula of prayer, church attendance and pious posing; and he clings hypocritically to the doctrine that "*faith* alone" may save him, for "*Good works* he careth nought about." Thus, whether Hopkins is genuinely a reactionary regarding religious matters, he is at least a conservative who laments liberalizing tendencies for what they have become and produced — hypocrisy. How widely his feelings were shared in 1793 we cannot say from only the evidence in *American Poems*, but at least E. H. Smith may have agreed, and we see his judgment that the poem was certainly an important enough statement to have been anthologized.

American Poems tells us all too little about science in the America of the period just preceding 1793. Franklin, quite naturally, is alluded to; Dwight, in his "Epistle," celebrates the inventor, Bushnell (primarily as a war hero), and Rittenhouse (also a prominent Revolutionary hero).

And in Mrs. Morton's poems James Bowdoin and the Harvard mathematician John Winthrop are commended. But in these allusions are constituted all the references to particular scientists in the anthology. (Barlow, in "The Prospect of Peace," alludes to scientific work in sound and atmospheric phenomena, but mentions no individuals.) Such names as Oliver Evans (1755-1819) and John Fitch (1743-1789), in invention and technology, are omitted. The same is true of the botanists Humphry Marshall (1722-1801) and Manasseh Cutler (1742-1823), and the botanist mathematician-philosopher Cadwallader Colden (1688-1776), the latter perhaps because of his materialistic philosophy. Neither are the Bartrams, John (1699-1777) and William (1739-1823), alluded to. All these figures had done important work prior to 1793. *American Poems*, then, seems only to represent poets who either had small knowledge of scientific and technological advances, and small interest in them, or who considered them inappropriate material for poetic allusion or eulogy; poets who celebrated scientists whose names were associated with nonscientific achievement (such as Revolutionary activity or, in Mrs. Morton's case, a personal friend, Bowdoin, and a leader at neighboring Harvard). That is, in the area of science, *American Poems* reflects only a lack of interest or actual ignorance on the part of the poets.

It is somewhat surprising that the same is true in the field of medicine, for the book's editor was a doctor, as was Lemuel Hopkins. Benjamin Rush, for example (under whom Smith had studied in 1790-91), perhaps the leading American medical figure of the day, is not mentioned even by his fellow Philadelphian, Hopkinson. Hopkinson's

poem (1789) does tell us, at least, that the necessary practice of dissection was yet held suspect, and that bodies for
the purpose were difficult to obtain.

It is Hopkins' poem "Epitaph on a Patient Killed by a
Cancer Quack" (1785) that affords the only valuable document concerning American medicine in *American Poems*.
The first American clinical picture of cancer, or medical
report on cancer, was written by Cadwallader Colden in
1751, and external cancers were commonly diagnosed and
treated by American doctors in that era. It is with the
quack, however, not the qualified medical man, that Hopkins deals. The poem clearly reflects the poet-doctor's life-
long efforts to raise medical standards. (E. H. Smith fought
the same battle along with Hopkins, even helping found
the first American medical journal in 1797.) Hopkins' poem
helps document in "small detail" the following generalizations asserted by Richard H. Shryock in his *Medicine
and Society in America, 1660-1860*: testimonials to easy
cures were commonly seen in eighteenth-century American periodicals; home "cures" were standard; quackery
was also common. And so, in spite of the fact that the
poems in the anthology allude very little to medical top-
ics, something of that very important aspect of American
civilization is documented in its pages.

In the area of politics the picture is simple: a Federalist bias predominates. The anthology shows us, that is,
little of the contemporary political scene, but much of the
politics of its contributors, and especially of its editor.
This is best illustrated in two ways. First, there is Smith's
deliberate exclusion of anti-Federalist or liberal poems.

The one small poem from Freneau, then America's leading poet, but also one of its leading democratic voices, is
a-political. And from Barlow, the apostate to New England conservatism, there are only his early poems, pieces
written before his alienation from the other Wits. Second,
the pieces from *The Anarchiad* reflect obvious attempts
to influence the Constitutional Convention delegates toward a strong central government, and Smith commemo-
rates the attempts in his selections. It might be added that
the very predominance of New England poets, mostly
known Federalists, shows the bias of the book's selections
in the area of politics.

This conservative bias is tempered, however, by an ex-
pression within the book of a blatant optimism. The
nationalistic poems, from Trumbull's "Elegy on the
Times" through Barlow's "vision" poems, reflect anything
but a conservative attitude toward the future glory of
America. The attitude is expansive, hopeful, even self-
assured as to the prospective greatness of the new United
States. Nationalism was an impulse that knew no faction-
al bounds, and Smith was, after all, young and forward
looking, not wedded to the status quo.

One of the most remarkable young men of his day, in
fact, was Elihu Hubbard Smith who, in the short twenty-
seven years of his life, became a second-generation Connecticut Wit, a poet, the editor of the first general anthology of American poetry, an operatic composer, a biographer,
and a leading medical figure.

Smith was born September 4, 1771, in Litchfield, Connecticut, where *American Poems* was eventually to be

published. He entered Yale College at the age of eleven, graduating in 1786. He spent the following two years at Timothy Dwight's Greenfield Academy, studying the classics and other literature. He then returned home to study medicine under his father, who was a doctor. He left Litchfield in 1790, spending the winter of 1790-91 in Philadelphia, where he attended medical lectures given by Benjamin Rush. He then settled in Wethersfield, Connecticut, to begin his practice of medicine. In the summer of 1793 he visited Litchfield, where he compiled *American Poems* and saw it published.

Later in 1793 Smith removed to New York City, where he spent most of the remainder of his life as a doctor and man of letters. In 1796 he was elected to the staff of a New York hospital. In the next year he became one of three doctors who began the first American medical journal, to which he was a frequent contributor. This was *The Medical Repository*. His opera, *The Banditti*, dedicated to his parents, appeared in 1797, but was a failure. In his last year Smith wrote a series of biographical essays about prominent American poets for the London *Monthly Magazine*, beginning with the life of Timothy Dwight (the series included sketches of Trumbull, Humphreys, Barlow, and Hopkins as well). Smith died of yellow fever September 19, 1798, at New York. He never married.

American Poems is, then, a most representative book of its time concerning the aspects of late eighteenth-century American culture discussed here. And this is true even though (at Smith's hand) a conservative, New England temperament predominates in the selections. For this temperament fails to exclude the optimistic visions of America so often expressed in its pages, fails to exclude an optimistic nationalism — fails to exclude, in fact, the kind of optimism about all things that is seen in the very scheme and act of publishing such a book. *American Poems* tells us of the poetic standards of its day in the forms and sentiments of its poems and in its very list of poets. It tells us of the poets' and readers' grasp of history in its time, of the events and heroes celebrated, and of the foes of freedom and decency as the poets saw them. It documents the years immediately preceding 1793 rather well, giving us much needed *detail* in our study of eighteenth-century American civilization. The book, a splendid landmark, has far from lost its value.

"Performances of this kind," to quote from Smith's Preface, "falling from the pens of persons not intent on literary fame ... are constantly liable to be forgotten and lost." But they should not be forgotten by the student of American civilization, by anyone, that is, who might make use of them to illuminate our study of the American panorama. For such a use the book is a fine "performance" indeed. *American Poems* is the product of a proud heritage and forms in turn a part of that heritage as it has come down to us.

WILLIAM K. BOTTORFF

State University College.
Geneseo, New York.

AMERICAN POEMS,

SELECTED AND ORIGINAL.

VOL. I.

LITCHFIELD:
PRINTED BY
COLLIER AND BUEL.

(THE COPY-RIGHT SECURED AS THE ACT DIRECTS.)

AMERICAN POEMS,

SELECTED AND ORIGINAL.

VOL. I.

LITCHFIELD:
PRINTED BY
COLLIER AND BUEL.

P R E F A C E.

IN the following pages, the Public, according to the
promife of the Publifhers, is prefented with a Volume
of American Poems; partly Selected, and partly Original.
In undertaking this Work, they have been actuated by a
variety of motives, and drawn onward by a number of objects. When looking round them, they faw many Poems,
written by the moft eminent American Authors, from the
loofe manner of their publifhment, known only to a few of
their particular acquaintance, and unheard of by the gene-
rality of their Countrymen. The value of the performances, and the regard which authors generally feel for their
literary offspring, left them no room to doubt, but that,
at fome future period, each perfon would think it not un-
worth the while to collect what he had fcattered. But
this period was uncertain; and the publifhers tho't that it
would not be rendering an unacceptable fervice to the Public, if they undertook the bufinefs of collecting, and arran-
ging each Author's productions in a volume, which from
its fize fhould claim a more univerfal attention.—Befide the
fmaller Poems of Gentlemen, diftinguifh'd for their poetical talents, many others, of very great merit, have appeared in the different Periodical publications of the United
States. Performances of this kind, falling from the pens
of perfons not intent on literary fame; or intent on reputation different from poetical reputation; or whofe names
have not yet been dignified by national applaufe; efpecial-

ly as many of them are adapted to particular and local occasions; notwithstanding their desert, are constantly liable to be forgotten and lost.   And the publishers have ob-
served it to be a matter of much regret, among persons of
reading and taste, that the frail security of an obscure news-
paper, was the only one they had for some of the handsom-
est specimens of American Poetry.   To afford a stronger,
and more durable security, is one of the objects of this
Publication.—Among other things, it did not appear to be
a matter altogether destitute of usefulness, to bring together, in one view, the several poetical productions of the different States.   By this means a more certain estimation
can be made of the comparative merit of their various wri-
ters; a more thorough acquaintance may be obtained of the
state of the belles-lettres in the individual parts of the Union; and hereby will be promoted a more intimate combi-
nation of literary interests.—It especially seemed a matter
of importance, to draw forth, for the amusement of the
lovers of poetry, those Poems which, for want of a Repository of this kind, alone, were withheld from the Public.
It was easy to foresee, that many persons, acting with a
proper regard to the worth of their own writings, would
readily give up that advantage, which news-papers bestow,
of having them known to every body; if they could by
means of a Work like the present one, secure them a certain
conveyance to the attention of the scientific and refined.
It was likewise the wish of the Publishers, to excite the
attention of those possessed of talents and leisure, to similar pursuits; by holding out to them a Work where, united with the like performances of the most celebrated
among their Countrymen, their Poems may be equally se-

cure of prefervation and notice.—Thefe have been the in-
tentions of the Publifhers.   How far their defign is accom-
plifhed, is not for them to determine.   That it fhould be
completely fo, was not to be expected.   This is but the beginning of an Undertaking; and they hope, not an un-
promifing one.   The Public alone, have the power to coun-
tenance and fupport them in its accomplifhment.—Should
the Volume, now publifhed, meet with that fuccefs which
the value of the Poems it contains feems to warrant, it is
the intention of the Publifhers to add another; and to con-
tinue the Collection as long as the *prefent fupply* of Materials, and *that* for which, in future, they may be indebt-
ed to the generofity of the literarty, will enable them.

They have, now, only to return, to their fubfcribers,
their moft unfeignedly grateful acknowledgments for the
generous fupport which they have afforded them ; and to
exprefs a hope, that tho' the publication owing to fome
unfortunate circumftances, has been delayed longer than
their firft purpofe, no other expectation, which they have
held forth, may be difappointed on a careful examination of
the Work.

Litchfield (Connecticut) June 1793.

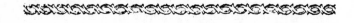

POSTSCRIPT.

IT is the intention of the Editors, as mentioned in the Preface, to purſue their deſign ; and, ſhould ſufficient encouragement appear, to publiſh a Second Volume, in the courſe of the next two years. —Many diſappointments, the ill health of one of the Editors, and other circumſtances, too complicated and painful to mention, have contributed to render their part of this Work leſs perfect than their expectations, and promiſes. They intend to finiſh the ſucceeding Volume, or Volumes, in a more elegant manner ; and, if a ſecond edition of the preſent volume ſhould be called for, it is their further intention to make it equal, in beauty, to the others ; to all of which ſuitable, and well-executed decorations ſhall be added.

C O N T E N T S.

SELECTED POETRY.

ORIGINAL POETRY.

AMERICAN POEMS.

SELECTED POETRY.

ELEGY on the TIMES.

Firſt printed at BOSTON, *Sept.* 20*th,* 1774*.*

By JOHN TRUMBULL, *Eſq.*

OH BOSTON! late with ev'ry pleaſure crown'd,
 Where Commerce triumph'd on the favoring gales,
And each pleas'd eye, that rov'd in proſpect round,
 Hail'd thy bright ſpires and bleſs'd thy op'ning ſails!

Thy plenteous marts with rich profuſion ſmil'd;
 The gay throng crouded in thy ſpacious ſtreets;
From either IND thy chearful ſtores were fill'd;
 Thy ports were gladden'd with unnumber'd fleets.

For there more fair than in their native vales,
 Tall groves of maſts aroſe in beauteous pride;
The waves were whiten'd by the ſwelling ſails,
 And plenty wafted on the neighb'ring tide.

Alas, how chang'd! the ſwelling ſails no more
 Catch the fair winds and wanton in the ſky;
But hoſtile beaks affright the guarded ſhore,
 And pointed thunders all acceſs deny.

C

Where the bold Cape its warning forehead rears,
 Where tyrant Vengeance waved her magic wand,
Far from the fight each friendly veffel veers,
 Calls the kind gales and flies the fatal ftrand.

The ruin'd Merchant turns his mournful eyes
 From the drear fhore and defolated way;
Thy filent marts unufual glooms furprize,
 And through thy ftreets the fons of rapine ftray.

Such the dread ftillnefs of the defert night,
 When brooding horror fettles on the groves;
While powers of darknefs claim their hateful right,
 And fierce for prey the favage tyger roves.

Along thy fields, which late in beauty fhone
 With lowing herds and graffy vefture fair,
The infulting tents of barbarous troops are ftrown,
 And bloody ftandards ftain the peaceful air.

Are thefe thy deeds, oh Britain? this the praife,
 That points the growing luftre of thy name?
Thefe glorious works that in thy latter days,
 Gild the bright period of thine early fame?

Shall thy ftrong fleets, with awful fails unfurl'd,
 On Freedom's fhrines the unhallow'd vengeance bend?
And leave forlorn the defolated world,
 Cruſh'd—every foe, and ruin'd—every friend!

And damp'd alas! thy foul-infpiring ray,
 Where Virtue prompted and where Genius foar'd,
Or quench'd in darknefs, and the gloomy fway
 Of Senates venal and the liveried Lord!

There shame sits blazon'd on the unmeaning brow,
　　And o'er the scene thy factious Nobles wait,
Prompt the mixt tumult of the noisy show,
　　Guide the blind vote and rule the mock debate.

To these how vain, in weary woes forlorn,
　　With fearful hands the fond complaint to raise,
Lift fruitless offerings to the ear of Scorn—
　　Of servile vows and well-dissembled praise!

Will the grim savage of the nightly fold
　　Learn from their cries the blameless flock to spare?
Will the deaf gods, that frown in molten gold,
　　Bless the dup'd hand, that spreads the prostrate prayer?

With what pleas'd hope before the face of Pride,
　　We rear'd our suppliant eyes with filial awe;
While loud Disdain with ruffian voice reply'd,
　　And Injury triumph'd in the garb of Law!

While Peers enraptur'd hail the unmanly wrong,
　　See Ribaldry, vile prostitute of shame,
Stretch the brib'd hand and prompt the venal tongue,
　　To blast the laurels of a FRANKLIN's fame!

But will the Sage, whose philosophic soul,
　　Controul'd the lightning in its fierce career,
Hear'd unappal'd the aerial thunders roll,
　　And taught the bolts of vengeance where to steer;—

Will he, while echoing to his just renown
　　The voice of kingdoms swells the loud applause;
Heed the weak malice of a Courtier's frown,
　　Or dread the coward insolence of laws?

See envying Britain rends the facred bays;
     Illuded Juſtice pens the mock decree;
While Infamy her darling ſcroll diſplays,
     And points well pleas'd, oh, WEDDERBURNE, to thee!

For nought avails the virtues of the heart,
     The vengeful bolt no Muſe's laurels ward;
From Britain's rage, and death's relentleſs dart,
     No worth can ſave us, and no fame can guard.

O'er hallow'd bounds ſee dire Oppreſſion roll;
     Fair Freedom buried in the whelming flood;
Nor charter'd rights the tyrant courſe controul,
     Though ſeal'd by Kings and witneſs'd in our blood.

No more ſhall Juſtice with unbiaſs'd hand,
     From lawleſs Rapine ſnatch her trembling prey,
While in her balance by *ſupreme* command
     Hang the dead weights of miniſterial ſway.

(For taught by pain, our injur'd boſoms feel
     The potent claims whence all our woes began,
And own *ſupreme* the power, that could repeal,
     Thoſe laws of heaven, that guard the rights of man.)

In vain we hope from Britain's haughty pride
     An hand to ſave us, or an heart to bleſs;
'Tis ſtrength, our own, muſt ſtem the ruſhing tide,
     And our own virtue yield the wiſh'd ſucceſs.

But, oh, my friends, the arm of blood* reſtrain!
     (No rage intemperate aids the public weal)
Nor baſely blend (too daring, but in vain)
     The aſſaſſin's madneſs with the patriot's zeal.

[*For the Note, ſee next page.*]

Shall the fields blufh, with vital crimfon ftain'd,
 When blind refentment marks the victim'd breaft?
Will reeking life, by vengeful hands prophan'd,
 Our wrongs relieve, or charm our woes to reft?

Ours be the manly firmnefs of the fage,
 From fhamelefs foes the ungrateful wounds to bear;
Alike remov'd from bafenefs and from rage,
 The flames of faction, and the chills of fear.

Check the vaft torrent of commercial gain,
 That buys our ruin at a price fo rare;
And while we fcorn Britannia's fervile chain,
 Difdain the livery of her marts to wear.

For fhall the luft of fafhions and of fhow,
 The curft idolatry of filks and lace,
Bid our proud robes infult our Country's woe,
 And welcome Slav'ry in the glare of drefs?

Will the blind dupe, in liveried tinfel gay,
 Boaft the fhamed trappings, that adorn the flave?
Will the fond mourner change his fad array,
 To attend in gorgeous pomp a parent's grave?

———————

* *This is not meant as a caution againft defending our rights with our blood, if we fhould be driven to that extremity; but only againft the impolitic zeal of thofe, who feem defirous to let loofe the rage of popular refentment, and bring matters immediately to a crifis in this Province.*

No ! the rich produce of our fertile foil,
    Shall cloath the neatnefs of our chearful train,
While heaven-born virtues blefs the pious toil,
    And gild the humble veftures of the plain.

No foreign labour in the Afian field
    Shall weave her filks to deck the wanton age,
But, as in Rome, the furrow'd vale fhall yield
    The unvanquifh'd Chieftain and paternal Sage.

And ye, whofe heaven in ermin'd pomp to fhine,
    To run with joy the vain, luxurious round,
Blefs the full banquet with the charms of wine,
    And roll the thundering chariot o'er the ground !

For this, while guis'd in fycophantic fmile,
    With hearts all mindlefs of your country's pain,
Your flattering falfhoods feed the ears of Guile,
    And barter freedom for the dreams of gain !

Are thefe the joys, on vaffal'd climes that wait—
    In downs of eafe luxuriant to repofe,
Quaff ftreams nectareous in the domes of ftate,
    And blaze in fplendor of imperial fhows ?

No—the hard hand, the tortur'd brow of Care,
    The thatch-roof'd hamlet and defencelefs fhed,
The tatter'd garb, that meets the inclement air,
    The famifh'd table, and the matted bed.—

Thefe are their fate—In vain the arm of toil
    With gifts autumnal crowns the bearded plain ;
In vain glad Summer prompts the genial foil,
    And Spring diffolves in foftening fhowers in vain ;

There favage Power extends his difmal fhade,
　　And chill Oppreffion, with her frofts fevere,
Sheds her dire blaftings o'er the fpringing blade,
　　And robs the expecting labours of the year.

So muft we fink ?—and at the ftern command
　　That bears the terrors of a tyrant's word,
Bend the crouch'd knee and raife the fuppliant hand,
　　The fcorn'd, dependant, vaffals of a Lord ?

The wintry ravage of the ftorm to meet,
　　Brave the fcorch'd vapours of the autumnal air,
Then pour the hard-earn'd harveft at his feet,
　　And beg fome pittance from our pains to fhare ?

But not for this, by heaven and virtue led,
　　From the mad rule of hierarchal pride,
From flavifh chains our injur'd fathers fled,
　　And follow'd freedom on the advent'rous tide ;

Dar'd the wild horrors of thefe climes unknown,
　　The infidious favage, and the crimfon'd plain,
To us bequeath'd the prize, their woes had won,
　　Nor deem'd they fuffer'd, or they bled in vain.

And think'ft thou, NORTH, the fons of fuch a race,
　　Where beams of glory bleft their purpled morn,
Will fhrink unnerv'd before a tyrant's face,
　　Nor meet thy louring infolence with fcorn ?

Look thro' the circuit of the extended fhore,
　　That checks the furges of the Atlantic deep !
What weak eye trembles at the frowns of pow'r ?
　　What leaden foul invites the bands of fleep ?

How Goodnefs warms each heaven-illumin'd heart!
    What generous gifts the woes of want affuage,
And fympathetic tears of pity ftart,
    To aid the deftin'd victims of thy rage!

No clamourous faction with unhallow'd zeal
    To wayward madnefs wakes the impaffion'd throng;
No thoughtlefs furies fheath their breafts with fteel,
    Or call the fword to avenge the oppreffive wrong.

Fraternal bands with vows accordant join;
    One guardian Genius, one enrapturing Soul
Nerves the bold arm, inflames the juft defign,
    Combines, infpirits, and illumes, the whole.

Now meet the Fathers of this weftern clime;
    Nor names more noble graced the rolls of fame,
When Spartan firmnefs brav'd the wrecks of time,
    Or Rome's bold virtues fann'd the heroic flame.

Not deeper thought th' immortal Sage infpir'd,
    On Solon's lips when Grecian fenates hung;
Nor manlier eloquence the bofom fir'd,
    When genius thunder'd from the Athenian tongue.

And hopes thy pride to match the patriot ftrain
    By the brib'd flave in penfion'd lifts enroll'd;
Or awe their councils by the voice prophane,
    That wakes to utterance at the calls of gold?

Can frowns of terror daunt the warrior's deeds,
    Where guilt is ftranger to the ingenuous heart?
Or Craft illude, where godlike Science fheds
    The beams of knowledge and the gifts of art?

Go,. raife thy hand, and with its magic pow'r
   Pencil with night the fun's afcending ray,
Bid the broad veil eclipfe the noon-tide hour,
   And damps of ftygian darknefs fhroud the day.—

(Such night as lours o'er Britain's fated land,
   Where raylefs fhades the darken'd throne furround;
Nor deeper glooms at Mofes' waving wand,
   Pour'd their thick horrors o'er the Memphian ground.)

Bid heav'ns dread thunders at thy voice expire;
   Or chain the angry vengeance of the waves;
Then hope thy breath can chill th' eternal fire,
   And free fouls pinion with the bonds of flaves.

Thou canft not hope—Attend the flight of days,
   View the bold deeds, that wait the dawning age,
Where Time's ftrong arm, that rules the mighty maze,
   Shifts the proud actors on this earthly ftage!

Then tell us, NORTH,—for thou art fure to know;
   For have not Kings and fortune made thee great?
Or lurks not genius in th' ennobled brow,
   And dwells not wifdom in the robes of ftate?

Tell how the pow'rs of luxury and pride,
   Taint thy pure zephyrs with their poifon'd breath;
How dark Corruption fpreads th' envenom'd tide,
   And Britain trembles on the verge of death.

And tell how, rapt by Freedom's deathlefs flame,
   And foft'ring influence of the fav'ring fkies,
This Weftern World, the laft recefs of fame,
   Sees in her wilds a new-born empire rife:

D

A new-born Empire, whose ascendant hour
   Defies the foes, that would its life destroy,
And like Alcides, with its infant power
   Shall crush those serpents, who its rest annoy.

Then look thro' time, and with extended eye,
   Pierce the deep veil of fate's obscure domain!
The morning dawns, th' effulgent star is nigh,
   And crimson'd glories deck her rising reign!

Behold afar beneath the cloud of days,
   Where rest the wonders of ascending fame;
What Heroes rise, immortal heirs of praise!
   What fields of death with conq'ring standards flame!

See her throng'd cities' warlike gates unfold!
   What tow'ring armies stretch their banners wide,
Where cold Ontario's icy waves are roll'd,
   Or far Altama's silver waters glide!

Lo from the groves, th' aspiring cliffs that shade,
   Ascending pines the surging ocean brave,
Rise in tall masts, the floating canvas spread,
   And rule the dread dominions of the wave!

Where her clear rivers pour the mazy tide,
   The laughing lawns in full luxuriance bloom,
The golden harvest spreads her wanton pride,
   The flow'ry garden breathes a glad perfume.

Her potent voice shall hush the storms of fate,
   Where the meads blossom or the billows roar;
And cities, gay with sumptuous domes of state,
   Stretch their bright turrets on the sounding shore.

There mark that Coaft, which feats of wealth furround,
  That haven, rich with many a flowing fail,
Where mighty fhips, from earth's remoteft bound,
  Float on the chearly pinions of the gale.

There BOSTON fmiles, no more the fport of fcorn,
  And meanly prifon'd by thy fleets no more ;
And far as ocean's billowy tides are borne,
  Lifts her fear'd enfigns of imperial power.

So fmile the fhores, where lordly Hudfon ftrays,
  (Whofe floods fair YORK and proud ALBANIA lave)
Or PHILADELPHIA's happier clime furveys
  Her glift ring fpires in Schuylkyll's lucid wave.

Or fouthward far extend thy wond'ring eyes,
  Where fertile ftreams the garden'd vales divide ;
And mid the peopled fields diftinguifh'd rife
  Virginian tow'rs, and Charleftown's fpiry pride.

Genius of arts, of manners and of arms,
  See deck'd with glory and the blooms of grace,
This Virgin-clime unfolds her brighter charms,
  And gives her beauties to thy fond embrace !

Hark, from the glades, and ev'ry lift'ning fpray,
  What heav'n-born Mufes wake th' enraptur'd fong !
The vocal fhades attune th' enchanting lay,
  And echoing vales harmonious ftrains prolong.

Thro' the vaft feries of defcending years,
  That lofe their currents in th' eternal wave,
Till heav'n's laft trump fhall rend th' affrighted fpheres,
  And ope each empire's everlafting grave ;

Propitious ſkies the joyous field ſhall crown,
    And robe her vallies in perpetual prime,
And ages bleſt of undiſturb'd renown,
    Beam their mild radiance o'er th' imperial clime.

And where is BRITAIN?—In the ſkirt of day,
    Where ſtormy Neptune rolls his utmoſt tide,
Where ſuns oblique diſſuſe a feeble ray,
    And lonely waves the fated coaſts divide;

Seeſt thou yon Iſle, whoſe deſert landſcape yields
    The mournful traces of the fame ſhe bore;
Where matted thorns oppreſs the cultur'd fields,
    And piles of ruin choak the dreary ſhore?—

From thoſe lov'd ſeats, the Virtues ſad withdrew,
    From fell Corruption's bold and venal hand;
Reluctant Freedom wav'd her laſt adieu,
    And Devaſtation ſwept the vaſſal d land.

On her white cliffs, the pillars once of fame,
    Her melancholy Genius ſits to wail;
Drops the fond tear, and o'er her lateſt ſhame,
    Bids dark Oblivion draw her ſable veil.

An ELEGY,

On the death of Mr. BUCKINGHAM ST. JOHN; *who was drowned in his passage from New-Haven to Norwalk, May 5th,* 1771.

BY THE SAME.

THE world now yeilds to night's returning sway;
    The deeper glooms lead on the solemn hour,
And call my steps, beneath the moon's pale ray,
    To roam in SADNESS on the sea-beat shore.

Now glide the inconstant shadows o'er the plain,
    The broad moon swimming thro the broken clouds,
The gleam of waters brightens on the main,
    And anchor'd navies lift their wavering shrouds.

Deep silence reigns; save on the moory ground,
    The long reed rustling to the passing gales,
The noise of dashing waves, and hallow sound
    Of rushing winds, that murmur thro the sails.

Far hence, ye pleasures of a mind at ease,
    The sprightly joys, that rural scenes can yeild,
When spring, led jocund by the softening breeze,
    Wakes the glad morn, and robes the dewy field!

Far be the giddy raptures of the gay,
    The midnight joys licentious youth can share,
When ruin, smiling o'er her destin'd prey,
    In sweet allurements hides the deadly snare.

Mine be the mufic of the rolling wave,
   The moonlight fhadows and furrounding gloom ;
Mine the dread haunts of contemplation grave,
   That lift the foul to fcenes beyond th. tomb.

Here while deep midnight holds her filent reign,
   And fancy bears the ravifh'd thought along,
Dark melancholy fpreads her airy train,
   And friendfhip calls, and grief infpires the fong.

As thro thefe mournful glooms I ftretch'd my fight,
   Mid founds of death, that bid the foul attend,
Mid empty forms, and fleeting fhapes of night,
   Slowly I view a white-rob'd fhade afcend,

That fays—" I once was St. John! from the bounds
   Of unknown realms beneath the dreary wave,
Where ever-reftlefs floods, in nightly rounds,
   Roll their dark furges o'er my watry grave ;

From feats, which ne'er to mortal fight difplay'd,
   The gates of dread eternity furround,
In night conceal'd, and death's impervious fhade,
   My voice afcends : attend the warning found !

Oh thou, attend ! who flufh'd with early bloom,
   In life's new fpring, and vernal fweetnefs gay,
Heedlefs of fate, that muft thy branch entomb,
   Spread'ft thy green bloffoms to the morning ray.

With thee how late, how like, alas ! to thee ;
   To mortal joys, by opening youth beguil'd,
I ftretch'd my airy wifh, and follow'd free,
   Where pleafure triumph'd, and where fancy fmil'd.

Then, while fond hope her glittering pinions ſpread,
 *Pointing to climes beyond the diſtant wave,
Even then, unnotic'd, o'er my deſtin'd head,
 Hung death's dire form, and ſeal'd me for the grave.

How vain the thought for many a joyous morn,
 To taſte of raptures unallay'd by woe !
At once from life and every pleaſure torn,
 From all I wiſh'd, and all I lov'd below.

The faithleſs morning, on our opening ſails,
 Smil'd out ſerene, and ſmooth'd our gliding way,
While the gay veſſel, fann'd by breathing gales,
 Play'd on the placid boſom of the ſea.

When lo, deſcending on the darkening wind,
 Burſt the dire ſtorm,—and feeble to ſuſtain
The ruſhing blaſts, in warring fury join'd,
 The frail ſkiff ſinks beneath the ſurging main.

And ſee, afar the oarleſs boat conveys
 The trembling ſailors to the diſtant ſhore ;
Alone, of aid bereft, with one laſt gaze,
 I ſunk in deeps : and ſunk to riſe no more.

In that ſad hour, what fearful ſcenes ariſe,
 What pangs diſtreſs, what unknown fears diſmay !
When future worlds diſcloſing on our eyes,
 The trembling ſoul forſakes the kindred day !

* *Mr. St. John was meditating a voyage to Europe.*

Before the awful bar, the Almighty throne,
 In dread I've stood the Eternal Judge to fee,
And fix'd in blifs, or doom'd to endlefs moan,
 Have heard the long, the unrevers'd decree :

Nor earth muft know the reft."——Where art thou now,
 In youthful joys my partner and my friend ;
Of thofe bleft hours thy fortune gave below,
 Of all our hopes is this the fatal end ?

Ah what avail'd that energy of mind,
 The heights of fcience, and of arts to explore,
That eaily led where genius unconfin'd,
 Spreads her glad feaft, and opes her claffic ftore !

Ah what avail'd, in earthly blifs fo frail,
 The fame gay-dawning on thy rifing years !
Ah what avail'd,—for what could then avail ?—
 Thy friend's deep forrows, or thy country's tears !

In pleafure's paths, by vivid fancy led,
 Mid every hope that blooming worth could raife,
The wings of death with fatal horror fpread,
 Blank'd the bright promife of thy future days.

So, from the louring weft, the darken'd clouds
 Rufh on the fun and dim his orient ray,
And hateful night in glooms untimely fhrouds
 The afcending glories of the vernal day.

Adieu, my friend, fo dear in vain, adieu,
 Till fome fhort days their fleeting courfes roll ;
Soon fhall our fteps thine earlier fate purfue,
 Mov'd in the race, and crowding to the goal.

The approaching hour ſhall ſee the ſun no more,
　Wheel his long courſe, or ſpread his golden ray ;
Soon the vain dream of mortal life be o'er,
　The brightneſs dawning of celeſtial day.

Then join'd in bliſs, as once in friendſhip join'd,
　May pitying Heaven our purer ſpirits raiſe,
Each crime atton'd, each virtue well reſin'd,
　To paſs a bleſt eternity of praiſe !——

***

A M B I T I O N.

An ELEGY.

BY THE SAME.

HENCE, gaudy Flattery, with thy ſiren ſong,
　Thy fading laurels, and thy trump of praiſe,
Thy magic glaſs, that cheats the wondering throng,
　And bids vain men, grow vainer, while they gaze.

For what the gain, tho nature have ſupplied
　A tender ſoul, to feel the ſting of pain ?
That fame how poor, that lifts our baſeleſs pride,
　And ſhews the heights our ſteps muſt ne'er attain !

E

How vain thofe thoughts that thro creation rove,
    Returning fraught with images of woe !
Thofe gifts how vain that pleafe not thofe we love !
    With grief opprefs'd, how fmall the gain to know !

And oh, that fate, in life's fequefter'd fhade,
    Had fix'd the limits of my filent way,
Far from the fcenes in noify pomp array'd,
    Where hope and fame but flatter to betray.

The lark had call'd me at the birth of dawn,
    My cheerful toils and rural fports to fhare ;
Nor, when mild evening glimmer'd on the lawn,
    Had fleep been frighted at the voice of care.

So the foft flocks in harmlefs pleafure ftray,
    Or fport in rapture on the flowery mead,
Enjoy the beauties of the vernal day,
    And no fad prefcience tells them they muft bleed.

Then wild ambition ne'er had fwell'd my heart,
    Nor had my fteps purfued the road to fame ;
Then ne'er had flander rais'd the envenom'd dart,
    Nor hung in vengeance o'er my hated name.

Nor views of blifs that never muft be mine,
    Urg'd the fond tear, or fwell'd the burfting figh ;
Nor tendereft pangs had bid my foul repine,
    Nor torture warn'd me that my hopes muft die.

Farewell, ye glittering phantoms of the mind,
    The golden vifion, or ambitious dream,
The fickle forms by fairy fancy join'd,
    The pride of laurels and the mufe's theme.

Vain hope, adieu! thou dear deluding cheat,
  Whofe magic charm can burft the bonds of pain;
By thee decoy'd, we clafp the gay deceit,
  And plan the fcenes of future joys in vain.

Come Sadnefs! come, mild fifter of Defpair,
  The helplefs fufferer's laft fupport and friend,
Lead to thofe fcenes that footh the wretch's care,
  Where life's falfe joys, and life itfelf, muft end!

Well pleas'd, I wander o'er the folemn ground,
  Where Death in horror holds his dread domain,
While night fits gloomy in the etherial round,
  And fwimming vapors cloud the dreary plain.

Ye ghofts, the tenants of the evening fkies,
  That fweep in fadnefs o'er the dufky vale,
Enrob'd in mifts, I fee your forms arife;
  I hear your voices founding in the gale!

Of life ye fpeak, and life's fantaftic toys,
  How vain the wifh, that grafps at things below!
How difappointment lours on all our joys,
  And hope bequeaths the legacy of woe!

Ye too, perhaps, while youth fupplied its beam,
  On fancy's pinions foaring to the fky,
Fed your deluded thoughts with many a dream,
  Of love and fame, and future fcenes of joy.

Like your's how foon our empty years fhall fade,
  Paft, like the vapors that in clouds decay,
Paft, like the forms that flit along the fhade,
  Ourfelves as worthlefs, and as vain as they!

Here the kind haven greets our weary fail,
   When the rude voyage of troubled life is o'er,
Safe from the ftormy blaft, the faithlefs gale,
   The gulphs that threaten, and the waves that roar.

The heart no more the pains of love fhall fhare,
   Nor torturing grief the wayward mind enflave,
Thro toil-worn years fatigued with reftlefs care,
   Peace, fought in vain, awaits us in the grave.

Nor peace alone! death breaks the fullen gloom,
   That dims the portals of eternal day,
Bids the freed foul her nobler powers affume,
   And wing from woes her heaven-directed way.

Fly hence ye fhades! ye brighter fcenes arife!
   Ye joys celeftial, opening on my view!
Vanifh, ye griefs, that dwell beneath the fkies,
   Ye ftreaming tears, ye fond complaints, adieu!

The PROPHECY of BALAAM.

Numbers: Chap. xxiii. 24.

An IRREGULAR ODE. *Written, Anno* 1773.

BY THE SAME.

I

ON lofty Peor's brow,
     That rears its forehead to the ſky,
     And ſees the airy vapours fly,
And clouds in bright expanſion ſail below,
     Sublime the Prophet ſtood.
          Beneath its pine-clad ſide,
The diſtant world her various landſcape yeilds;
Winding vales and lengthening fields,
     Streams in ſunny maze that flow'd;
          Stretch'd immenſe in proſpect wide
          Foreſts green in ſummer's pride;
     Waving glory gilds the main,
The dazzling ſun aſcending high;
     While earth's blue verge at diſtance dimly ſeen,
Spreads from the aching ſight, and fades into the ſky.

II.

Beneath his feet along the level plain,
     The hoſt of Iſrael ſtretch'd in deep array;
Their tents roſe frequent on the enamell'd green;
     Bright to the winds the colour'd ſtreamers play.

Red from the flaughter of their foes,
In awful fteel the embattled heroes ftood;
High o'er the fhaded ark in terror rofe
The cloud, the dark pavilion of their God.
Before the Seer's unwilling eyes,
The years unborn afcend in fight.
He faw their opening morn arife,
Bright in the fun fhine of the favoring fkies;
While from the unfufferable light,
Fled the dire demons of oppofing night.
No more, elate with Stygian aid,
He waves the wand's enchanted power,
And baleful thro the hallow'd glade,
His magic footfteps rove no more.
Fill'd with prophetic fire, he lifts his hand,
O'er the dim hoft in deep array;
And aw'd by Heaven's fupreme command,
Pours forth the rapture of the living lay.

III.

Fair, oh Ifrael, are thy tents!
Bleft the banners of thy fame!
Bleft the dwelling of the faints,
Where their God difplays his name!
Fair as thefe vales, that ftretch their lawns fo wide,
As gardens fmile, in flowery meadows fair,
As rifing cedars on the ftreamlet's fide,
That lift their branches to the fragrant air!
Vain is magic's deadly force,
Vain the dire enchanter's fpell,
Waving wand, or charmed curfe,
Vain the pride, the rage of hell!

From Peor's lofty brow,
I fee the eternal powers reveal'd,
And all the lengthen'd plains below
O'erfhrouded by the Almighty fhield!
God, their guardian God, defcends,
And o'er the favor'd hoft Omnipotence extends.

IV.

And fee, bright Judah's ftar afcending
Fires the eaft with crimfon day,
Aweful o'er his foes impending,
Pours wide the lightning of his ray,
And flames deftruction on the oppofing world!
Death's broad banners, dark, unfurl'd,
Wave o'er his blood-encircled way!
Scepter'd king of Moab, hear,
Deeds, that future times await,
Deadly triumph, war fevere,
Ifrael's pride, and Moab's fate!
What echoing terrors burft upon my ear!
What aweful forms in ghaftly horror rife!
Empurpled rage, pale ruin, heart-ftruck fear,
In fcenes of blood afcend, and fkim before my eyes!

V.

Dimly on the fkirt of night
O'er thy fons the cloud impends,
Louring ftorm with wild affright
Loud the aftonifh'd ether rends.
Long hofts, emblaz'd with fun-bright fhields appear,
And victory fevere

Sits on their lightening fwords : along the fhores,
　　Arm'd with the bolts of fate,
　　Impending navies wait ;
Above, around, the fhout of ruin roars.
For nought avails, that clad in fpiry pride,
Thy rifing cities glitter'd on the day ;
　　The vengeful arms wave devaftation wide,
And give thy pompous domes to mouldering flames a prey.

VI.

Edom bows her lofty head ;
　　Seer fubmits her vanquifh'd bands ;
Amalek, of hofts the dread,
　　Sinks beneath their wafting hands.
See, whelm'd in fmoky heaps, the ruin'd walls,
　　Rife o'er thy fons' unhappy grave ;
Low their blafted glory falls ;
　　Vain the pride that could not fave !
Ifrael's fwords arreft their prey ;
Back to fwift fate thy frighted ftandards turn ;
　　Black defolation rolls along their way ;
War fweeps in front, and flames behind them burn :
　　And death, and dire difmay,
Unfold their univerfal grave, and ope the mighty urn.

The DOWNFALL of BABYLON.

*An Imitation of sundry passages in the thirteenth and fourteenth
Chapters of the Prophecy of Isaiah, and the eighteenth
Chapter of the Revelations of St. John.*

Written, anno 1775.

BY THE SAME.

'TWAS now the day, devote to blest repose,
    From realms of darkness, when the Saviour rose,
In Patmos's Isle, with sacred light inspir'd,
The great Apostle from the world retir'd;
Before his eyes eternal wonders roll,
And future visions open on his soul,
Unfolding skies the scenes of fate display,
And Heaven descending in the beam of day.

He saw with joy the promis'd Church arise,
Fam'd thro the earth, and favor'd from the skies;
A starry crown invests her radiant head,
Around her form the solar glories spread,
Her power, her grace, by circling realms approv'd,
By angels guarded, and by Heaven belov'd:
Till mystic Babel, with blaspheming pride,
For idol forms the eternal power defied;
Then martyr'd blood the holy offering seal'd,
And persecution dyed the carnag'd field,
Religion sunk in superstitious lore,
And Heaven-built temples swam with sainted gore.

F

But not in reft, till virtue fhould expire,
Slept the juft vengeance of eternal ire.
The Seer beheld, till God's avenging hand
Smote the proud foe, and fwept the guilty land;
Then pious rapture triump'd on his tongue,
And infpiration breath'd the exulting fong.

" What fudden fall hath dimm'd thy boafted ray,
Son of the Morn! bright Phofphor of the day!
How funk in death, a victim of the grave,
Thy pride fo vaunting, and thy arm fo brave!
Where now the haughty boaft?"　Above the fkies,
O'er the ftarr'd arch my towering fteps fhall rife,
To Heaven's high walls my glories fhall afcend,
My throne be 'ftablifh'd, and my power extend,
O'er the wide world to ftretch my arm abroad;
A God in fplendor, and in might a God."

Behold from rage the bold oppreffor ceas'd;
Thy glory wan, and all thy treafures wafte!
Eternal wrath, awaken'd o'er thy land,
Tears the weak fceptre from the injurious hand;
Heaven gives its captive fons a kind releafe,
And earth fmiles, joyous, at the fongs of peace.

Lo, at thy fall, in realms of night below,
Hell greets thine entrance to the worlds of woe!
See from their thrones along the infernal fhade,
Rife the dark fpectres of the mighty dead,
Friends to thy fway, and partners in thy crimes,
Kings once on earth, and tyrants in their times!
" And art thou fall'n?"—their looks of wonder crave—
" Swept, undiftinguifh'd, to the darkfome grave?

O'er thy pale cheek funereal damps are fpread,
And fhrouds of fable wrap thee with the dead;
What aw'd the world oblivion's fhadows hide,
And glad worms revel on the wrecks of pride.

   Is this the Power, whofe once tremendous eye
Shook the wide earth, and dar'd the avenging fky,
Oppofing kingdoms from their fceptres hurl'd,
And fpread fad ruin o'er the vanquifh'd world?
Is this the Power, that rofe in boafted ftate,
Proud judge of thrones, and arbiter of fate?
The Power, whofe forceries, us'd in every clime,
Stain'd the dark annals of recording time,
While perfecution taught the infernal lore,
And zeal was fated with the martyr's gore?—
Lo! clos'd thine eyes that wont the Heavens to brave,
Expos'd thou ly'ft, an outcaft from the grave;
No fplendid urn thy funeral duft contains,
Nor one kind turf conceals thy fad remains;
For thee no marble lifts its tablet high,
Where kings deceas'd in mournful glory lie;
For juft renown divides thee from the bleft,
Nor decks the clods that lull thy bones to reft."

   And fee Deftruction from the Almighty hand,
Sweeps her broad befom o'er thy guilty land;
Careering flames attend her dreadful way,
And rifing darknefs intercepts the day;
The dim fun finks in fearful fhades of night,
The moon and planets veil their trembling light,
O'er thy doom'd walls the louring ftorms afcend,
And fate's dread omens mark thy haftening end.

See mid the o'erarching canopy of shade,
An angel-form, in robes of blood array'd,
Lifts his red arm, that bids the tempest rise,
Wing'd with the etherial vengeance of the skies;
And calls the wintry winds, that all around,
Roll on the storms, and sweep the delug'd ground,
And far beneath, where direful earthquakes sleep,
Bursts the dark chambers of the affrighted deep!
Lo! Heaven avenging pours the fiery tide;
Thy whelm'd walls sink, thy tottering turrets slide,
Thy glittering domes sulphureous torrents lave,
And doom thy seats, a desart and a grave!

For there no more shall gay assemblies meet,
Crowd thy full marts, and throng thy spacious street;
No more the bridegroom's cheerful voice shall call
The viol, sprightly in the sounding hall;
No more the lamp shall yeild her cheerful light,
Gild thy lone roofs and sparkle thro the night.
Each morn shall view thy desolated ground,
With falling domes and shatter'd spires around,
And clad in weeds, in wild confusion thrown,
The marble trophy, and the sculptur'd stone.
No future age thy glories shall recall,
Thy turrets lift, or build thy desart wall;
Where the gilt palace pierc'd the admiring skies,
The owl shall stun thee with funereal cries,
The baleful dragon thro thy gardens rove,
And wolves usurp the consecrated grove.
No shepherd there the wandering flock shall spread,
Nor, tir'd, repose beneath the tented shed;

No ftranger there with devious footfteps ftray,
Where circling horrors guard the fated way ;
Eternal Ruin rears her ftandard wide,
And vengeance triumphs o'er the realms of pride."

THE SPEECH OF
PROTEUS to ARISTÆUS,
CONTAINING THE STORY OF ORPHEUS AND EURIDICE ;
Tranflated from the fourth Book of Virgil's Georgics.

A Collegiate Exercife : Written, Anno 1770.

BY THE SAME.

A GOD purfues' thee with immortal hate,
By crimes provok'd that prompt the wrath of fate.
In guiltlefs woe the haplefs Orpheus died,
And calls the powers to avenge his injur'd bride.

Along the ftreams, with flying fteps fhe ftrove,
To fhun the fury of thy lawlefs love ;
Unhappy fair ! nor on the fated way
Saw the dire fnake that ambufh'd for her prey.

Her fifter Dryades wail'd the fatal wound ;
The lofty hills their melting cries refound ;
Then wept the rocks of Rhodope, the towers
Of high Pangæus, and the Rhefian fhores ;
The mournful founds the Attic lands convey,
And Hebrus rolls in fadden'd waves away.

He, on his lyre, effay'd with tuneful art,
To footh the ceafelefs anguifh of his heart ;
Thee, his fair bride, to lonely grief a prey,
Thee fung at rifing, and at falling day :
Then fought the realms of death and Stygian Jove,
Thro black'ning horrors of the infernal grove,
Mid direful ghofts, and powers of deep defpair,
Unknown to pity, and unmov'd by prayer.
From hell's dark fhores, to Orpheus' melting fong,
On every fide the gloomy nations throng ;
Thin, airy fhades, pale fpectres void of light,
Like fancied forms that glide athwart the night.
As flitting birds in fummer's chequer'd fhade,
Dance on the boughs, and flutter thro the glade,
Or feek the woods when night defcends amain,
And pours in ftorms along the wintry plain :
Men, matrons, round the fweet mufician prefs'd,
The fpoufelefs maidens, and the youths unbleft,
Snatch'd from their parents' eyes, or doom'd to yeild
To war's dire combats on the bloody field ;
Whom the deep fens, that drain the moory ground,
And black Cocytus reedy lake furround,
Where baleful Styx her mournful margin laves,
And deadly Lethe rolls the oblivious waves.

Hell heard the fong ; and fix'd in deep amaze,
On the fweet bard the fnaky Furies gaze ;
Grim Cerberus hung entranc'd ; and ceas'd to reel
The giddy circle of Ixion's wheel.

Thefe dangers 'fcap'd, he feeks the upper air,
Elate with joy, and follow'd by the fair :

Such law the Fates impos'd : but doom'd to prove
The fudden madnefs of ill-omen'd love !
Could fate relent, or melt at human woe,
A venial crime, were venial aught below !
Light gleam'd at hand ; the Stygian fhades retire ;
With wifhes wild, and vanquifh'd with defire,
His fears forgot, he turn'd ; his lovely bride
Given to his hope, with trembling glance efpy'd.
There end his joys, and vanifh'd into air
His fancied raptures and his fruitlefs care,
Broke is the league—and thrice tremendous roars
The diftant thunder on the infernal fhores.

What rage, fhe cried, hath dafh'd our joys again,
Pair'd in fad fates, and doom'd to endlefs pain.
I hear the voice that calls me back to woes,
My fwimming eyes eternal flumbers clofe.
A laft farewel ! the infernal glooms arife,
And, wrapt in night, my parting fpirit flies ;
Vain my weak arms, extended to reftore
The bridal hand, that muft be thine no more.

She faid, and vanifh'd inftant from his eye,
Like melting fmoke that mingles with the fky.
No kind embrace, his deepening grief to allay,
No farewel word, tho much he wifh'd to fay,
Nor hope remain'd. Stern Charon now no more
Confents to waft him to the infernal fhore.
Forever fnatch'd from all his foul could love,
What prayers, what tears, what fongs, the Fates could move?
Her, breathlefs, pale, to manfions of the grave,
The bark bore floating on the Stygian wave.

In gelid caves, with horrid glooms array'd,
Where cloud-topt hills project an awful shade;
Along the margin of the desert shore,
Where lovely Strymon's rushing waters roar,
Seven hapless months he wail d his fatal love,
His ravish'd bride, and blam'd the hand of Jove.
Stern tygers soften d at the tuneful sound,
The thickets move, the forests dance around :
So in some poplar's shade, with soothing song,
Sad Philomela mourns her captive young ;
When some rude swain hath found the unfeather'd prey,
Her nest despoil'd, and borne the prize away ;
Thro the long night she breathes her plaintive strain,
The slow, deep moan resounds, and echoes o'er the plain.

Pleasure no more his soul estrang'd could move,
The charms of beauty, or the joys of love.
Alone he stray'd, where wintry Tanais flows,
Thro deserts whiten'd with eternal snows.
Mourn'd his lost bride, the infernal powers' deceit,
And curs'd the vain, illusive, gifts of fate.

When Bacchus' Orgies stain'd the midnight skies,
Their proffers scorn'd, the Thracian matrons rise ;
Their hopeless rage the bleeding victim tore,
His sever'd limbs are scatter'd on the shore ;
Rent from his breathless corse, swift Hebrus sweeps
His gory visage to the distant deeps.

Yet when cold death sate trembling on his tongue,
With fainting soul, Euridice he sung,
Ah dear, ah lost Euridice, he cries,
Euridice, the echoing shore replies.

THE TRIAL OF FAITH.*

BY TIMOTHY DWIGHT, D. D.

PART I.
DANIEL, CHAP. I.

BENEATH the dawn, o'er Babel's fruitful plain,
  In proud effulgence mov'd the conquering train.
Full on the fun's broad beam their buckler's ray
Streak'd the glad fields, and gave a mimic day.

G

---

* THIS Poem is reprinted from the New-Haven Gazette, and the Connecticut Magazine, published by Meigs
and Dana, for the year 1786;—where it forms three Numbers of a Periodical Paper, undertaken by Dr. Dwight—
and is introduced by the following Preface, viz.——" The
' inclosed Poem is handed you for publication. I have
' long thought that the Bible furnished many subjects for
' poetry, far more deserving the ambition and efforts of
' genius, than those to which it is commonly dedicated. I
' do not mean merely that they are subjects more friendly
' to virtue, but to poetry. They are more sublime, novel,
' beautiful, agreeable, and in every way interesting.——
' Perhaps this experiment may not have been so happily
' made, as to elucidate the truth of this opinion. But as
' it is, it is submitted to the judgment of your readers.
' Should it have the happy influence to induce even one
' person of poetical talents, to apply those talents to this
' method of ornamenting his own character, and that of
' his country, I shall think my labours not unhappily di-
' rected."

With ſpiry ſplendor varying ſtandards glow'd ;
In pomp ſublime majeſtic chieftains rode ;
The ſilver clarions gave a ſolemn ſound,
And cars unnumber'd, thundering ſhook the ground.

There JUDAH's ſpoils in proud diſplay were borne ;
There purple veſture mock'd the riſing morn ;
There ſacred veſſels, rich from Ophir's mine,
Beam'd their ſtrong light, and imag'd art divine ;
There mov'd the prince, the queen, the lord, the ſage,
And hapleſs captive throngs of every age.

High-thron'd, the monarch from his golden car,
Survey'd the trophies of ſucceſsful war.
Majeſtic, tall, the mighty hero roſe,
Born to command, and dreadful to his foes :
His loſty limbs, enrob'd in rich attire
Of ſteel, and gold, were circled round with fire :
His pride, his ſoul, expanded at the ſight,
And his glad eye-balls warm'd with living light.

As o'er the captive train he caſt his eyes,
And heard, unmov'd, their mingled groans and cries,
Four youths, companions, ſilent paſs'd along,
By form diſtinguiſh'd from the vulgar throng.
Fair o'er them trembled beauty's purple flame ;
Their eyes, as angels', caſt a ſunny beam ;
Sublime their port ; ſerene their ſolemn look ;
By fear unaw'd, by heavieſt woes unbroke ;
To ills ſuperior ; earth and time above ;
But touch'd with kindred woe, and yearning love.
The monarch gaz'd.—His fierce and hardy mind
Then firſt with ſweet and tender thoughts refin'd ;

He felt each nerve with ftrange emotion thrill,
And down each cheek new tears in filence fteal.
No more the hoft, no more the·fpoils appear'd ;
No more the trump's infpiring voice was heard ;
Fix'd as he gaz'd, to foft compaffion won,
The pomp was buried, and the triumph gone.

  To Arioch then, his favor'd, faithful flave,
The turning prince his fovereign pleafure gave :
" Seeft thou, my Arioch, thofe bright, youthful forms ;
" What grace furrounds them, and what beauty warms !
" With what fair pride, magnificently great,
" They move fuperior to their humble fate !
" For arms, for empire, not for bondage made,
" They win my foul, and claim imperial aid.
" Go then, my Arioch, go, their fteps purfue ;
" With gentle fympathy their fouls fubdue ;
" Their monarch's favour to their hearts enfure ;
" Win them from grief ; difrobe their rags impure ;
" Their courfe immediate to the palace bend ;
" Let faithful Ashpenaz their fteps attend ;
" Superior far to all in every grace,
" Among the chofen youths appoint the place."

  The monarch fpake. The faithful chief obey'd,
And to the palace ftrait the youths convey'd.
There Ashpenaz, the eunuch's prince, receiv'd,
To hope reftor'd them, and from want reliev'd.
Cheer'd with kind words, their every wifh obey'd,
And thus, with foft and tender accent, faid :——

  " All-lovely youths ! attir'd with every grace,
' The beft, and brighteft, of your haplefs race,

' Think not, from war's dire scenes, the Assyrian mind,
' To love imp rvious, or to misery blind.
' Even the great prince, our mighty realm who sways,
' Train'd in fierce wars, and nurs'd in bloody ways,
' Though proudly borne on Conquest's lofty wings,
' Lord of a world, and king of countless kings,
' Yet bade me kindly every want supply,
' No hope extinguish, and no joy deny.

 ' By his command, on kingly dainties fed,
' Serv'd by his slaves, and in his palace bred,
' In every art, in every mystery train'd,
' By lords approv'd, by royal love sustain'd.
' Your lives, in peace serene, shall glide away,
' New joys returning with returning day.

 ' For me, my bosom, not of stubborn steel,
' Well knows to love, and long has learn'd to feel.
' Your woes, O Youths, your nation's fate severe,
' Pierce my sad soul, and prompt the tender tear.
' Each gentle act, that marks a parent's hand,
' From faithful ASHPENAZ assur'd command;
' From earliest years, to youths a constant guide,
' 'Tis joy to bless them, and to serve is pride.''

 Thus spoke the prince. With meek, but solemn grace,
The elder youth return'd this sad address:
' O Prince of Eunuchs, soothing friend of woe!
' Thy gentle solace bids our sorrows flow:
' With love, with gratitude, our bosoms burn,
' But, pierc'd with grief, our hapless nation mourn.
' For ah! her sons, of every good forlorn,
' Waste with dire want, or shrink from piercing scorn;

' Or rage, in flaughter bids them weltering roll ;
' Or gloomy flavery blafts the wither'd foul ;
' Her childlefs mothers fpread the reeking ground ;
' Her babes, unpitied, glut the hungry hound ;
' Levell'd in duft, her heaven-built Temple lies,
' And SALEM's fmoking ruins fill the fkies.
' More dread thefe fplendors fhew the fearful doom,
' As day more deeply fhades the darkfome tomb :
' Then, mid all joys, permit our hearts to mourn,
' Nor think thy goodnefs meets a bafe return."

He fpoke.   The prince, to chambers proud and fair,
Led the fad youths, and footh'd their rifing care,
Their graceful forms in fplendid garments drefs'd,
And kindly cheer'd their troubled minds to reft.

As now all-fragrant fpread the rich repaft,
Cates of all climes, and wines of every tafte ;
Deep cares revolving in his troubled breaft,
His chofen friends the elder youth addrefs'd :——

   " O youths, refin'd in fierce affliction's flame,
' Like gold, refulgent with undroffy beam !
' Now new alarms your virtuous minds affail,
' New dangers tempt, and untried foes prevail.
' As icy rocks, by winter beat in vain,
' Yeild to mild funs, and melt in vernal rain,
' So the firm heart, no cruelty could move,
' May lofe each virtue in the beams of love.
' Thofe cates, compos'd of all things rich and rare,
' Cull'd with nice art, and drefs'd with fkilful care,
' From truth's fair path our footfteps foftly charm,
' Our prayers enfeeble, and our faith difarm.

' To pureſt food the ſacred law confin'd,
' The taſte luxurious, and the wandering mind.
' Fix'd be our hearts its high beheſts to obey,
' Nor let vain banquets lure our feet aſtray.
' From humble pulſe ſereneſt peace ſhall ſpring,
' Health nerve the limbs, and lift the mental wing;
' The ſoul, the form, with health and beauty bloom,
' And heaven complacent grant a milder doom.''

Thus ſpoke the youth.   With ſmiles of pure delight,
In duty's path the aſſenting friends unite,
To heaven the feaſt, the roving wiſh reſign'd,
And gain'd the banquet of the obedient mind.

The courteous prince, by ſoft intreaties led,
Indulg'd their prayer, and gave the humble bread.
Heaven bleſs'd its ſons.—As mid the inferior grove,
Four beauteous pines aſcend the clouds above,
Mid heats, and droughts, and ſtorms, and froſt, and ſnow,
Through the full year with living verdure grow,
O'er every wood, with pride majeſtic, reign,
And wave exulting round the adjacent plain :
In port, in ſtature, thus, with thoughts ſublime,
And worth, ſuperior to the aſſaults of time,
Their gentle manners, great beyond diſguiſe,
Friendly to man, and faithful to the ſkies,
The favour'd captives grew, and learn'd to ſoar
Through all the myſteries of Chaldean lore ;
Learn'd how the ſtars in ſolemn ſplendor roll ;
How countleſs realms compoſe one mighty whole ;
What arts, what mazes, through the ſyſtem run ;
How hoſts are marſhall'd, and how fields are won.

THE TRIAL OF FAITH.

BY THE SAME.

PART II.
DANIEL, CHAP. II.

THUS rofe the youths, by lords and kings approv'd,
By earth exalted, and by Heaven belov'd,
When, loft in flumbers as the fovereign lay,
What time fair Phofphor fings the approach of day,
Full to his eyes a vifion rofe fublime,
Big with dread myfteries of afcending time.
Alarm'd, awak'd, he left the thorny bed;
His fleep all vanifh'd, and the vifion fled :
In vain he tried the wonders to reftore,
The fleeted phantom met his eyes no more.

Then deep convulfions fhook his ftormy mind,
That knew no croffes, and no wifh refign'd.
At once he fummon'd all the learn'd and wife,
Skill'd to explain, and artful to difguife,
Practis'd to bode, in words of foothing guile,
New feats, new triumphs, and new realms of fpoil.
And thus the king —— "Let every fage and feer,
Dreamer of dreams, and ftar-taught prophet hear!
This night, as funk in fleep, your monarch lay,
When truth's clear dreams attend approaching day,

Before my eyes a folemn vifion rofe,
Clear, full, diftinct, as morn's full fplendor glows;
Fill'd with dread fcenes, with acts of mighty name,
With change of empires, and with years of fame.
I wak'd—I rofe—but all the events of night
Fled from my view, and took their final flight.
Then hear, ye fages; borne by fkill fublime,
Thro' the dark ages of afcending time,
Explore the vifion, make the wonders known;
And tell what changes wait the Affyrian throne.''

    The Hero fpoke. Around the fpacious room
The ftrange command diffus'd a folemn gloom;
When thus a hoary fage——" O king divine,
Be endlefs life, and power, and honour thine!
Thy high behefts our hearts delight to obey;
We own thy glory, and we blefs thy fway.
But, O dread Prince, thy vifions to reveal,
Tranfcends the efforts of terreftial fkill.
Could ft thou, by memory's aid, the fcenes reftore,
Eafy thy feers the myftery would explore;
Would teach, for thee what crowns of triumph bloom,
Or what new nations meet the general doom.
The Gods alone, to whofe unbounded eye
Spread, in clear fight, all realms beneath the fky,
In obvious view the ftars immenfely roll,
Or on fleet pinions roves the wandering foul,
Can bid the eventful fcenes of night return,
Or ope the vanifh'd vifions of the morn.
A new command, a labour yet undone,
Thy will enjoins us, and thy voice makes known,

Nor lord requir'd, nor prophet e'er divin'd,
The secret motions of the mazy mind."

The monarch heard.   With sudden anger bright,
From his fierce eye-balls flash'd a withering light:
Sternly he cried,——"Base, impious wretches, hear
What wrath betides you, and what fate is near.
If, taught by heaven, your hearts the dream divine,
Wealth waits your steps, and crowns before you shine:
Prophets of truth, your race shall then be seen,
Lov'd by the Gods, and precious gifts to men.
But if this feat your purblind skill denies,
Each wretch, who soils the robe of wisdom, dies.
Mock'd by your boasts, my soul, no longer tame,
Shall rouse to sense, and bid just vengeance flame;
Each pamper'd carcase this right hand shall tear,
Glut the rob'd wolves, and feast the fowls of air.
Your hosts, your houses, give to flames a prey,
And sweep the nuisance from the world away."

He spoke: the seers withdrew.—The realm around,
From voice to voice diffus'd the dismal sound.
From ARIOCH, ASHPENAZ the tidings knew!
With thoughts all anxious to the youths he flew,
Rehears'd the tale——and "You, by worth betray'd,
Must soon," he cried, "be number'd with the dead."
"Fear not, O Prince,"—the elder youth reply'd:
"While heaven commands no ills the just betide.
Virtue refines, beneath affliction's power,
As gold runs beauteous from dissolving ore.
To light the dream shall rise, or, if the sky
Ordains our death, 'tis highest gain to die.

H

Unmov'd, our hearts, that thousand deaths have known
In Judah's woes, will meet the pangs of one;
From toil, and grief, and shame, unpinion'd rise,
And mix with angels in their native skies.
But haste, ah haste, and faithful ARIOCH bring,
E're he commence the vengeance of the king;
This night, shall Heaven the vanish'd scenes restore,
And save the prophets from vindictive power."

The Prince to ARIOCH flew, and, bath'd in tears,
Rehears'd the tale of mingled hopes, and fears.
He came: And pleas'd to stay the monarch's rage,
Led to the throne the young, unbearded sage.
With mild regard, the softening sovereign view'd,
While worth, and beauty, half his wrath subdued,
Heard him, with modest mien, his hope propose,
That Heaven, ere morn, the vision would disclose,
And bade glad ARIOCH vengeance dire delay,
'Till the wish'd hour should ope the promis'd day.

Those hours, the youths consum'd in fasts severe,
And the pure fervence of effectual prayer.
The God of worlds, to whom, with beam divine,
Fairer than morn the sons of Zion shine,
With love all bounteous bade the vision rise,
Dread, full, and clear, to DANIEL's slumbering eyes.

At earliest dawn, the youths, in bright array,
Toward the new palace bent their early way;
Through rows of lords, and rows of kings they pass'd,
While eyes of wonder thousands on them cast;
For round the court had spread the fearful doom,
That mark'd the guiltless Magi to the tomb.

Before the throne the beardlefs prophets ftood ;
Round their fair forms the grace of virtue glow'd ;
Pleas'd, the great monarch view'd : With fofter ray,
His eye-balls fmil'd their fiercer flames away ;
His fettling vifage loft its wrathful form,
As Spring looks fair behind a wintery ftorm.

" O KING of kings?" the elder youth began—
" Thy dread requeft tranfcends the power of man.
In vain thy feers the vifion would regain ;
Like ours, their wifhes, toils, and tears, are vain.
'Tis God alone the wonders can difplay,
The God, who form'd the heaven, the earth, and fea ;
Naked, and clear, before whofe fearching eye,
The foul, the thoughts, and deep affections lie ;
He brought the eventful vifion to thy fight,
And he again commands it into light.

" What time the dew of peace around thy bed
The filent flumbers of the morning fpread,
Dread to thine eyes a wonderous image fhone,
Awful in form, in fplendor like the fun.
Its head of flaming gold, its arms and breaft,
Of filver fair, inferior worth confefs'd ;
Its thighs and belly glow'd with brazen light ;
Its legs, of iron, mark'd refiftlefs might ;
Its iron feet, commix'd with miry clay,
Difplay'd unfolid power, to time a prey.
When lo ! fpontaneous, from the mountains rent,
A ftone came thundering down, with fwift defcent ;
Full on the form, with mighty force it burft,
Crufh'd all its limbs, and ground its frame to duft ;

Borne by the winds, thou faw'ſt its ruins fly,
Like chaff, when whirlwinds ſweep the ſummer ſky.
And as a riſing cloud, but juſt beheld,
Approaching, widens o'er the aerial field,
Expands, aſcends, and, ſlow thro ether driven,
Sails thro the immenſe, and fills the bounds of heaven :
So the ſmall cliff to riſe, and ſwell, began,
Spread thro' the fields, the neighbouring groves o'er-ran,
O'er towns, o'er realms, o'er mountains, left the eye,
Uproſe beyond the clouds, and heav'd the boundleſs ſky.

" 'Tis thus, O king ! the Lord of Heaven declares,
What ſcenes roll onward with the tide of years.
By us, his ſovereign voice to thee makes known,
And tells what changes wait the Aſſyrian throne.

" Thou art this head of gold : Thy power ſublime,
Rules thouſand kings, and ſpreads thro every clime.
But ſoon thy glory haſtens to decay,
Soon the bright arms commence a humbler ſway :
That too ſhall fail ; the brazen kingdom riſe,
Like ocean, ſpreading to ſurrounding ſkies.
As iron then an empire ſtrong ſhall ſpring,
Subdue each realm, and vanquiſh every king :
Beneath its wonderous power, all nature yeilds,
Europe's lone wilds, and Aſia's cultur'd fields.
Hence various kings, to art, and force, a prey,
As iron potent, yet diſſolv'd like clay :
Unſound, unſolid, ſhall their empire riſe,
Varying, as clouds their changes in the ſkies.
In thoſe far diſtant days, o'er every land,
Shall God's dread ſceptre rear its high command :

Before its power, refifting powers decay;
Nations, and kings, and empires, melt away;
Through unknown wilds the vaft dominion roll,
Extend its conquering force from pole to pole;
From morn's far regions reach the fhores of even,
Fill earth, and time, and rear its pomp to heaven.
Thus, King of kings! the heavens thy dream reftore,
And teach the changes of terreftial power."

The monarch heard, and look'd, when heavenly flame,
Round the fair youths fhould caft a golden beam;
Or d'er their limbs inftinctive lightnings run;
Or rainbow'd pinions lift them to the fun.
Proftrate to earth he fell: and,—" Oh!" he cries,
" Your God is Lord of gods, and worlds, and fkies:
He, only he, could make thefe vifions known;
Let praife, and glory, wait his heavenly throne."

To DANIEL, then the raptur'd hero bade
Incenfe be fir'd, and rich oblations paid;
O'er his prime lords his favourite place ordain'd,
A prince to every king, and every land:
While, high o'er BABEL's realm, his partners fate
In kingly favour, and judicial ftate.

Where'er they pafs'd, purfuing wonder came;
The Magi blefs'd, the children lifp'd their name;
To them were Judah's prayers and bleffings given,
And the poor mark'd them as the fons of Heaven.

THE TRIAL OF FAITH.

BY THE SAME.

PART III.
DANIEL, CHAP. III.

A ND now once more, the fpacious empire round,
    War's fearful clarion ceas'd its fhrilling found ;
Her voice harmonious, on fubfiding gales,
Sweet peace refounded through the glad'ening vales :
When lo, new fears the faithful friends await,
And other trials lour'd approaching fate.
Long through the monarch's foul the project ran,
(Grateful to proud and heaven-dethroning man)
To bind the foul, the confcience to enchain,
And force one worfhip through his wide domain.
Fir'd with the fond defign, an image fair,
Rich with pure gold, and gem'd with many a ftar.
He form'd, fair image of the morning fun,
Acknowledg'd guardian of th' Affyrian throne.
To this, his foul decreed mankind fhould bow,
Each victim burn, and rife each facred vow,
And bade his mighty lords direct their way
To meet their fovereign, on th' appointed day.
North of proud Babel's walls, from fky to fky,
The plain of Dura left the labouring eye :

There willows wav'd o'er Tygris flowery fide :
There broad Euphrates roll'd his mighty tide.
This the dread fcene the monarch's will ordain'd ;
And hither throng'd the lords of many a land.
As now the deftin'd morn her luftre fhed,
Here o'er the fields a hoft immenfely fpread ;
Kings, nobles, chieftains, every fage and feer,
And hofts of flaves, and warriors gather'd here.

   Bright rofe, in pomp divine, the imperial fun ;
Light, life, and joy danc'd round his golden throne ;
The heavens unclouded fmil'd a fairer blue ;
Reviving beauty cloath'd the world anew ;
As on old ocean glows the fun's broad ray,
And lights his glafly fields with mimic day ;
So, kindled by his beams, around the plain,
A new morn trembled o'er the unnumber'd train ;
From helms, and fhields, and fteeds, and cars, afpires
A general glory of immingling fires :
The Tygris brighten'd in the golden beam,
And fweeter murmurs foften'd o'er the ftream.
On a tall pedeftal, before them fhone
The facred image of the rifing fun ;
In folemn pomp, a hero rofe fublime,
His eye deep piercing through the fcenes of time.
When firft the orb, afcending from the main,
Caft his far level'd beams along the plain,
The form fuperb with every fplendor fhone,
Streak'd the gay fields, and feem'd another fun.
There the deep ruby pour'd a crimfon ray ;
The funny topaz fhed a rival day :

Of every hue the mimic rainbow came,
And join'd its varied lights in one tranfcendant flame.
Far round the plain the throng unnumber'd ftood,
And gaz'd in filence on the imag'd god,
When thus the heralds cried, "With reverent ear
Your Monarch's voice, ye kings and nations, hear,
What time the notes of mingled mufic roll,
With magic influence on th' enraptur'd foul,
Before you golden form, ye fuppliants all
Proftrate on earth, with facred homage, fall.

They fpoke : as, borne thro' fome far winding vale,
The voice of ocean leads the fpringing gale ;
More loud, more folemn from the diftant fhore,
The flow, deep murmurs rife, and fwell, and roar ;
Propp'd on his ftaff, the hoary feaman ftands,
And calls back happier times, and other lands ;
Through his limbs thrills the youth-renewing charm,
And fkies, and winds, and waves, his bofom warm :
So fudden, from ten thoufand pipes and ftrings,
Loud, full and clear, the voice of mufic fprings :
O'er the glad plain, the breathing founds exhale,
And fwell, and wanton in the rifing gale ;
Now deep, majeftic in dread pomp they roll ;
Now foftly languifh on the yeilding foul ;
Now folemn awe, now lively zeal infpire,
Wake heavenly dreams, and light romantic fire :
Now funk on earth, the unnumber'd fuppliants lie,
And fmoking altars cloud the fragrant fky.

'Mid the vaft throng, the friends of **Daniel** ftood,
Nor bent the knee before the golden god.

Alone they stood; for at the palace gate,
So the king bade, in judgement Daniel sate,
The Magi saw, and straight, by envy led,
Flew to the king, and thus impatient said——
(For tho' the youths preserv'd from death their race,
Their bosoms sicken'd at their rivals' place)
O prince! regardless of thy dread decree,
The Jews, so honor'd, lov'd and bless'd by thee,
Before yon golden God refuse to bow,
Present the prayer, or pay the solemn vow.
They slight thy gods, despise thy glorious name,
Nor heed the vengeance of the fearful flame.

Fir'd at the tale, before their sovereign king
He bade fierce guards the sons of Judah bring.
Serene they came. And dare your hearts, he cries,
Against the terrors of my anger rise?
Dare ye refuse before yon god to bow,
Present the prayer, and pay the solemn vow?
Then know from me, vain youths, repenting know,
Before you flames of fearful vengeance glow.
Nor hope to 'scape. What man, what god can save,
When I command you to the burning grave?
Be warn'd; be wise, your monarch's god adore;
Nor tempt the dangers of resistless power.

He spoke. As cherubs, dress'd in robes of light,
To earth, on heaven's high errands, wing their flight,
With solemn, sweet, complacent smile appear,
And blossom in immortal beauty here:
So, rosy splendor purpling o'er his face,
With **meekly dignity and matchless grace,**

I

Whilſt on the king he caſt a heavenly look,
That half revers'd the ſentence ere he ſpoke.
His lifted eye ſerene with ſolemn pride,
With gentle voice, the elder* youth replied,
Well pleas'd, O prince! our hearts confeſs thy ſway,
And all thy juſt commands with joy obey ;
Faithful and patient, every toil ſuſtain,
Unaw'd by danger, and unmov'd by pain.
But the great God who form'd the earth and ſeas,
Firſt claims our homage, firſt demands our praiſe :
To him alone our knees in worſhip bend ;
To him our praiſes and our prayers aſcend ;
His mighty arm his faithful ſons ſhall ſave
From all the terrors of the burning grave ;
Or bid the flames with harmleſs fury glow ;
Or crown with endleſs bliſs the tranſient woe.
But know, Aſſyrian prince! ſhould ills moſt dire
Rend our rack'd hearts, and bid our lives expire ;
Should virtue yeild to unrelenting power,
And heaven forſake us in the dreadful hour ;
Still to his throne our ſacred thoughts ſhall riſe,
Nor heed the gods that dwell beneath the ſkies.

  He ſpoke : Again, with ecſtaſies of ire,
The king's full viſage flaſh'd infernal fire ;
Fiercely he bade his guards the offenders bind,
And bear them forth, their feet and arms confin'd,
Through the wide hoſt their guilt and fate proclaim,
And light the furnace with a ſeven-fold flame.

* Shadrach.

The guards obey'd.   As near the feat of woe,
Their eyes beheld the fearful vengeance glow,
They claim'd, with fervent prayers, the pitying fky,
And fix'd their fouls to fuffer and to die.
Serene, they faw the dark and dreadful fires,
Felt the fierce heat, and ey'd the gloomy fpires;
Serene, they heard the long, deep murmurs roar,
As diftant, rifing whirlwinds rend the fhore.

Forth to the flames the unfriended youths they caft;
Nor 'fcap'd the eager guards the fcorching blaft:
Far round them fhot a long, infolding fpire,
And wrap'd them helplefs in the mantling fire.

Mean time the king, the ftorm of vengeance o'er,
His wrath provok'd, his will oppos'd no more,
Felt other thoughts, and paffions more refin'd
Compofe the fettling tumult of his mind.
Softening, he thought on all their conduct paft,
Their virtue fpotlefs, and their wifdom vaft,
The wondrous dream, to them, with Daniel, given,
And all their pillar'd confidence in heaven.
His will they brav'd, of pains nor death afraid;
But ftill with mildeft meeknefs difobey'd;
With fuch firm truth, fuch peaceful words denied,
As fpoke the foul of virtue, not of pride.
Who knows, he whifper'd, but their well taught mind,
Serves nobler gods, with worfhip more refin'd?
Who knows but he who could the dream reftore,
May fave his favourites from the furnace' power?

As thus he fpoke, with wand'ring courfe and flow,
He turn'd his footfteps towards the feat of woe:

'Till, with unguided, heedlefs feet he came
Where full before him burn'd the difmal flame.
When lo, dread fcenes amaz'd his wilder'd fight :
The youths walk'd peaceful through the horrid light :
Harmlefs around them climb'd the circling fpires,
And mild as zephyrs play'd the lambent fires.
Hymns of fweet praife the adoring prophets fung,
And mid hoarfe murmurs raptur'd warblings rung.

He gaz'd : at once, with light and beauty new,
Through the dread cavern fudden fplendor flew ;
A new dawn brighten'd o'er the dreary tomb,
Drown'd the dark flames and quench'd the fullen gloom.
So when the morn's bright face, in fair attire,
Through orient windows ftrikes the wintry fire,
The red flames wither in the etherial ray,
And all their earthly luftre dies away.

He gaz'd ; when lo ! a form of bodied light,
Sprung from the fun and like the parent bright,
In flow and ftately grandeur, trod the fcene,
And the dread cavern fmil'd, a Heaven within.
Fair ftars his wondrous crown, his ftrange attire
The lucid rainbow's many-colour'd fire ;
Like threads of burnifh'd filver, round his head,
His twinkling locks in folemn glory play'd ;
In pomp divine above his fhoulders borne,
And dipt in rofeate beams of rifing morn,
His long wings waving, fell : beneath his feet,
The unnumber'd ftreams of fpringing light'nings meet.
Full on the friends he beam'd a fun-bright fmile,
Tranfcendent meed of all their faith and toil !

Complacence pure, all thoughts, all minds above,
That op'd the yearnings of redeeming love.
Such ſmiles ſalute th' unbòdied ſoul forgiven ;
Such ſmiles improve the ſainted race of Heaven ;
Such ſmiles ſerene, with unextinguiſh'd ray,
Purpled the opening morn of endleſs day.
At once ſoft ſounds of gratulation rung ;
Strange muſic play'd, unſeen muſicians ſung ;
The ſolemn ſounds with more than mortal fire,
Wav'd with mild warblings, o'er th' etherial lyre :
Marbled, on earth the proſtrate monarch lay,
And ſwoon'd his vanquiſh'd ſenſe and ſoul away.

At length reſummon'd from the gloomy dead,
His opening eyes beheld the viſion fled.
With ſtrong, but plaintive voice, amaz'd he cried,
Sons of the ſky and earth's tranſcendent pride !
Forth from thoſe dreary flames triumphant come,
And quit the manſions of the deſtin'd tomb.

Forth came the youths ; unſing'd their fair attire,
Their limbs unconſcious of the potent fire ;
The king, the nobles mark'd with ſolemn gaze,
And ſighs and ſilence own'd their deep amaze.

Round the wide plain the ſaddening pomp decay'd ;
The muſic died, the vaſt aſſembly fled ;
The knee unbent, the image ceaſ'd to adore ;
The extinguiſh'd altars ſhed perfumes no more ;
The golden form apart forſaken ſtood,
And not a ſuppliant hail'd the ſlighted god :
Round the wide circuit brooding ſilence lay,
And clouds of deepeſt gloom o'ercaſt the day.

Then through his boundless empire Heaven's great name,
The humbl d monarch bade his criers proclaim.
To Heaven s great God, they cried, your honors pay,
Let kings and nations own his sovereign sway ;
With power divine to earth his angel came,
And sav'd his prophets from the sevenfold flame.

To Babel's walls return'd the royal train :
Their wonted honors cloth'd the youths again.
With transport, Daniel heard his friends relate
Their glorious triumph o'er the destin'd fate ;
The flames by heavenly power innoxious made ;
The solemn glories on the angel shed ;
In dreams the labor'd pomp forever gone ;
The tyrant vanquish'd and his god o'erthrown.

Belov'd, rever'd, the sons of virtue shin'd,
Heirs of the skies, and patrons of mankind.
Through all th' Assyrian world their bounty spread ;
All Judah triumph'd ; all oppression fled ;
Their glad approach, instinctive homage bless'd ;
Crouds bent before them, lords and kings caress'd ;
To them the songs of every realm were given,
And ceaseless round them glow'd the light of heaven.

ADDRESS

OF THE

GENIUS of COLUMBIA,

To the Members of the Continental Convention.

BY THE SAME.

FROM weſtern ſkies, a cloud of glory came,
 A ſmall, dim ſpot, a torch of lambent flame;
Aſcending, widening, flow the ſkirts unroll'd,
Rainbow'd with fire, and warm'd with glowing gold.
There, borne by ſummon'd winds, in pomp ſublime,
His look far-piercing down the vaſt of time,
Where the long, narrowing vale deſerts the eye,
Unboſom'd dimly on the eternal ſky,
The Genius ſate. He ſaw, when faction ſpent,
No more with war his darling kingdom rent,
The ſtream of kindred blood forbore to flow,
And morn faint trembled o'er the night of woe,
Call'd from each ſiſter realm, the wiſe and great,
In Penn's fair walls, and awful council ſate;
Pois'd in their hands, Columbia's mighty ſway,
And tottering laws, and rights, and freedom, lay.

 He ſaw, when fairer than the glow of even,
And bright as viſions of diſcloſing heaven,
Full in his face a ſacred ſplendor ſhone,
And the weſt kindled with another ſun.

" All hail, my fons," he cried, " my voice attend,
Your country's genius, guardian, guide, and friend:
The counfels mark, that faithful friend fupplies,
Attend, and learn the dictates of the fkies.
Before you, lo! what fcenes of glory fpread,
The faireft, brighteft, nobleft, heaven has made:
Their home, where freedom, fcience, virtue, find,
The laft receffes of oppreff'd mankind.
The immenfe of empire here, amaz'd, defcry,
Where realms are loft, and hidden oceans lie;
Where Perfia's vaft would fink in fhades conceal'd,
And Rome's proud world diminifh to a field.
See, from the pole, where frozen fountains rife,
And pour their waters under torrid fkies,
Where Rhines and Danubes, rills and ftreamlets play,
To fwell the pomp of Miffifippi's fea;
Where a zone's breadth majeftic woods extend,
And other Andes o'er the ftorms afcend;
Where meadows bound the morn and evening rays;
Where plains are kingdoms, and where lakes are feas.

See thro all climes the unmeafur'd empire run,
And drink each influence from the lingering fun;
Pure fkies unbofom'd, days fereneft roll,
And gales of health, from Darien fan the pole.

In each blefs'd clime, to crown induftrious toil,
See every product fpring from every foil,
Here the fur whitens in the frozen fhade;
Here flocks unnumber'd crowd the paftur'd glade;
Here threatening famine double harvefts fcorn—
Europe's rich grains, and India's ufeful corn—

Virginia's fragrant pride, huge fleets convey,
And fields of rice float cumbrous o'er the sea,
While all its wealth, the world of waters yeilds,
And treasures fill the subterranean fields.
These goods to waft where'er expands the wind,
To bless and to sustain the human kind,
See, stretch'd immense from Cancer to the pole,
On either side contending oceans roll;
O'er this, all Europe wings her haughty sails;
O'er that, all India wafts on spicy gales;
While bays, and streams, and lakes, her realms explore,
And land each product at each happy door.

   To fill these realms, a generous race behold,
Of happiest genius, and of firmest mould;
In thoughts, in arts, in life, in language join'd,
One faith, one worship, one politic mind,
Patient, serene, in toils and dangers dire,
Their nerves of iron, and their souls of fire:
Call'd from all realms, these chosen sons have join'd
Expansive manners, and a genial mind,
The liberal sentiment, the adventurous thought,
With greatness teeming, and with goodness fraught;
Chain'd to no party; by no system bound;
Confining merit to no speck of ground;
Nor Britons, Frenchmen, Germans, Swiss, or Huns,
Of earth the natives, and of heaven the sons,
Regarding, loving, all the great and good,
Of every rank, clime, party, sect, and blood.

K

The swain, with blifs to Europe's climes unknown,
His wife, his house, his lands, his flock, his own,
Treads, independent, on the subject soil,
Prepar'd for every danger, every toil;
Prepar'd to see antarctic oceans roll,
To circle earth, and search the lonely pole;
Or thro the immense of science wind his way;
Or lift poetic wings beyond the day;
The ridgy front of death for freedom dare,
Or, round all regions, hush the voice of war.

Heaven from all climes this happy realm conceal'd,
While wolves and Indians roam'd the bloody field,
Till human rule a soft'ning aspect wore,
Till war's black chariot ceas'd to roll in gore,
Till bigot zeal resign'd his scarlet sway,
And his dread thunders puff'd in smoke away.

Thus oh how blefs'd the era of her fate,
How bright the morning, and how long the date!
For now each fair improvement of the mind,
Each nobler effort lifts the human kind;
Vast means of blifs mechanic arts combine;
All liberal arts the rugged soul refine;
Freedom, and right, and law, their reign assume,
Stern Power resist, and cheer the world's sad doom;
On nature's ocean, science lifts her sails,
Finds other stars, and catches nobler gales;
While dawning virtue beams from yonder sky,
And brighter suns arise on human joy.

Such scenes of blifs, ye sages, blefs your eyes:
For men, for realms like these, your plans devise.

Be then your counfels, as your fubject, great,
A world their fphere, and time's long reign their date.

Each party-view, each private good, difclaim,
Each petty maxim, each colonial aim ;
Let all Columbia's weal your views expand,
A mighty fyftem rule a mighty land ;
Yourfelves her genuine fons let Europe own,
Not the fmall agents of a paltry town.

Learn, cautious, what to alter, where to mend ;
See to what clofe projected meafures tend.
From preffing wants the mind averting ftill,
Thinks good remoteft from the prefent ill :
From feuds anarchial to oppreffion's throne,
Mifguided nations hence for fafety run ;
And through the miferies of a thoufand years,
Their fatal folly mourn in bloody tears.

Ten thoufand follies thro Columbia fpread ;
Ten thoufand wars her darling realms invade.
The private intereft of each jealous ftate ;
Of rule the impatience, and of law the hate.
But ah ! from narrow fprings thefe evils flow,
A few bafe wretches mingle general woe.
Still the fame mind her manly race pervades,
Still the fame virtues haunt the hallow'd fhades.
But when the peals of war her center fhook,
All private aims the anxious mind forfook.
In danger's iron-bond her race was one :
Each feparate good, each little view unknown.
Now rule, unfyftem'd, drives the mind aftray ;
Now private intereft points the downward way :

Hence civil difcord pours her muddy ftream,
And fools and villains float upon the brim ;
O'er all, the fad fpectator cafts his eye,
And wonders where the gems and minerals lie.

But ne'er of freedom, glory, blifs, defpond :
Uplift your eyes thofe little clouds beyond ;
See there returning funs, with gladdening ray,
Roll on fair fpring to chafe this wintry day.

Tis yours to bid thofe days of Eden fhine :
Firft, then, and laft, the federal bands entwine :
To this your every aim and effort bend :
Let all your efforts here commence and end.

O'er ftate concerns, let every ftate prefide ;
Its private tax controul ; its juftice guide ;
Religion aid ; the morals to fecure ;
And bid each private right thro time endure.

Columbia's interefts public fway demand,
Her commerce, impoft, unlocated land ;
Her war, her peace, her military power ;
Treaties to feal with every diftant fhore ;

To bid contending ftates their difcord ceafe ;
To fend thro all the calumet of peace ;
Science to wing thro every noble flight ;
And lift defponding genius into light.

Thro every ftate to fpread each public law,
Intereft muft animate, and force muft awe.
Perfuafive dictates realms will ne'er obey ;
Sway, uncoercive, is the fhade of fway.

Be then your task to alter, aid, amend;
The weak to strengthen, and the rigid bend;
The prurient lop; what's wanted to supply;
And graft new scions from each friendly sky.

Slow, by degrees, politic systems rise;
Age still refines them, and experience tries.
This, this alone consolidates, improves;
Their sinews strengthens; their defects removes;
Gives that consistence time alone can give;
Habituates men by law and right to live;
To gray-hair'd rules increasing reverence draws;
And wins the slave to love e'en tyrant laws.
But should Columbia, with distracted eyes,
See o'er her ruins one proud monarch rise;
Should vain partitions her fair realms divide,
And rival empires float on faction's tide;
Lo fix'd opinions 'gainst the fabric rage!
What wars, fierce passions with fierce passions wage!
From Cancer's glowing wilds, to Brunswick's shore,
Hark, how the alarms of civil discord roar!
" To arms," the trump of kindled warfare cries,
And kindred blood smokes upward to the skies.
As Persia, Greece, so Europe bids her flame,
And smiles with eye malignant, o'er her shame.
Seize then, oh! seize Columbia's golden hour;
Perfect her federal system, public power;
For this stupendous realm, this chosen race,
With all the improvements of all lands its base,
The glorious structure build; its breadth extend;
Its columns lift, its mighty arches bend!

On freedom, ſcience, arts, its ſtories ſhine,
Unſhaken pillars of a frame divine ;
Far o'er the Atlantic wild its beams aſpire,
The world approves it, and the heavens admire ;
O'er clouds, and ſuns, and ſtars, its ſplendors riſe,
Till the bright top-ſtone vaniſh in the ſkies.''

COLUMBIA.

BY THE SAME.

COLUMBIA, Columbia, to glory ariſe,
    The queen of the world, and child of the ſkies !
Thy genius commands thee ; with rapture behold,
While ages on ages thy ſplendors unfold.
Thy reign is the laſt, and the nobleſt of time,
Moſt fruitful thy ſoil, moſt inviting thy clime ;
Let the crimes of the eaſt ne'er encrimſon thy name;
Be freedom, and ſcience, and virtue, thy fame.

To conqueſt, and ſlaughter, let Europe aſpire ;
Whelm nations in blood, and wrap cities in fire ;
Thy heroes the rights of mankind ſhall defend,
And triumph purſue them, and glory attend.
A world is thy realm : for a world be thy laws,
Enlarg'd as thine empire, and juſt as thy cauſe ;
On Freedom's broad baſis, that empire ſhall riſe,
Extend with the main, and diſſolve with the ſkies.

Fair Science her gates to thy fons fhall unbar,
And the eaft fee thy morn hide the beams of her ftar.
New bards, and new fages, unrival'd fhall foar
To fame, unextinguifh'd, when time is no more ;
To thee, the laft refuge of virtue defign'd,
Shall fly from all nations the beft of mankind ;
Here, grateful to heaven, with tranfport fhall bring
Their incenfe, more fragrant than odours of fpring.

Nor lefs fhall thy fair ones to glory afcend,
And Genius and Beauty in harmony blend ;
The graces of form fhall awake pure defire,
And the charms of the foul ever cherifh the fire ;
Their fweetnefs unmingled, their manners refin'd
And virtue's bright image, inftamp'd on the mind,
With peace, and foft rapture, fhall teach life to glow,
And light up a fmile in the afpect of woe.

Thy fleets to all regions thy pow'r fhall difplay,
The nations admire, and the ocean obey ;
Each fhore to thy glory its tribute unfold,
And the eaft and the fouth yeild their fpices and gold,
As the day-fpring unbounded, thy fplendor fhall flow,
And earth's little kingdoms before thee fhall bow,
While the enfigns of union, in triumph unfurl'd,
Hufh the tumult of war, and give peace to the world.

Thus, as down a lone valley, with cedars o'erfpread,
From war's dread confufion I penfively ftray'd—
The gloom from the face of fair heav'n retir'd ;
The winds ceas'd to murmur ; the thunders expir'd ;

Perfumes, as of Eden, flow'd sweetly along,
And a voice, as of angels, enchantingly sung :
" Columbia, Columbia, to glory arise,
The queen of the world, and the child of the skies."

The SEASONS Moralized.

BY THE SAME.

BEHOLD the changes of the skies,
  And see the circling seasons rise ;
Hence, let the moral truth refin'd,
Improve the beauty of the mind.

Winter, late with dreary reign,
Rul'd the wide, unjoyous plain ;
Gloomy storms with solemn roar
Shook the hoarse, resounding shore,

Sorrow cast her sadness round,
Life and joy forsook the ground,
Death, with wild imperious sway,
Bade the expiring world decay.

Now cast around thy raptur'd eyes,
And see the beauteous spring arise ;
See, flow'rs invest the hills again,
And streams re-murmur o'er the plains.

Hark, hark, the joy-infpiring grove
Echoes to the voice of love ;
Balmy gales the found prolong,
Wafting round the woodland fong.

Such the fcenes our life difplays,
Swiftly fleet our rapid days ;
The hour that rolls forever on,
Tells us our years muft foon be gone.

Sullen Death, with mournful gloom
Sweeps us downwards to the tomb ;
Life, and health, and joy decay,
Nature finks, and dies away.

But the foul in gayeft bloom,
Difdains the bondage of the tomb ;
Afcends above the clouds of even,
And, raptur'd, hails her native heaven.

Youth, and peace, and beauty there
Forever dance around the year ;
An endlefs joy invefts the pole,
And ftreams of ceafelefs pleafure roll.

Light, and joy, and grace divine
With bright and lafting glory fhine :
Jehovah's fmiles, with heav'nly ray,
Diffufe a clear, unbounded day.

K

A HYMN,

Sung at the PUBLIC EXHIBITION of the SCHOLARS, belonging to the Academy in Greenfield, May 2d, 1788.

BY THE SAME.

HAIL child of light, returning Spring,
    Fair image, foretaste sweet, of heaven!
In thee our hearts thy Maker sing,
    By whose blest bounty thou wast given.

From thee the wintry glooms retire,
    The skies their purest beams display,
And winds, and showers, and suns conspire,
    To clothe the world with life and May.

Hail knowlege, hail, the moral spring
    That wakes the verdure of the mind!
To man, thy rays indulgent bring
    All fragrant flowers, and fruits refin'd.

Thy progress with the morn began,
    Before thee every region smil'd;
The savage brighten'd into man,
    And gardens blossom'd in the wild.

All hail fair Virtue, noblest good,
    The bliss and beauty of the skies!
By whom, to yonder blest abode,
    The humble, and the faithful rise.

While here fair Learning fmiles benign,
  And Spring leads on the genial year,
From realms of life and peace divine,
  Defcend, and bloom, and flourifh here.

And O thou fount of good fupreme,—
  The fun that lights eternal fpring,
At once of knowledge fource and theme,
  Thee firft, and laft, our voices fing !

Virtue, in every charm array'd,
  For this dark world, thy fufferings won ;
Thofe charms thy matchlefs life difplay'd,
  When here the incarnate fplendor fhone.

As dews refrefh, as funs revive,
  When clear and cloudlefs fhines the day,
Command our rifing race to live,
  And win them from the world away.

With thee, the fource of every grace,
  Our fong fhall end, as it began ;
Our hope, our truft, our joy, and praife,
  The Saviour, and the Friend of Man.

A SONG.

BY THE SAME.

LOOK, lovely maid, on yonder flow'r,
  And fee that bufy fly,
Made for the enjoyment of an hour,
  And only born to die.

See, round the rofe he lightly moves,
  And wantons in the fun,
His little life in joy improves,
  And lives, before 'tis gone.

From this inftinctive wifdom, learn,
  The prefent hour to prize;
Nor leave to-day's fupreme concern,
  'Till morrow's morn arife.

Say, lovlieft fair, canft thou divine
  That morrow's hidden doom?
Know'ft thou, if cloudlefs fkies will fhine,
  Or heaven be wrapt in gloom?

Fond man, the trifle of a day,
  Enjoys the morning light,
Nor knows, his momentary play
  Muft end, before 'tis night.

The prefent joys are all we claim;
  The paft are in the tomb;
And, like the poet's dream of fame,
  The future never come.

No longer then, fair maid, delay
   The promis'd fcenes of blifs;
Nor idly give another day,
   The joys affign'd to this.

If *then* my breaft can foothe thy care,
   'Twill *now* that care allay;
If joy this hand can yield, my fair,
   'Twill yield that joy to-day.

Quit then, oh quit! thou lovely maid,
   Thy bafhful, virgin pride;
To-day the happy plot be laid,
   The bands, to-morrow, tied!

The pureft joys fhall be our own,
   That e'er to man were giv'n;
And thofe bright fcenes, on earth begun,
   Shall brighter fhine in heaven.

THE CRITICS.*

A FABLE.

Written September 1785.

'*To every general rule there are exceptions.*'—Common Sense.

***

BY THE SAME.

***

'TIS said of every dog that's found,
    Of mongrel, spaniel, cur, and hound;
That each sustains a doggish mind,
And hates the new, sublime, refin'd.
'Tis hence the wretches bay the moon,
In beauty throned at highest noon;
Hence every nobler brute they bite,
And hunt the stranger-dog with spite;
And hence, the nose's dictates parrying,
They fly from meat to feed on carrion.
'Tis also said, the currish soul
The critic race possesses whole;
As near they come, in tho'ts and natures,
As two legg'd can, to four legg'd creatures;
Alike the things they love and blame,
Their voice, and language, much the same.

***

  * This Poem is reprinted from *The Gazette of the United States,* of July 13, 1791; where it was first published.

The Mufe this fubject made her theme,
And told me in a morning dream.
Such dreams you fages may decry ;
But Mufes know they never lie.
Then hear, from me, in grave narration,
Of thefe ftrange facts, the ftrange occafion.

In Greece Cynethe's village lay,
Well known to all, who went that way,
For dogs of every kindred famed,
And from true doggifh manners named.
One morn, a greyhound pafs'd the ftreet ;
At once the foul-mouth'd conclave met,
Huddling around the ftranger ran,
And thus their fmart *review* began.
" What tramper" with a grinning fneer,
Bark'd out the clumfy cur, " is here ?
No native of the town, I fee ;
Some foreign whelp of bafe degree.
I'd fhew, but that the record's torn,
We true Welfh curs are better born.
His coat is fmooth ; but longer hair
Would more become a dog by far.
His flender ear, how ftrait and floping
While ours is much improved by *cropping.*"

" Right," cried the blood-hound, " that ftrait ear
Seems made for nothing, but to hear ;
'Tis long agreed, thro' all the town,
That handfome ears, like mine, hang down ;
And tho' his body's gaunt, and round,
'Tis no true rawboned gaunt of hound.

How high his nose the creature carries!
As if on bugs, and flies, his fare is;
I'll teach this strutting, stupid log,
To smell's the business of a dog."

"Baugh-waugh!" the shaggy spaniel cried,
"What wretched covering on his hide!
I wonder where he lives in winter;
His strait, sleek legs too, out of joint are;
I hope the vagrant will not dare
His fledging with my fleece compare.
He never plung'd in pond or river,
To search for wounded duck and diver;
By kicks would soon be set a skipping,
Nor take, one half so well a whipping."

"Rat me," the lap-dog yelp'd, "thro' nature,
Was ever seen so coarse a creature?
I hope no lady's sad mishap
E'er led the booby to her lap;
He'd fright PRIMRILLA into fits,
And rob FOOLERIA of her wits;
A mere barbarian, Indian whelp!
How clownish, countryish, sounds his yelp!
He never tasted bread and butter,
Nor play'd the petty squirm and flutter;
Nor e'er, like me, has learn'd to fatten,
On kisses sweet, and softest patting."

"Some parson's dog, I vow," whined puppy;
"His rusty coat how sun-burnt! stop ye!"
The beagle call'd him to the wood.
The bull-dog bellowed, "Zounds! and blood!"

The wolf-dog and the maſtiff were,
The Muſe ſays, an exception here;
Superior both to ſuch foul p'ay,
They wiſh'd the ſtranger well away.

From *ſpleen* the *ſtriƈtures* roſe to *fury*,
" Villain," growl'd one, " I can't endure you."
" Let's ſeize the truant," ſnarl'd another,
Encored by every foul-mouth'd brother.
" 'Tis done," bark'd all, " we'll mob the creature,
And ſacrifice him to ill-nature."

The greyhound, who deſpiſed their breath,
Still tho't it beſt to ſhun their teeth.
Eaſy he wing'd his rapid flight,
And left the ſcoundrels out of ſight.

Good JUNO, by the ancients holden,
The genuine *notre-dame* of ſcolding,
Sate pleaſed, becauſe there'd ſuch a fuſs been,
And in the hound's place wiſh'd her huſband;
For here, even pleaſure bade her own,
Her ladyſhip was once out-done.
" Hail dogs," ſhe cried, " of every kind!
Retain ye ſtill this ſnarling mind,
Hate all that's good, and fair, and new,
And I'll a goddeſs be to you.

Nor this the only good you prove;
Learn what the fruits of JUNO's love.
Your ſouls, from forms, that creep all four on,
I'll raiſe, by ſyſtem Pythagorean,

M

To animate the human frame,
And gain my favorite tribe a name.
Be ye henceforth (fo I ordain)
Critics, the genuine curs of men.
To fnarl be ftill your higheft blifs,
And all your criticifm like this.
Whate'er is great, or juft, in nature,
Of graceful form, or lovely feature ;
Whate'er adorns the ennobled mind,
Sublime, inventive, and refin'd ;
With fpleen, and fpite, forever blame,
And load with every dirty name.
All things of nobleft kind and ufe,
To your own ftandard vile reduce,
And all in wild confufion blend,
Nor *heed* the *fubject, fcope,* or *end.*
But chief, when *modeft young beginners,*
'Gainft *critic laws,* by *nature* finners,
Peep out in verfe, and dare to run,
Thro' towns and villages your own,
Hunt them, as when yon ftranger dog
Set all your growling crew agog ;
Till ftunn'd, and fcared, they hide from view,
And leave the country clear for you."

This faid, the goddefs kind careffing,
Gave every cur a double bleffing.
Each doggifh mind, tho' grown no bigger,
Henceforth affumed the human figure,
The body walk'd on two ; the mind
To four, ftill chofe to be confin'd ;

Still creeps on earth, still scents out foes,
Is still led onward by the nose;
Hates all the good, it used to hate,
The lofty, beauteous, new, and great;
The stranger hunts with spite quintessent,
And snarls, from that day to the present.

EPISTLE to Col. HUMPHRYES.

GREENFIELD, 1785.

BY THE SAME.

FROM realms, where nature sports in youthful prime,
   Where Hesper lingers o'er his darling clime,
Where sunny genius lights his sacred flame,
Where rising science casts her morning beam,
Where empire's final throne in pomp ascends,
Where pilgrim freedom finds her vanish'd friends,
The world renews, and man from eastern fires,
Phœnix divine, again to Heaven aspires,
Health to my friend this happy verse conveys,
His fond attendant o'er the Atlantic seas.

   Health to my friend let every wish prolong;
Be this the burden of each artless song;
This in the prayer of every morn arise;
Thou angel guardian, waft it to the skies!

His devious courfe let fostering Heaven furvey;
Nor ills betide, nor foes arrest his way.

Nor health alone——may blifs thy path attend;
May truth direct thee, and may peace befriend;
From virtue's fount thy taintlefs actions flow;
The fhield of confcience blunt the dart of woe;
To rifing blifs refin'd above alloy,
Where budding wifhes blossom into joy,
Where glory dwells, where faints and feraphs fing,
Let Heaven, in profpect, tempt thy lifted wing.

Me the fame views, the fame foft tide of cares,
Bear gently onward down the ftream of years,
Still the fame duties call my courfe along;
Still grows, at times, the pain-deluding fong;
Still fcenes domeftic earthly joys refine,
Where bleft Maria mingles cares with mine;
The fame fond circle ftill my life endears,
Where Fairfield's elms, or Stamford s groupe appears;
Or where, in rural guife, around me fmile
Manfions of peace, and Greenfield's beauteous hill;
Still to my cot the friend delighted hies,
Aud one lov'd parent waits beneath the fkies.

To thee, far fummon'd from each native fcene,
With half the breadth of this wide world between,
How blefs'd the news my happy verfe conveys,
Of friends, divided by interfluent feas?
Health, peace, and competence, their walks furround,
On the bright margin of yon beauteous Sound;
Where Hartford fees the firft of waters glide,
Or where thy Avon winds his filver tide.

Yet thou muſt mourn a friend,* a brother dear,
And o'er departed merit drop a tear.
Him ſenſe illum'd, the hero's warmth inſpir'd,
Grace taught to pleaſe, and patriot virtue fir'd;
Alike in peace, in war, at home, abroad,
Worth gain'd him honor, where his footſteps trode;
Yet all in vain: his laurel'd garlands bloom;
But waſte their beauty on the untimely tomb.

Meantime, invited o'er the Atlantic tide,
Where arts refin'd allure thy feet aſide,
May'ſt thou, unmov'd by ſplendor's painted charms,
And ſteel'd, when pleaſure ſmiling ſpreads her arms,
The great ſimplicity of ſoul retain,
The humble fear of Heaven, and love of man.
When round thy courſe temptations ſweetly throng,
When warbling ſirens chant the luſcious ſong,
When wealth's fair bubble beams its hues afar,
When grandeur calls thee to her golden car,
When pleaſure opes the boſom bright of joy,
And the dy'd ſerpent gazes to deſtroy;
Oh! may the heavenly Guide thy paſſions warm,
Up virtue's hills thy feet reſiſtleſs charm,
Shew thee what crowns reward the glorious ſtrife,
And quicken fainting duty into life.

Oft has thine eyes, with glance indignant ſeen
Columbia's youths, unfolding into men,

---

* Major Elijah Humphreys, brother to Col. Humphreys,
who died in the Weſt-Indies, in 1785.

Their minds to improve, their manners to adorn,
To Europe's climes by fond indulgence borne;
Oft haft thou feen thofe youths, at cuftom's fhrine,
Victims to pride, to folly, and to fin,
Of worth bereft, of real fenfe forlorn.
Their land forget, their friends, their freedom fpurn;
Each noble caufe, each folid good defert,
For fplendor happinefs, and truth for art;
The plain, frank manners of their race defpife,
Fair without fraud, and great without difguife;
Where, thro the life the heart uncover'd ran,
And fpoke the native dignity of man.

For thefe, the gain let Virtue blufh to hear,
And each fad parent drop the plaintive tear!
Train'd in foul ftews, impoifon'd by the ftage,
Hoyl'd into gaming, Keyfer'd into age,
To fmooth hypocrify by Stanhope led,
To truth an alien, and to virtue dead,
Swoln with an Englifh butcher's four difdain,
Or to a Fribble dwindled from a man,
Homeward again behold the jackdaw run,
And yield his fire the ruins of a fon!

What tho' his mind no thought has e'er perplex'd,
Converfe illum'd, or obfervations vex'd;
Yet here, in each debate, a judge he fhines,
Of all, that man enlarges, or refines;
Religion, fcience, politics, and fong;
A prodigy his parts; an oracle his tongue.
Hift! hift! ye mere Americans, attend;
Ope wide your mouths; your knees in homage bend;

While Curl difclofes to the raptur'd view
What Peter, Paul, and Mofes, never knew;
The light of new-born wifdom fheds abroad,
And adds a * leanto to the word of God.
What Creole wretch fhall dare, with home-made foils,
Attack opinions, brought three thoufand miles;
Senfe, in no common way to mortals given,
But on Atlantic travellers breath'd by Heaven;
A head, *en queue,* by Monfieur Frizzle drefs'd;
Manners, a Paris Taylor's arts inveft;
Pure criticifm, form'd from *acted* plays;
And graces, that would even a Stanhope grace?
Commercial wifdom, merchants here inhale
From him, whofe eye hath feen the unfinifh'd bale;
Whofe feet have pafs'd the fhop, where pins were fold,
The wire was filver'd, and the heads were roll'd!
Conven'd, ye lawyers, make your humbleft leg!
Here ftands the man has feen Lord Mansfield's wig!
Phyficians hufh'd, hear Galen's lips diftil,
From Buchán's contents, all the Art to heal!
Divines, with reverence ceafe your fcripture whims,
And learn this male Minerva's moral fchemes;
Schemes theologic found in Drury-lane,
That prove the bible falfe, and virtue vain!
Heavens! fhall a child in learning, and in wit,
O'er Europe's climes, a bird of paffage flit;

---

* An awkward addition to a dwelling-houfe, very common
in New-England.

There, as at home, his stripling self unknown,
By novel wonders stupified to stone,
Shut from the wise, and by no converse taught,
No well-read day, nor hour of serious thought,
His head by pleasure, vice, and hurry, turn'd,
All prudence trampled, all improvements spurn'd;
Shall he, with less of Europe in his cap,
Than satchell'd school-boy guesses from the map,
On every subject struttingly decree,
Ken the far shore, and search the unfathom'd sea,
Where learning has her lamp for ages oil'd,
Where Newton ponders, and where Berkeley toil'd?
Of all the plagues, that rise in human shape,
Good Heaven, preserve us from the travell'd Ape!
* " Peace to all such :" but were there one, whose mind
Bold genius wing'd, and converse pure, refin'd,
By nature prompted science' realms to roam,
And both her Indies bring with rapture home;
Who men, and manners, search'd with eagle eye,
Exact to weigh, and curious to descry;
Himself who burnish'd with the hand of care,
Till kings might boast so bright a gem to wear;
Should he, deep plung'd in Circe's sensual bowl,
Imbrue his native manliness of soul,
With eye estrang'd, from fair Columbia turn,
Her youth, her innocence, and beauty scorn;
To that foul harlot, Europe, yield his mind,
Witch'd by her smiles, and to her snares resign'd;

* Pope's prologue to the Satires.

To nature's bloom prefer the rouge of art,
A tinsell'd outside to a golden heart,
Show, to the bliss by simple freedom given,
To virtue, Stanhope, and Voltaire to Heaven;
Who but must wish, the apostate youth to see?
Who but must agonize, were Humphreys he?
But all thy soul shall 'scape, the escape to aid,
Fair to thy view be every motive spread.
Of each gay cause the dire effects survey,
And bring the painted tomb disclos'd to day.
Tho' there proud pomp uprears his throne on high;
Tho' there the golden palace lights the sky;
Tho' wealth unfolds her gay, Edenian seats,
Her walk of grandeur, and her wild of sweets;
The stage, the park, the ring, the dance, the feast,
Charm the pall'd eye, and lure the loathing taste;
Yet there fierce war unceasing sounds alarms;
Pride blows the trump, and millions rush to arms;
See steel and fire extinguish human good!
See realms manur'd with corses, and with blood!
At slaughter's shrine expires the new-born-joy,
And all Jehovah's bounty fiends destroy.
See the huge jail in gloomy grandeur rise,
Low'r o'er mankind, and mock the tempted skies!
Hear the chain clank! the bursting groan attend!
And mark the neighboring gibbet's pride ascend.
See earth's fair face insatiate luxury spoils!
For one poor tyrant, lo, a province toils!
To brothels, half the female world is driven,
Lost to themselves, and reprobates of heaven.

N

There too refinement glances o'er the mind;
And nought but vice, and outfide, is refin'd;
To vice aufpicious, brilliant manners blend,
The waxen faint, and finner, foe and friend,
Melt from the foul each virtue, as they fhine,
And warm the impoifon'd bloffom into fin.
In fair Columbia's realms, how chang'd the plan;
Where all things bloom, but, firft of all things, man!
Lord of himfelf, the independent fwain,
Sees no fuperior ftalk the happy plain:
His houfe, his herd, his harveft, all his own,
His farm a kingdom, and his chair a throne.
Unblench'd by foul hypocrify, the foul
Speaks in her face, and bids his accents roll;
(Her wings unclipp'd) with fire inftinctive warms,
Strong pulfes feels, and bold conceptions forms;
At nobleft objects aims her flight fupreme,
The purpofe vaft, and enterprize extreme.
Hence round the pole her fons exalt the fail,
Search fouthern feas, and roufe the Falkland whale;
Or on bold pinions hail the Afian fkies,
And bid new ftars in fpicy oceans rife.
Hence in bright arms her chiefs fuperior flame,
Even now triumphant on the fteep of fame,
Where Vernon's Hero mounts the throne fublime,
And fees no rival grace the reign of time.
Hence countlefs honours rifing Med'cine claims;
Hence Law prefents her conftellated names;
The Sacred Science fees her concave bright
Inftarr'd, and beauteous, with the fons of light;

Hence Edwards cheer'd the world with moral day,
And Franklin walk'd, unhurt, the realms where lightnings
Mechanic genius hence exalts his eye,   [play.
All powers to meafure, and all fcenes defcry,
Bids Rittenhoufe the heavenly fyftem feign,
And Bufhnell fearch the chambers of the main.
Hence too, where Trumbull leads the ardent throng,
Afcending bards begin the immortal fong :
Let glowing friendfhip wake the cheerful lyre,
Bleft to commend, and pleas'd to catch the fire.
Be theirs the fame, to bards how rarely given !
To fill with worth the part affign'd by Heaven ;
Diftinguifh'd actors on life's bufy ftage,
Lov'd by mankind, and ufeful to the age ;
While fcience round them twines her vernal bays,
And fenfe directs, and genius fires their lays.
While this fair land commands thy feet to roam,
And, all Columbian, ftill thou plan'ft for home,
From thofe bright fages, with whofe miffion join'd,
Thou feek'ft to build the interefts of mankind,
Experience, wifdom, honour, may'ft thou gain,
The zeal for country, and the love of man.
There thro' the civil fcience may'ft thou run ;
There learn how empires are preferv'd, or won ;
How arts politic wide dominions fway ;
How well-train'd navies bid the world obey ;
How war's imperial car commands the plain,
Or rolls majeftic o'er the fubject main ;
Thro' earth, how commerce fpreads a fofter fway,
And Gallia's fons negociate realms away.

Then, crown'd with every gift, and grace, return,
To add new glories to the weſtern morn ;
With ſages, heroes, bards, her charms diſplay,
Her arts, arms, virtues, and her happy ſway ;
Bid o'er the world her conſtellation riſe,
The brighteſt ſplendor in the unmeaſur'd ſkies,
Her genial influence thro' all nations roll,
And huſh the ſound of war from pole to pole.

And oh, may he, who ſtill'd the ſtormy main,
And lightly wing'd thee o'er the glaſſy plain,
Thro' life's rough-billow'd ſea, with kinder gales,
With ſkies ſerener, and with happier ſails,
Each ſhoal eſcap'd, afar each tempeſt driven,
And nought but raptures round the enchanted Heaven,
To bliſs, fair ſhore, thy proſperous courſe convey,
And join my peaceful bark, companion of thy way.

THE PROSPECT OF PEACE.*

BY JOEL BARLOW, ESQUIRE.

THE closing scenes of Tyrants' fruitless rage,
　　The opening prospects of a golden age,
The dread events that crown th' important year,
Wake the glad song, and claim th' attentive ear.

　Long has Columbia rung with dire alarms,
While freedom call'd her injur'd sons to arms;
While various fortune fir'd th' embattled field,
Conquest delay'd, and victory stood conceal'd;
While closing legions mark'd their dreadful way,
And millions trembled for the dubious day.

　In this grand conflict heaven's Eternal Sire,
At whose dread frown the sons of guilt expire,
Bade vengeance rise, with sacred fury driven,
On those who war with Innocence and Heaven.

　Behold, where late the trembling squadrons fled,
Hosts bow'd in chains, and hapless numbers bled,
In different fields our numerous heroes rouse,
To crop the wreath from Britain's impious brows.

———

* This Poem is reprinted from the 12mo edition, printed by Thomas and Samuel Green, New-Haven, 1788,—and was delivered, by the Author, in Yale-College, at the Public Examination of the Candidates for the Degree of Bachelor of Arts; July 23, 1778.

Age following age fhall thefe events relate
'Till Time's old empire yield to deftin'd Fate;
Hiftoric truth our guardian chiefs proclaim,
Their worth, their actions, and their deathlefs fame;
Admiring crouds their life-touch'd forms behold
In breathing canvafs, or in fculptur'd gold,
And hail the Leader of the favorite throng,
The rapt'rous theme of fome heroic fong.

And foon, emerging from the orient fkies,
The blifsful morn in glorious pomp fhall rife,
Wafting fair Peace from Europe's fated coaft;
Where wand'ring long, in mazy factions loft,
From realm to realm, by rage and difcord driven,
She feemed refolv'd to reafcend her heaven.

This LEWIS view'd, and reach'd a friendly hand,
Pointing her flight to this far-diftant land;
Bade her extend her empire o'er the Weft,
And Europe's balance tremble on her creft!

Now, fee the Goddefs mounting on the day,
To thefe fair climes direct her circling way,
Willing to feek, once more, an earthly throne,
To cheer the globe, and emulate the fun.
With placid look fhe eyes the blifsful fhore,
Bids the loud-thundering cannon ceafe to roar;
Bids Britifh navies from thefe ports be toft,
And hoftile keels no more infult the coaft:
Bids private feuds her facred vengeance feel,
And bow fubmiffive to the public weal;
Bids long, calm years adorn the happy clime,
And roll down bleffings to remoteft time.

Hail! heaven-born Peace, fair Nurse of Virtue hail!
Here, fix thy fceptre and exalt thy fcale;
Hence, thro' the earth extend thy late domain,
'Till Heaven's own fplendor fhall abforb thy reign!

What fcenes arife! what glories we behold!
See a broad realm its various charms unfold;
See crouds of patriots blefs the happy land,
A godlike fenate and a warlike band;
One friendly Genius fires the numerous whole,
From glowing Georgia to the frozen pole.

Along thefe fhores, amid thefe flowery vales,
The woodland fhout the joyous ear affails;
Induftrious crouds in different labours toil,
Thofe ply the arts, and thefe improve the foil.
Here the fond merchant counts his rifing gain,
There ftrides the ruftic o'er the furrow'd plain,
Here walks the ftatefman, penfive and ferene,
And there the fchool boys gambol round the green.

See ripening harvefts gild the fmiling plains,
Kind Nature's bounty and the pride of fwains;
Luxuriant vines their curling tendrils fhoot,
And bow their heads to drop the cluftering fruit;
In the gay fields, with rich profufion ftrow'd,
The orchard bends beneath its yellow load,
The lofty boughs their annual burden pour,
And juicy harvefts fwell th' autumnal ftore.

Thefe are the bleffings of impartial heaven,
To each fond heart in juft proportion given.
No grafping lord fhall grind the neighbouring poor,
Starve numerous vaffals to increafe his ftore;

No cringing slave shall at his presence bend,
Shrink at his frown, and at his nod attend;
Afric's unhappy children, now no more
Shall feel the cruel chains they felt before,
But every State in this just mean agree,
To bless mankind, and set th' oppressed free.
Then, rapt in transport, each exulting slave
Shall taste that Boon which God and nature gave,
And, fir'd with virtue, join the common cause,
Protect our freedom and enjoy our laws.

At this calm period, see, in pleasing view,
Art vies with Art, and Nature smiles anew:
On the long, winding strand that meets the tide,
Unnumber'd cities lift their spiry pride;
Gay, flowery walks salute th' inraptur'd eyes,
Tall, beauteous domes in dazzling prospect rise;
There thronging navies stretch their wanton sails,
Tempt the broad main and catch the driving gales;
There commerce swells from each remotest shore,
And wafts in plenty to the smiling store.

To these throng'd seats the country wide resorts,
And rolls her treasures to the op'ning ports;
While, far remote, gay health and pleasure flow,
And calm retirement cheers the laboring brow.
No din of arms the peaceful patriot hears,
No parting sigh the tender matron fears,
No field of fame invites the youth to rove,
Nor virgins know a harsher sound than love.

Fair Science then her laurel'd beauty rears,
And foars with Genius to the radiant ftars.
Her glimmering dawn from Gothic darknefs rofe,
And nations faw her fhadowy veil difclofe ;
She cheer'd fair Europe with her rifing fmiles,
Beam'd a bright morning o'er the Britifh ifles,
Now foaring reaches her meridian height,
And bleft Columbia hails the dazzling light !

Here, rapt in tho't, the philofophic foul
Shall look thro' Nature's parts and grafp the whole,
See Genius kindling at a FRANKLIN's fame,
See unborn fages catch th' electric flame,
Bid hovering clouds the threatening blaft expire,
Curb the fierce ftream and hold th' imprifon'd fire !

See the pleas'd youth, with anxious ftudy, rove,
In orbs excentric thro' the realms above,
No more perplex'd, while RITTENHOUSE appears
To grace the mufeum with the rolling fpheres.

See that young Genius, that inventive foul,
Whofe laws the jarring elements control :
Who guides the vengeance of mechanic power,
To blaft the watery world and guard the peaceful fhore.

And where's the rifing Sage, the unknown name,
That new advent'rer in the lifts of fame,
To find the caufe, in fecret nature bound,
The unknown caufe, and various charms of found ?
What fubtil medium leads the devious way ,
Why different tenfions different founds convey ;

O

Why harſh, rough tones in grating diſcord roll,
Or mingling concert charms th' enraptur'd ſoul.

And tell the cauſe why ſluggiſh vapors riſe,
And wave, exalted, thro' the genial ſkies ;
What ſtrange contrivance nature forms to bear
The ponderous burden thro' the lighter air.

Theſe laſt Diſplays the curious mind engage,
And fire the genius of the riſing age ;
While moral tho'ts the pleas'd attention claim,
Swell the warm ſoul, and wake the virtuous flame ;
While Metaphyſics ſoar a boundleſs height,
And launch with EDWARDS to the realms of light.

See the bleſt Muſes hail their roſeate bowers,
Their manſions blooming with poetic flowers ;
See liſtening Seraphs join the epic throng,
And unborn JOSHUAS riſe in future ſong.

Satire attends at Virtue's wakening call,
And Pride and Coquetry and Dulneſs fall.

Unnumber'd bards ſhall ſtring the heavenly lyre,
To thoſe bleſt ſtrains which heavenly themes inſpire ;
Sing the rich Grace on mortal Man beſtow'd,
The Virgin's Offspring and the *filial God ;*
What love deſcends from heaven when JESUS dies !
What ſhouts attend him riſing thro' the ſkies !

See Science now in lovelier charms appear,
Grac'd with new garlands from the blooming Fair.
See laurel'd nymphs in poliſh'd pages ſhine,
And Sapphic ſweetneſs glow in every line.

No more the rougher Mufe fhall dare difgrace
The radiant charms that deck the blufhing face;
But rifing Beauties fcorn the tinfel fhow,
The powder'd coxcomb and the flaunting beau;
While humble Merit, void of flattering wiles,
Claims the foft glance, and wakes th' enlivening fmiles.
The opening luftre of an angel-mind,
Beauty's bright charms with fenfe fuperior join'd,
Bid Virtue fhine, bid Truth and Goodnefs rife,
Melt from the voice, and fparkle from the eyes;
While the pleas'd Mufe the gentle bofom warms,
The firft in genius, as the firft in charms.
Thus age and youth a fmiling afpect wear,
Aw'd into virtue by the leading Fair;
While the bright offspring, rifing to the ftage,
Conveys the bleffings to the future age.

These are the views that Freedom's caufe attend;
These fhall endure 'till Time and Nature end.
With Science crown'd, fhall Peace and Virtue fhine,
And bleft Religion beam a light divine.
Here the pure Church, defcending from her God,
Shall fix on earth her long and laft abode;
Zion arife, in radiant fplendors drefs'd,
By Saints admir'd, by Infidels confefs'd;
Her opening courts, in dazzling glory, blaze,
Her walls falvation, and her portals praife.

From each far corner of th' extended earth,
Her gathering fons fhall claim their promis'd birth.
Thro' the drear waftes, beneath the fetting day,
Where prowling natives haunt the wood for prey,

The ſwarthy Millions lift their wond'ring eyes,
And ſmile to ſee the Goſpel morning riſe :
Thoſe who, thro' time, in ſavage darkneſs lay,
Wake to new light, and hail the glorious day !
In thoſe dark regions, thoſe uncultur'd wilds,
Freſh blooms the roſe, the peaceful lilly ſmiles ;
On the tall cliffs unnumber'd *Carmels* riſe,
And in each vale ſome beauteous *Sharon* lies.

From this fair Mount th' excinded ſtone ſhall roll,
Reach the far Eaſt and ſpread from pole to pole ;
From one ſmall Stock ſhall countleſs nations riſe,
The world repleniſh and adorn the ſkies.
Earth's blood-ſtain'd empires, with their Guide the Sun,
From orient climes their gradual progreſs run ;
And circling far, reach every weſtern ſhore,
'Till earth-born empires riſe and fall no more.
But ſee th' imperial GUIDE from heaven deſcend,
Whoſe beams are Peace, whoſe kingdom knows no end ;
From calm Veſperia, thro' th' etherial way,
Back ſweep the ſhades before th' effulgent day ;
Thro' the broad Eaſt, the brightening ſplendor driven,
Reverſes Nature and illumines heaven ;
Aſtoniſh'd regions bleſs the gladdening ſight,
And Suns and Syſtems own ſuperior light.

As when th' afterial blaze o'er Bethl'em ſtood,
Which mark'd the birth-place of th' incarnate God ;
When eaſtern prieſts the heavenly ſplendor view'd,
And numerous crouds the wonderous ſign purſu'd ;
So eaſtern kings ſhall view th' unclouded day
Riſe in the Weſt and ſtreak its golden way :

That signal spoke a Savior's humble birth,
This speaks his long and glorious reign on earth!

THEN Love shall rule, and Innocence adore,
Discord shall cease, and Tyrants be no more;
'Till yon bright orb, and those celestial spheres,
In radiant circles, mark a thousand years;
'Till the grand *fiat* burst th' etherial frames,
Worlds crush on worlds, and Nature sink in flames!
The Church elect, from smouldering ruins, rise,
And sail triumphant thro' the yielding skies,
Hail'd by the Bridegroom! to the Father given,
The Joy of Angels, and the Queen of Heaven!

SELECTED POETRY.

A POEM,*

Spoken at the PUBLIC COMMENCEMENT at YALE-COL-
LEGE, in NEW-HAVEN, Sept. 12, 1781.

BY THE SAME

ONCE more, thou facred Seat, the changing year
    Hath circled heaven and bid the day appear,
That opes thy portals, gilds thy fpiry dome,
And calls thy children from their joyous home.

---

    * This Poem is reprinted from the Hartford Edition;
to which the following Advertifement was prefixed.——
" It may not be amifs to inform the fubfcribers for the
" following performance, that a copy was not given at
" the time it was requefted, on account of its containing
" feveral paffages taken from a larger work which the au-
" thor has by him, unfinifhed. Upon farther confidera-
" tion however, it is thought not improper to prefent to
" the Public a fpecimen of that work, in this incorrect
" manner, that a conjecture may be formed what fuccefs
" it may meet, when the whole fhall make its appearance.
" The paffages are thofe that refpect the affairs of America
" at large, and the future progrefs of Society. As to the
" other parts of the Poem which are confined to the ftate
" of education in Connecticut, although the fubject may
" be thought too particular to be relifhed beyond the lim-
" its of a Commencement Auditory, yet if they fhould
" ferve to turn the attention of any part of the Public to
" the real fituation of Yale College, it may juftify the
" publication."

Thro' seven long years hath war's terrific power
Rang'd every town and crimson'd every shore,
Pursu'd fair Science from each happy seat,
Rav'd in her domes and forc'd her last retreat,
And oft, Yalensia, doom'd thy final fall,
While thy sad Genius trembled for thy wall.
Now see, at last, the venerable train,
Thine elder sons ascend thy courts again!
We joy the reverend, happy throng to see,
We wake thy own blest Muse, and bid her sing to thee.

Long have we liv'd beneath thy nurturing care,
And joy and friendship crown'd our labors there;
No more within those blissful haunts we dwell,
To all thy train we bid a long farewel;
One gentle grasp, one silent, sorrowing tear,
And joys and friends forever disappear;
Fate calls us hence the world's broad stage to tread,
Act a short part, and mingle with the dead.
We go——but may thy glory still ascend,
Thy fame, thy virtues thro' the world extend;
Thy future sons, a calm, delightful throng,
As following years shall lead their steps along,
To peace, to happiness, to glory rise,
Shine thro' the earth and brighten in the skies.
No ruffian force that treads the distant shore,
Shall dare invade thy peaceful labors more;
While the proud foes beneath our standards yield,
And our brave brethren claim the crimson field,
Within thy courts shall pride and slaughter cease,
And genius dignify the walks of peace.

And oh! may some blest hand regard thy cries,
Some great, some liberal benefactor rise,
Whose soul awakes at thy inspiring call,
To lift thy spires, enlarge thy scanty wall,
Who joys to aid the Muse's feeble voice,
And bid bright learning in her sons rejoice,
Bid wealth and dignity thy steps attend,
And rival arts and rival virtues blend,
O'er all the happy land thy beauties shine,
And every joy, and every wish be thine.

Ye patriot worthies, whom these strains assail,
Ye Reverend Sires, and all ye Sons of Yale,
Behold our seat, by former bounty given,
Pride of our land and favorite child of heaven,
Whence liberal arts and liberal thoughts ye drew,
When few her children and her wants were few;
Now see, the narrow bounds can scarce contain
Half the throng'd numbers of her joyous train,
While every friend averts the unconscious eye,
And power, and interest, pass unheeding by.

As late, when war's grim terrors sought repose,
And evening mists and distant fires arose,
Far in a gloomy grove I pensive stray'd,
Where death's pale phantoms walk'd the midnight shade,
Thin clouds of sickening damps, o'er ether driven,
Obscur'd the stars and shut the eye from heaven;
Unwonted sighs within my bosom rose,
Cities o'erturn'd and all my country's woes
Pour'd on my heart; but chief thy feeble cries,
Neglected Science, bade my griefs arise.

I faw, from Briton's Ifle, thy genius flown,
In thefe fair climes to fix a nobler throne,
While here thy fons the peaceful myrtle yield,
To pluck the crimfon laurel of the field.
I faw thy feats to fcenes of flaughter turn'd,
Thy walls defac'd, thy faireft labours burn'd;
E'en Yale, thy lovlieft handmaid, now no more,
Knew the gay fmiles of youth fhe knew before,
Her funds decreas'd, her ftrength, her int'reft fled,
Her friends neglected, and her HOSMER dead.

Now a calm fplendor burft the faddening gloom,
And gales etherial breath'd a glad perfume,
Mild in the midft a form celeftial fhone,
Rob'd in the veftments of the rifing fun;
Tall rofe his ftature, dignity and grace
Mov'd in his limbs and wanton'd in his face,
His folding mantle flow'd in eafy pride,
His harp divine lay ufelefs by his fide,
His locks in curls from myrtle chaplets hung,
And founds melodious melted from his tongue.

" Mortal, attend, behold before thee ftand
Learning's bright Genius, guardian of the land;
Let grief no more awake the piteous ftrain,
Nor think fair Science left her heaven in vain.
Awhile my fkill muft guide the wild affray,
Range the red field and fweep thy foes away,
Soon fhall this arm a milder fceptre bear,
And bleft Yalenfia prove my favorite care.
Mean time her friends her glory fhall attend,
Enlarge her ftores and bid her walls afcend;

P

Bid every art from that pure fountain flow,
All that the Mufe can fing or man can know;
The various branches various teachers claim,
And univerfal knowledge lift her fame.

And fee! ere long in that delightful feat,
Her fons and friends, a numerous concourfe, meet;
Once more to view her, greet her youthful train,
And hear her feeble, faddening voice complain.
Go thou, in pride of youth attend them there,
And thefe commands in ftrains melodious bear.
Say 'tis for them to ftretch the liberal hand,
While war's dread tumults yet involve the land,
Suftain her drooping, rear her radiant eyes,
And bid her future fame begin to rife.
Tell them the wild commotions foon fhall ceafe,
And bleft Columbia hail the charms of peace,
Where reft the future deeds on earth defign'd
To raife, to dignify and blefs mankind.

While Europe's numerous courts my caufe attend,
And mutual intereft fix the mutual friend,
Behold, from each far realm, what glories fhine!
Their power, their commerce and their fcience mine.
And here, what roving views before them fpread!
Where this new empire lifts her daring head!
What wide extent her waving enfigns claim!
Lands yet unknown and ftreams without a name.
Where the deep gulph unfolds Floridia's fhore,
To where Ontario bids hoarfe Laurence roar;
Where Miffifippi's waves their fources boaft,
Where groves and floods and realms and climes are loft,

To where the mild Atlantic's length'ning tide,
Laves numerous towns, and swells their naval pride.
And see! by nature's hand o'er all bestow'd,
The last pure polish of the forming God.
What various grandeur strikes the gladdening eyes!
Bays stretch their arms and mountains lift the skies;
The lakes, unfolding, point the streams their way,
The plains, the hills their lengthening skirts display,
The vales draw forth, fair wave the glimmering wilds,
And all the majesty of nature smiles.

On this broad theatre, unbounded spread,
In different scenes, what countless throngs must tread!
Soon as the new form'd empire, rising fair,
Calms her brave sons now breathing from the war,
Unfolds her harbours, spreads the genial soil,
And welcomes freemen to the chearful toil.
What numerous sages must exalt her name!
What numerous bards must tell the world her fame!
What numerous chiefs beneath my forming care,
Must blaze in arms and ward the waste of war!
While every art and all the graces meet,
To form her thousands to the cares of State,
To heal pale sickness, bid diseases cease,
And found the tidings of eternal peace.

Those must arise the present age to lead,
And following millions hail the paths they tread.

Such gladdening views will ope the bounteous store,
The grasp of interest and the pride of power,
Yalensia's friends shall thus attend her call,
And youths unnumber'd bless the favorite wall.

And tho' thou feeft the rage of flaughter roll,
And different views thy wayward race controul,
Tho' ftill oppos'd their intereft, and their laws,
And every fceptre leads a different caufe,
Yet thro' the whole the fame progreffive plan,
Which draws, for mutual fuccour, man to man,
From men to tribes, from tribes to nations fpreads,
And private ties to public compact leads,
Shall rife by flow degrees, and ftill extend,
Their power, their intereft, and their paffions, blend;
Their wars grow milder, policies enlarge,
Increafing nations feel the general charge,
Form broad alliances for mutual aid,
Mingle their manners and extend their trade,
Till each remoteft realm, by friendfhip join'd,
Link in the chain and harmonize mankind,
The union'd banner be at laft unfurl'd,
And wave triumphant round the accordant world.

Already now commencing glories rife,
The work begins beneath yon northern fkies;
The Ruffian forefts to the deep advance,
The ports unfold, the glimmering navies dance,
For commerce arm'd, the different powers combine,
And heaven approving aids the bleft defign.
Tho' rival regions ftill the combat wage,
And hold in bickering ftrife the unfettled age,
Yet no rude war, that fweeps the crimfon plain,
Shall dare difturb the labors of the main;
For heaven, impartial to the earth born race,
Bade one broad circling deep their fhores embrace,

Spread to all realms the same wide, watry way,
Liberal as air and unconfin'd as day,
That every diftant land the wealth might fhare,
Exchange their wants and fill their treafures there,
Their fpeech affimilate, their empires blend,
And laws and mildnefs thro' the world extend.
Raife now thine eye, the haftening years fhall roll,
And thefe glad fcenes delight thy rifing foul."

We then beheld, 'till where in lonely pride,
The far, blue Baltic pours his laboring tide;
At once in gathering fquadrons, from the north,
The mingling ftreamers lead the nations forth;
From different fhores unnumber'd mafts arife,
And wave their peaceful curtains to the fkies;
Broader and broader ftill the wings unfold,
All Europe's coafts the ftreaming pomp behold,
From Gallia's ports, from Albion's hoary height,
United flags are pointed into fight;
Where broad Hifpania's ftrand two oceans lave,
And the rich Tagus mingles with the wave,
The countlefs navies lift their banners wide,
And ftream their glories o'er the foamy tide;
While thro' the glimmering Strait, in long array,
Pour'd from the fleets that croud the midland fea,
The fails look forth and fwell their beauteous pride,
With wider waves and bolder barks to glide;
While far, far diftant, where the watry way
Spreads the blue borders of defcending day,
The mifty fails advance in lengthening fweep,
Pride of the weftern world and daughters of the deep.

From all the bounds that meet the Atlantic wave,
While to our view the crouded fquadrons heave,
In fign of union, each advancing line,
Leads a calm nation, bids their banners join,
Till far as pole from pole, the cloudlike train
Skirts the dim heavens and fhades the whitening main.

We faw, in other feas and other fkies,
With equal pomp unnumber'd ftreamers rife;
Where Afia's ifles and utmoft fhores extend,
Like rifing funs the fheeted mafts afcend,
Sweep from all ports that cleave the orient ftrand,
Load every ocean, compafs every land,
For peaceful commerce join the friendly train,
No more to combat on the watry plain.

We faw new barks to new difcoveries roll,
Where unknown waves falute each diftant pole;
Far in the north, where feas Pacific pour,
And ope Columbia from the Afian fhore,
The daring fails th' unmeafur'd flight purfue,
And ifles and countlefs nations rife to view.
While fome bold Sage, Columbus like, defign'd
By other ftars and waves to lead mankind,
With confcious pride and philofophic eye,
Treads the lone borders of the fouthern fky,
With perfevering toil the deeps explores,   [fhores.
Till there a new found world extends her length'ning

We faw, from each new realm, new arts afcend,
New manners rife, new wealth and power extend,
Allure the hero, feed the enquiring fage,
Enlarge the genius, dignify the age,

Till laws and empires fwell their rifing reign,
And their own navies whiten on the main.

Such views around us fpread, when thus the guide,
" Thefe are my works that load the fweeping tide;
Nor lefs my power the walks of fcience claim,
In this fair land to raife her nobleft name.
No more fhall war difturb her peaceful reign,
And call to fields of death her youthful train,
No more her views by wealth and power immur'd.
To rage alone and fcenes of blood inur'd,
To teach the lance to thirft for human gore,
To teach pale Avarice to fwell the ftore,
To teach the milder arts the prize to yield,
Teach her own mufe the clangor of the field,
From ruin'd regions fill the voice of fame,
And call celeftial fire to blaze a tyrant's name.
No more in bolder breafts, to dwell confin'd,
And hold her feat in half the human mind,
O'er gentler paffions fpread a harfh controul,
And light the glare of grandeur in the foul;
But fofter virtues now demand her care,
And her own laurels grace the rifing fair.
Each rival fex to rival arts afpires,
Each aids alike the univerfal quires;
This bids bold commerce load the laboring main,
Or rear the peaceful harveft of the plain;
That leads the hours of calm domeftic toil,
And cheers the houfhold with an evening fmile,
To each fond heart an equal tafk affign'd,
And equal virtues raife the mutual mind.

While daring thoughts and deeper tracts of truth
Thro' philofophic mazes lead the youth,
The fofter arts demand a fofter care,
And loves and graces dignify the fair.
While ftates and empires, policies and laws,
Lure the firm patriot in the bolder caufe,
To ftem the tide of power or ward the war,
Like me to fuffer and like me to dare.
Behold, with equal dignity and grace,
The matron virtues guide her peaceful race;
A pleafing tafk her tender bofom warms,
The infant care now fmiling in her arms,
Now ripening features, as the form improves,
Speak the dear image of the man fhe loves;
She lures the rifing wifh to thoughts refin'd,
And her own virtues fwell the opening mind,
The prattling throng to lifping reafon grown,
To ape her lovelinefs improve their own;
The fire beholds the living beauties bloom,
Pride of his life and hope of years to come,
Aids every virtue taught by her to rife,
Joins the delightful tafk, and trains them for the fkies.

Thus different arts their kindred cares employ,
In fields of action or domeftic joy,
Then, rifing from the ufeful to the fine,
Their mingling fouls with rival glory fhine.
From each pure tafte confenting graces blend,
When the tall pillars of the dome afcend,
The walls heave ftately, arches bend on high,
And full proportion meets the roving eye.

Or when the garden to the impaffion'd heart,
Unfinifh'd lies and afks the rural art,
With juft defign their equal fancies play,
From each alike the rambling beauties ftray,
Till thro' the whole the different fcenes prevail,
Here flows the fountain and there draws the dale,
The laughing lawn, the frowning footlefs grove,
And all the feats of innocence and love.

Nor lefs their power the living canvas warms,
And breathes the pencil'd paffion into charms;
Heroes and beauties hear the wakening call,
And diftant ages fill the ftoried wall.

Two kindred arts the fwelling ftatue heave,
Wake the dead wax and teach the ftone to live;
The daring chiffel claims the bolder ftrife,
To roufe the fceptred marble into life,
While fairer hands the livelier fire controul,
And into fofter figures fhed the foul.
In hearts attun'd the voice of mufic dwells,
Steals o'er the lip and into paffion fwells,
Swept by th' alternate hand the living lyre,
To mutual rapture wakes the floating fire,
Till all the magic melody of found,
Pours in delightful harmony around.

And when the breath of heaven from **Angel quires,**
With life divine the joyous Mufe infpires,
In rival bofoms, fee the Goddefs glow!
And bind her bays on each confenting brow.

Q

The foaring bard awakes the trembling ftring,
Virtues and loves and heavenly themes to fing;
No more of vengeful chiefs and bickering Gods,
Where ocean crimfons and Olympus nods,
Or heavens, convulfing rend the dark profound,
To chain fierce Titans to the groaning ground,
But, fir'd by milder themes, and charms refin'd,
Beam'd from the beauties of the fair one's mind,
His foul awakes the peace infpiring fong,
And life and happinefs the ftrain prolong;
To moral beauties bids the world attend,
And jarring realms in focial compact blend;
Bids laws extend and commerce ftretch the wing,
Far diftant fhores their barter'd tributes bring;
He fees the nations join, their blifs increafe,
(Leagu'd in his lays) and fings them into peace.
While pleas'd, the Mufe divides her equal care,
And the fame ardor warms the liftening fair;
From his pure breath fhe lights a bolder flame,
The fame her genius and her flight the fame,
In mutual fmiles the borrow'd graces play,
In mutual fweetnefs flide the hours away,
In mutual aid the borrow'd numbers roll,
And fwell'd to rapture breathes the mutual foul.

From their own loves, thus foften'd and refin'd,
The general wifh extends to all mankind,
The neighbour's cares, the family, the friend
Pour on the heart, and in the bofom blend;
The poor, the ftranger find a welcome home,
The vagrant foot is pointed where to roam,

The eye of anguiſh, when no help is near,
Looks the fond wiſh and finds the mingling tear ;
E'en to their foes their equal goodneſs bends,
And hoſtile minds are ſoften'd into friends.

And when their lays have pour'd the bounteous mind,
In warm benevolence, to all their kind,
They lift the bolder note, the raptures glow,
To loves pure ſource whence all her ſtreamlets flow.
Rapt into viſion of the bright abode,
From angel harps they catch th' inſpiring God ;
Thro' heavens, o'er-canopy'd by heavens, they ſoar,
Where floods of light in boundleſs beauty pour,
Seraphs and ſyſtem'd worlds innumerous move,
Link'd in the chain of harmonizing love ;
Thence following down, th' effulgent glory trace,
Which brought ſalvation to their kindred race.

Thus, on the ſtream of life, with gentle ſweep,
They roll delightful to the welcome deep,
Where, unconfin'd, their ſpirits gently fail,
View happier climes and taſte a purer gale ;
Thro' ether's boundleſs realms together riſe,
And claim their kindred manſions in the ſkies ;
There fill the rapture of th' adoring throng,
Whoſe lays on earth prelude the heavenly ſong."

An ELEGY

On the late honorable TITUS HOSMER, Efq. one of the
Counfellors of the State of Connecticut, a Member of
Congrefs, and a Judge of the Maritime Court of Appeals
for the United States of America.

INSCRIBED TO
MRS. LYDIA HOSMER,
Relict of the late honorable TITUS HOSMER, *Efq.*

As a teftimony of the Author's veneration for the many
amiable virtues which rendered her the delight and
ornament of fo worthy a Confort, and ftill render
her an honour to a very numerous and
refpectable acquaintance.

BY THE SAME.

COME to my foul, O fhade of HOSMER, come,
   Tho' doubting fenates afk thy aid in vain ;
Attend the drooping virtues round thy tomb,
   And hear a while the orphan'd Mufe complain.

The Mufe which thy indulgence bade afpire,
   And dare purfue thy diftant fteps to fame ;
At thy command fhe firft affum'd the lyre,
   And hop'd a future laurel from thy name.

How did thy fmiles awake her infant fong !
   How did thy virtues animate the lay !
Still fhall thy fate the dying ftrain prolong,
   And bear her voice with thy loft form away.

Come to my soul thou venerable Sage,
   In all the sheeted majesty of night,
Snatch the bold quill, control the noble rage,
   And seize the raptur'd fancy in her flight.

Come in the form that shadowy spirits dress,
   When death's dim veil hath shrouded all their pride,
While yon tall cloud but emulates thy face,
   Where the lone moon-beam trembles thro' its side.

Come on the gale that listening midnight heaves,
   When glare-ey'd phantoms, bending with a bier,
Stalk thro' the mist, ascend the sounding graves,
   And wake wild wonders in the startled ear.

In this dread scene no more the wonted fires
   Kindle my breast, or ope a wish within,
The soul, distracted, from herself retires,
   And sighs to mingle and to soar with thine.

And where, thou blest immortal, art thou flown!
   Can these deep shades detain thy willing ear?
Canst thou from loaded breezes hear a groan?
   Or stain thy spotless mantle with a tear!

Can ought on earth thy flight hath left behind,
   Borne in the music of a once lov'd strain,
Approach the unbody'd mansion of the mind?
   Or bend one pitying look to earth again?

Can thence no thought to that fair seat descend?
   The seat once joyous in thy joys below,
Where robes of sable sadness now depend,
   And all the still solemnities of woe.

Can the dear partner of thy tender years,
   Sad as the mifty fading face of even,
With all the wafted treafure of her tears,
   Avert no fmile nor bribe a care from heaven?

While that young throng, that dear deferted train,
   Where thy lov'd image foften'd fweetnefs wears,
Swell with new tendernefs each following pain,
   And add unnumber'd, undivided cares.

Around the fair one fee their beauties bloom,
   (Or wilt thou not the moving fair one heed?)
How their keen anguifh points the diftant tomb,
   Where all their joys and every hope is fled!

So lonely Cynthia, on her evening throne,
   And all her young-ey'd planetary train,
In languid luftre feek their fire the fun,
   Down the ftill chambers of the weftern main.

Yet that broad fplendor from his nightly race,
   With rifing radiance fhall the day reftore;
Another fpring renews fair nature's face,
   And years and ages die to waken more.

But thou, alas! no more on earth wilt tread,
   Nor one fhort hour thy bleft employments leave,
Tho' the fad knell, that hail'd thee to the dead,
   Had doom'd thy helplefs country to her grave.

Thy country, whofe ftill fupplicating moan,
   Implores thy counfels with an infant cry;
And loads the fame ftern Angel with a groan,
   Which bore thy kindling fpirit to the fky.

Wilt thou (since nothing here can bribe thy stay,
   And nothing here can tempt thee from on high,
Since tears of innocence must idly stray,
   And grateful millions breathe the fruitless sigh;

Since every tender tie that mortals prize,
   And all that fame's immortal children gain,
Yield to the untimely mandate of the skies,
   And ask thy kind continuance still in vain :)

Wilt thou in seats of blessedness above,
   Where cares of empire claim the eternal ear,
Among thy country's guardian seraphs prove
   The hand to cherish and the heart to hear?

There, while the dread sublimity of soul
   O'er all the star-ey'd heaven exalts thy throne,
While worlds beneath immeasurably roll,
   And shew the well-known circuit of thine own,

Wilt thou remark the bluely-bending shore?
   Where hills and champaigns stretch abroad their pride,
Where opening streams their lengthiest currents pour,
   And heaps of heroes swell the crimson tide.

Wilt thou recognize that confus'd uproar?
   Towns curl'd in smoaky columns mounting high,
Mix'd with the clarion's desolating roar;
   Rending and purpling all the nether sky.

Amid the tumult, wilt thou see afar
   Our laurel'd heroes striving for the day?
While clouds, unfolding, ope the wings of war,
   Where the grim legions sweep the foes away.

And while their deeds thy bleſt approvance claim,
 While crouds of rival chiefs thy guidance ſhare,
Behold that firſt, that finiſh'd heir of fame,
 And be the beſt of heroes ſtill thy care.

That hero whoſe illuminating ſword
 Lights death and victory through the darken'd field,
Bids realms and ages waken at his word,
 Their ſire, their ſoul, their ſaviour and their ſhield.

Behold that Senate, whoſe delightful ear
 With thy bold eloquence hath often rung,
Where trembling realms, for many a doubtful year,
 Have learnt their ſure ſalvation from thy tongue.

While cares of empires ſit upon their brow,
 And all th' increaſing counſels of an age,
Demand, alike, bold virtue's warmeſt glow,
 And the wide walks of ſcience in the ſage ;

Let thy own wiſdom's ever beaming light
 Illume their well-known dignity of ſoul,
Let thy benevolence their hearts unite,
 And every voice, and every wiſh controul.

Lift the deep curtain from the vale of time,
 Where unborn years their future circles wind,
Where the broad intereſts of a growing clime
 Spread to all realms and regulate mankind.

Unfold to their keen penetrating view,
 What to the infant empire ſhould be known,
That worlds' and ages' happineſs or woe,
 Hang on th' important iſſue of their own.

And sure thou wilt that honor'd realm revere,
   Where first thine early steps began their fame,
Where thy lov'd memory, ever doubly dear,
   Awakes a tenderer tribute to thy name.

Canst thou forget, when youthful years began,
   Where opening science kindled every grace,
And smil'd to see, ascending in the man,
   The friend, the pride, the glory, of his race?

Where civil rights, the dignity of men,
   And all the extensive privilege of laws,
Roll'd from thy voice or brighten'd from thy pen,
   Compel'd attention and secur'd applause.

Where rising worth thine early name enroll'd
   Among the first fam'd fathers of the age,
And bade the untarnish'd characters of gold
   Flame in the front of glory's deathless page.

Attentive still to virtue's noble aim,
   And greatly strenuous to advance her cause,
Lead thou her counsels, animate her flame,
   Sire of her sons, and guardian of her laws.

And see! aloft in that sublime retreat,
   Where injur'd rights obtain their last appeal,
How pensive justice o'er thy vacant seat,
   With faltering hand suspends her turning scale.

If chance some Hosmer, with an even eye,
   And skill'd like thee to poize the trembling weight,
Should chear the nymph, thine honor'd place supply,
   And bless the nations with a longer date;

R

When from all bounds of this extensive land,
   Or where wide oceans spread their coasts abroad,
Dark causes rise, demanding from his hand,
   Th' impartial deep discernment of a god;

Then in his breast may all thy virtues rise,
   And all thy dignity around him shine,
Then drop thy own blest mantle from the skies,
   And make the person as the place, divine.

He will, my friends——th' unbodied life above,
   With every virtue brighten'd and refin'd,
That glow'd below, with patriotic love,
   The love of happiness and human kind,

Will burn serener in a purer sky,
   Where broader views and bolder thoughts unroll,
Where universal Being fills the eye,
   And swells the unbounded wishes of the soul.

No tender thought by heaven's own breath inspir'd,
   Which taught the gentle bosom here to glow,
Which the warm breast with patriot ardor fir'd,
   Or stole the secret tear for silent woe;

No tender thought by heaven's own will approv'd,
   Can e'er forsake the mansion first assign'd;
But reaches still the object once belov'd,
   And lives immortal in th' immortal mind.

Fix'd in a brighter sphere, with surer aim,
   Tho' greater scenes his growing views employ,
Yet Hosmer kindles with an Hosmer's flame,
   And his dear country feeds his noblest joy.

He fees our rifing, all-involving caufe,
   Spread like the morn to every diftant clime,
Awake the mild magnificence of laws,
   And roll down bleffings on the ftream of time.

Nor think, O haplefs fair one, tho' awhile,
   From thy fond arms his happier fpirit rove,
That foaring innocence can ceafe to fmile,
   Or his Seraphic bofom ceafe to love.

In Heaven's own breaft the felf-exiftent fires,
   E'er time began, illum'd th' eternal flame,
Lit from the beam, the Archangellic quires
   Preferve th' unchanging ardor ftill the fame.

And fhall the heaven-born fpirit after death,
   Robb'd of its virtues from its nature fly,
Or lofe in climes of blifs the afpiring breath,
   Which wing'd its paffage to its kindred fky?

Think, in the chambers of eternal morn,
   Where beauty blooms along the vernal vale,
Where loves and virtues every fmile adorn,
   And hymns of Angels fwell the floating gale;

Think how his well-known fympathy of foul
   Views every pain thy tendernefs can know;
Counts the full tears in filence as they roll,
   And learns the tale of every fpeaking woe.

Thou know'ft, while here, he joy'd to give relief,
   To call dark merit to the eye of day,
To rob the filent orphan of her grief,
   And breathe the figh from innocence away.

How did the trembling visage of the poor,
  With grateful glow embolden at his smile !
And learn, well pleas'd, within his wonted door,
  Its joys to cherish, and its cares beguile.

Thou know'st his early wish began to prize
  The bliss that wayward mortals seldom find,
That lifts the frequent suppliant to the skies,
  While answ'ring blessings fill the raptur'd mind.

Know then, fair mourner, from the climes of day,
  (While these drear shades of solitude you tread)
His unseen hand companion of thy way,
  Thro' the dark paths thy wandering steps shall lead.

While all thy virtues rise before the throne,
  And all thy griefs be number'd in his sight,
Those shall refine and ripen with his own,
  And these be hush'd in everlasting night.

Thy children too, his images below,
  Fair as young plants, and smiling as the morn,
With thy own loveliness shall learn to glow,
  And all thy graces brighten and adorn.

Short is the date that virtue from its home,
  In these deep shades, can suffer and refine ;
And when kind heaven relieves it from the doom,
  Ours be the choice to tremble, and resign.

Vain were the task, the daring thought were vain,
  To check the sun's bold circuit as he flies ;
Nor think the cling of fondness can detain
  The soaring seraph from his kindred skies.

Then ceafe, fond partner of his earthly joys,
   And leave behind each unavailing care ;
Think what a fcene his happier flight employs,
   And hafte to meet him and to mingle there.

An ELEGY

On the burning of FAIRFIELD, *in* CONNECTICUT.

Written on the fpot,—anno 1779.

BY COL. DAVID HUMPHREYS.

YE fmoking ruins, marks of hoftile ire,
   Ye afhes warm, which drink the tears that flow,
Ye defolated plains my voice infpire,
   And give foft mufic to the fong of woe !

How pleafant, Fairfield, on th' enraptur'd fight
   Rofe thy tall fpires, and op'd thy focial halls !
How oft my bofom beat with pure delight,
   At yonder fpot, where ftand the darken'd walls !

But there the voice of mirth refounds no more,
   A filent fadnefs through the ftreets prevails,
The diftant main alone is heard to roar,
   And hollow chimnies hum with fullen gales;

Save where fcorch'd elms th' untimely foliage fhed,
   Which ruftling hovers round the faded green;
Save where at twilight mourners frequent tread,
   'Mid recent graves o'er defolation's fcene.

How chang'd the blifsful profpect, when compar'd
    Thefe glooms funereal with thy former bloom :
Thy hofpitable rights when Tryon fhar'd,
    Long ere he feal'd thy melancholly doom.

That impious wretch, with coward voice decreed
    Defencelefs domes and hallow'd fanes to duft,
Beheld with fneering fmile the wounded bleed,
    And fpurr'd his bands to rapine, blood and luft.

Vain was the widow's, vain the orphan's cry,
    To touch his feelings or to footh his rage ;
Vain the fair drop that roll'd from beauty's eye,
    Vain the dumb grief of fupplicating age.

Could Tryon hope to quench the patriot flame,
    Or make his deeds furvive in glory's page ?
Could Britons feek of favages the fame,
    Or deem it conqueft thus the war to wage ?

Yes, Britons fcorn the councils of the fkies,
    Extend wide havoc, fpurn the infulted foes !
Th' infulted foes to tenfold vengeance rife,
    Refiftance growing as the danger grows.

Red in their wounds and pointing to the plain,
    The vifionary fhapes before me ftand ;
The thunder burfts, the battle burns again,
    And kindling fires encrimfon all the ftrand.—

Long dufky wreaths of fmoke, reluctant driven,
    In blackening volumes o'er the landfcape bend ;
Here the broad fplendor blazes high to heaven,
    There umber'd ftreams in purple pomp afcend.

In fiery eddies round the tott'ring walls,
   Emitting fparks, the lighter fragments fly;
With frightful crafh the burning manfion falls,
   The works of years in glowing embers lye.

Tryon! behold thy fanguine flames afpire,
   Clouds ting'd with dyes intolerably bright!
Behold well pleaf'd the village wrap'd in fire;
   Let one wide ruin glut thy ravifh'd fight!

Ere fades the grateful fcene, indulge thine eye,
   See age and ficknefs tremuloufly flow,
Creep from the flames—fee babes in torture dye—
   And mothers fwoon in agonies of woe.

Go, gaze, enraptured with the mother's tear,
   The infant's terror, and the captive's pain,
Where no bold bands can check thy curft career;
   Mix fire with blood on each unguarded plain.

Thefe be thy triumphs! this thy boafted fame!
   Daughters of mem'ry, raife the deathlefs fongs!
Repeat through endlefs years, his hated name,
   Embalm his crimes and teach the world our wrongs!

AN ELEGY
ON LIEUTENANT DE HART,*
Vol. Aid to Gen. Wayne.

BY THE SAME.

WHEN autumn all humid and drear
    With darkneſs and ſtorms in his train
Announcing the death of the year,
    Deſpoil'd of its verdure the plain :
When horror congenial prevail'd,
    Where graves are with fearfulneſs trod,
De Hart by his ſiſter was wail'd,
    His ſiſter thus ſigh'd o'er his ſod :

" Near Hudſon, a fort, on theſe banks,
    " Its flag of defiance unfurl'd :
" He led to the ſtorm the firſt ranks ;
    " On them, iron tempeſts were hurl'd.
" Tranſpierc'd was his breaſt with a ball—
    " His breaſt a red fountain ſupply'd,
" Which, guſhing in waves ſtill and ſmall,
    " Diſtain'd his white boſom and ſide.

" His viſage was ghaſtly in death,
    " His hair, that ſo laviſhly curl'd,
" I ſaw, as he lay on the heath,
    " In blood, and with dew-drops impearl'd.

* This young warrior was killed in the attack on the
block-houſe, near Fort Lee, 1780.

" How dumb is the tongue, that could fpeak
    " Whate'er could engage and delight!
" How faded the rofe on his cheek!
    " Thofe eyes, how envelop'd in night!

" Thofe eyes, that illumin'd each foul,
    " All darken'd to us are now grown :
" In far other orbits they roll,
    " Like ftars to new fyftems when gone.
" My brother, the pride of the plain,
    " In vain did the graces adorn ;
" His bloffom unfolded in vain,
    " To die like the bloffom of morn.

" Oh war, thou haft wafted our clime,
    " And tortur'd my bofom with fighs :
" My brother, who fell ere his prime,
    " Forever is torn from my eyes.
" To me, how diftracting the ftorm,
    " That blafted the youth in his bloom!
" Alas, was fo finifh'd a form
    " Defign'd for fo early a tomb ?

" How bright were the profpects that fhone!
    " Their ruin 'tis mine to deplore—
" Health, beauty, and youth were his own,
    " Health, beauty, and youth are no more.
" No bleffings of nature and art,
    " Nor mufic that charm'd in the fong,
" Nor virtues that glow'd in the heart ,
    " Dear youth, could thy moments prolong!

S

" Thrice fix times the fpring had renew'd
  " Its youth and its charms for the boy ;
" With rapture all nature he view'd,
  " For nature he knew to enjoy.
" But chiefly his country could charm :
  " He felt—'twas a generous heat—
" With drums and the trumpet's alarm,
  " His pulfes in confonance beat.

" Ye heroes, to whom he was dear,
  " Come weep o'er this forrowful urn,
" Come eafe the full heart with a tear—
  " My hero will never return :
" He died in the dawn of applaufe,
  " His country demanded his breath ;
" Go, heroes, defend the fame caufe,
  " Avenge with your country his death."

So fung on the top of the rocks,
  The virgin in forrow more fair ;
In tears her blue eyes ; and her locks
  Of auburn flew loofe on the air.
I heard, as pafs'd down the ftream ;
  The guards of the foe were in view :—
To enterprize fir'd by the theme,
  I bade the fweet mourner adieu.

MOUNT VERNON:
An Ode.

BY THE SAME.

BY broad Potowmack's azure tide,
   Where Vernon's mount, in sylvan pride,
     Displays its beauties far,
Great Washington, to peaceful shades,
Where no unhallow'd wish invades,
     Retir'd from fields of war.

Angels might see, with joy, the sage,
Who taught the battle where to rage,
     Or squench'd its spreading flame,
On works of peace employ that hand,
Which wav'd the blade of high command,
     And hew'd the path to fame.

Let others sing his deeds in arms,
A nation sav'd, and conquest's charms:
     Posterity shall hear,
'Twas mine, return'd from Europe's courts,
To share his thoughts, partake his sports,
     And sooth his partial ear.

To thee, my friend, these lays belong:
Thy happy seat inspires my song,
     With gay, perennial blooms,
With fruitage fair, and cool retreats,
Whose bow'ry wilderness of sweets
     The ambient air perfumes.

Here spring its earliest buds displays,
Here latest on the leafless sprays,
  The plumy people sing;
The vernal show'r, the rip'ning year,
Th' autumnal store, the winter drear,
  For thee new pleasures bring.

Here lapp'd in philosophic ease,
Within thy walks, beneath thy trees,
  Amidst thine ample farms,
No vulgar converse heroes hold,
But past or future scenes unfold,
  Or dwell on nature's charms.

What wond'rous era have we seen,
Plac'd on this isthmus, half between
  A rude and polish'd state !
We saw the war tempestuous rise,
In arms a world, in blood the skies,
  In doubt and empire's fate.

'The storm is calm'd, seren'd the heav'n,
And mildly o'er the climes of ev'n,
  Expands th' imperial day :
" O God, the source of light supreme,
" Shed on our dusky morn a gleam,
  " To guide our doubtful way !

" Restrain, dread pow'r, our land from crimes !
" What seeks, tho' blest beyond all times,
  " So querulous an age ?
" What means to freedom such disgust,
" Of change, of anarchy the lust,
  " The fickleness and rage ?'

So fpake his country's friend, with fighs,
To find that country ftill defpife
    The legacy he gave—
And half he fear'd his toils were vain,
And much that man would court a chain,
    And live through vice a flave.

A tranfient gloom o'ercaft his mind:
Yet, ftill on providence reclin'd,
    The patriot fond believ'd,
That pow'r benign too much had done,
To leave an empire's tafk begun,
    Imperfectly achiev'd.

Thus buoy'd with hope, with virtue bleft,
Of ev'ry human blifs poffeft,
    He meets the happier hours;
His fkies affume a lovelier blue,
His profpects brighter rife to view,
    And fairer bloom his flow'rs.

AN ODE.

ADDRESSED TO LAURA.

——————

BY THE SAME.

——————

OH, lovely Laura, may a youth,
 Infpir'd by beauty, urg'd by truth,
  Difclofe the heart's alarms,
The fire in raptur'd breafts that glows,
Th' impaffion'd pang on love that grows,
  And dare to fing thy charms!

Enough with war my lay has rung;
A fofter theme awakes my tongue;
  'Tis beauty's force divine:
Can I refift that air, that grace,
The harmony of form and face?
  For ev'ry charm is thine.

Of health, of youth th' expanding flufh,
Of virgin fear the flying blufh,
  With crimfon ftain thy cheek:
The bee fuch nectar never fips,
As yield the rofe-buds of thy lips,
  When fweetly thou doft fpeak.

'Tis thine the heavieft heart to cheer,
Thofe accents, drank with eager ear,
  So mufically roll:

Where fwells the breaft, the fnow-white fkin
Scarce hides the fecret thoughts within,
  Nor needs difguife that foul.

With thee, of cloudnefs days I dream;
Thy eyes, in morning fplendors, beam
  So exquifitely fair—
What tafte! as o'er thy back and breaft,
In light-brown ringlets neatly dreft
  Devolves a length of hair.

Unblam'd, oh, let me gaze and gaze,
While love-fick fancy fondly ftrays,
  And feafts on many a kifs;—
For us let tides of rapture roll,
And may we mingle foul with foul,
  In extacies of blifs!

THE GENIUS OF AMERICA.
A SONG.
Tune,—The watry God, &c.

BY THE SAME.

WHERE fpirits dwell and fhad'wy forms
  On Andes' cliffs mid black'ning ftorms,
 With livid lightnings curl'd:
The awful genius of our clime,
In thunder rais'd his voice fublime,
 And hufh'd the lift'ning world.

" In lonely waves and waftes of earth,
" A mighty empire claims its birth,
    " And heav'n afferts the claim;
" The fails that hang in yon dim fky,
" Proclaim the promis'd era nigh,
    " Which wakes a world to fame.

" Hail ye firft bounding barks that roam,
" Blue-tumbling billows topp'd with foam,
    " Which keel ne'er plough'd before!
" Here funs perform their ufelefs round,
" Here rove the naked tribes embrown'd,
    " Who feed on living gore.

" To midnight orgies, off'ring dire,
" The human facrifice on fire,
    " A heav'nly light fucceeds—
" But, lo! what horrors intervene,
" The toils fevere, the carnag'd fcene,
    " And more than mortal deeds!

" Ye FATHERS, fpread your fame afar,
" 'Tis yours to ftill the founds of war,
    " And bid the flaughter ceafe;
" The peopling hamlets wide extend,
" The harvefts fpring, the fpires afcend,
    " Mid grateful fongs of peace.

" Shall fteed to fteed, and man to man,
" With difcord thund'ring in the van,
    " Again deftroy the blifs?
" Enough my myftic words reveal,
" The reft the fhades of night conceal,
    " In fate's profound abyfs."

An EPISTLE to Dr. DWIGHT.*
On board the Courier de l'Europe, July 30, 1784.

BY THE SAME.

FROM the wide watry wafte, where nought but fkies
   And mingling waves falute the aching eyes ·
Where the fame moving circle bounds the view,
And paints with vap'ry tints the billows blue ;
To thee, my early friend! to thee, dear Dwight ?
Fond recollection turns, while thus I write ;
While I reflect, no change of time or place,
The impreffions of our friendfhip can efface ;
Nor peace, nor war, tho' chang'd for us the fcene,
Tho' mountains rife, or oceans roll between ;
Too deep that facred paffion was impreft
On my young heart, too deep it mark'd your breaft ;
Your breaft which afks the feelings of your friend,
What chance betides him, or what toils attend?
Then hear the mufe, in fea-born numbers tell
In mind how cheerful, and in health how well ;
And ev'n that mufe will deign to let you know,
What things concur to make and keep him fo.

T

---

* For Dr. Dwight's letter to Col. Humphreys, fee
page 75.

We go, protected by supernal care,
With cloudless skies, and suns serenely fair;
While o'er the unruffled main the gentle gale
Consenting breathes, and fills each swelling sail;
Conscious of safety in the self-same hand,
Which guides us on the ocean or the land.

Of thee, fair bark! the muse prophetic sings,
" *Europe's swift Messenger!* expand thy wings,
" Rear thy tall masts, extend thine ample arms,
" Catch the light breeze, nor dread impending harms.
" Full oft shalt thou, if aught the muse avails,
" Wing the broad deep with such delightful gales;
" Full oft to either world announce glad news,
" Of allied realms promote the friendly views;
" So shall each distant age assert thy claim,
" And *Europe's Messenger* be known to fame!"

What tho' this plain so uniform and vast,
Illimitably spreads its dreary waste;
What tho' no isles, nor vales, nor hills, nor groves,
Meet the tired eye that round the horizon roves;
Yet, still collected in a narrow bound,
Ten thousand little pleasures may be found.

Here we enjoy accommodations good,
With pleasant liquors, and well-flavor'd food,
Meats nicely fatten'd in Columbian fields,
And luscious wines, that Gallia's vintage yields,
On which you bards ('twas so in former days)
Might feast your wit, and lavish all your praise.

Within our ship, well-furnish'd, roomy, clean,
Come see the uses of each different scene.

Far in the prow, for culinary ufe,
Fires, not poetic, much good cheer produce;
The ovens there our daily bread afford,
And thence the viands load our plenteous board.

See various landfcapes fhade our dining hall,
Where mimic nature wantons round the wall,
There no vain pomp appears, there all is neat,
And there cool zephyrs fanning, as we eat,
Avert the fervors of the noon-tide ray,
And give the mildnefs of the vernal day.

See the great cabin nigh, its doors unfold,
Shew fleeting forms from mirrors fix'd in gold!
O'er painted ceilings brighter profpects rife,
And rural fcenes again delight our eyes:
There oft from converfe or from focial fports,
We drink delight lefs dafh'd than that of courts.

But when more fober cares the hour requires,
Each to his cell of folitude retires;
His bed, his books, his paper, pen and ink,
Prefent the choice, to reft, to read, or think.

Yet what would all avail to prompt the fmile,
Cheer the fad breaft, or the dull hour beguile;
If well-bred paffengers, difcreet and free,
Were not at hand to mix in focial glee?
Such my companions,—fuch the mufe fhall tell,
Him firft, whom once you knew in war fo well,
Our Polifh friend,* whofe name ftill founds fo hard,
To make it rhyme would puzzle any bard;

---

* General Kofciufzko.

That youth, whom bays and laurels early crown'd,
For virtue, science, arts, and arms, renown'd.
Next him, behold, to grace our watry scene,
An honest German lifts his generous mien;
Him Carolina sends to Europe's shore,
Canals and inland waters to explore;
From thence return'd, she hopes to see her tide,
In commerce rich, thro' ampler channels glide.
Next comes the bleak Quebec's well-natured son;
And last our naval chief, the friend of fun;
Whose plain, frank manners, form'd on fickle seas,
Are cheerful still, and always aim to please:
Nor less the other chiefs their zeal display,
To make us happy as themselves are gay.

  Sever'd from all society but this,
Half way from either world we plough the abyss:
Save the small sea-bird and the fish that flies,
On yon blue waves no object meets my eyes.
Nor has the insidious hook, with lures, beguil'd
Of peopled ocean scarce a single child.
Yet luckless Dolphin, erst to Arion † true,
Nought could avail thy beauteous, transient hue;
As o'er the deck, in dying pang you roll'd,
Wrapt in gay rain-bows and pellucid gold.

  Now see that wand'rer bird, fatigued with flight
O'er many a watry league, is forc'd to light

---

† Ille sedet, citharamque tenet, pretiumque vehendi
Cantat, et æquoreas carmine mulcet aquas.
               Ovid. Fast. 2.

High on the maſt,—the bird our ſeamen take,
Tho' ſcar'd, too tir'd its refuge to forſake:
Fear not ſweet bird, nor judge our motives ill,
No barb'rous man, now means thy blood to ſpill,
Or hold thee cag'd; ſoon as we reach the ſhore,
Free ſhalt thou fly, and gaily ſing and ſoar!

Another grateful ſight now cheers the eye,
At firſt a ſnow-white ſpot in yon clear ſky;
Then thro' the optic tube a ſhip appears,
And now diſtinct athwart the billows veers:
Daughter of ocean, made to bleſs mankind!
Go, range wide waters on the wings of wind;
With friendly intercourſe far climes explore,
Their produce barter, and increaſe their ſtore;
Ne'er ſaw my eye ſo fair a pageant ſwim,
As thou appear'ſt, in all thy gallant trim!

Amus'd with trivial things, reclin'd at eaſe,
While the ſwift bark divides the ſummer ſeas;
Your bard (for paſt neglect to make amends)
Now writes to you, anon to other friends.

Anon the ſcene, in Europe's poliſh'd climes,
Will give new themes for philoſophic rhymes,
Ope broader fields for reaſon to explore,
Improvements vaſt of ſcientific lore!

Thro' nations bleſt with peace, but ſtrong in arms,
Refin'd in arts, and apt for ſocial charms,
Your friend will ſtray, and ſtrive, with ſtudious care,
To mark whate'er is uſeful, great, or rare;

Search the small shades of manners in their lives,
What policy prevails, how commerce thrives ;
How morals form of happiness the base,
How others differ from Columbia's race ;
And, gleaning knowlege from the realms he rov'd,
Bring home a patriot heart, enlarg'd, improv'd.

———————

A SONG.

Tranflated from the French.

—————

BY THE SAME.

———————

IT rains, it rains, my fair,
　　Come drive your white sheep fast ;
To shelter quick repair,
　　Haste, shepherdess, make haste.

I hear—the water pours,
　　With patt'ring on the vines :
See here ! see here ! it lours—
　　See there the lightning shines.

The thunder dost thou hear ?
　　Loud roars the rushing storm :
Take (while we run, my dear)
　　Protection from my arm.

I see our cot, ah hold!
  Mama and sister Nance,
To open our sheep-fold,
  Most cheerily advance.

God bless my mother dear,
  My sister Nancy too!
I bring my sweet-heart here,
  To sleep to night with you.

Go, dry yourself, my friend,
  And make yourself at home—
Sister, on her attend:
  Come in, sweet lambkins, come.

Mama, let's take good care
  Of all her pretty sheep;
Her little lamb we'll spare
  More straw whereon to sleep.

'Tis done—now let us haste
  To her;—you here, my fair!
Undress'd, oh what a waist!
  My mother, look you there.

Let's sup; come take this place,
  You shall be next to me;
This pine-knot's cheerful blaze
  Shall shine direct on thee.

Come taste this cream so sweet,
  This syllabub so warm;
Alas! you do not eat:
  You feel ev'n yet the storm.

'Twas wrong—I prefs'd too much
    Your fteps, when on the way :
But here, fee here your couch—
    There fleep till dawn of day

With gold the mountain tips :—
    Good night, good night, my dove :
Now let me on your lips,
    Imprint one kifs of love.

Mama and I will come,
    When morn begins to fhine,
To fee my fweet-heart home,
    And afk her hand for mine.

EPITAPH

On a Patient killed by a Cancer Quack.

By Dr. Lemuel Hopkins.

HERE lies a fool flat on his back,
   The victim of a Cancer Quack;
Who loft his money and his life,
By plaifter, cauftic, and by knife.
The cafe was this—a pimple rofe,
South-eaft a little of his nofe;
Which daily reden'd and grew bigger,
As too much drinking gave it vigour:
A fcore of goffips foon enfure
Full three fcore diff'rent modes of cure;
But yet the full-fed pimple ftill
Defied all petticoated fkill;
When fortune led him to perufe
A hand-bill in the weekly news;
Sign'd by fix fools of diff'rent forts,
All cur'd of cancers made of warts;
Who recommend, with due fubmiffion,
This cancer-monger as magician;
Fear wing'd his flight to find the quack,
And prove his cancer-curing knack;
But on his way he found another,—
A fecond advertifing brother:

U

But as much like him as an owl
Is unlike every handfome fowl;
Whofe fame had rais'd as broad a fog,
And of the two the greater hog:
Who us'd a ftill more magic plaifter,
That fweat forfooth, and cur'd the fafter.
This doctor view'd, with moony eyes
And fcowl'd up face, the pimple's fize;
Then chriften'd it in folemn anfwer,
And cried, " This pimple's name is CANCER."
" But courage, friend, I fee you're pale,
" My fweating plaifters never fail;
" I've fweated hundreds out with eafe,
" With roots as long as maple trees;
" And never fail'd in all my trials—
" Behold thefe famples here in vials!
" Preferv'd to fhew my wond'rous merits,
" Juft as my liver is—in fpirits.
" For twenty joes the cure is done—"
The bargain ftruck, the plaifter on,
Which gnaw'd the cancer at its leifure,
And pain'd his face above all meafure.
But ftill the pimple fpread the fafter,
And fwell'd, like toad that meets difafter.
Thus foil'd, the doctor gravely fwore,
It was a right rofe-cancer fore;
Then ftuck his probe beneath the beard,
And fhew'd them where the leaves appear'd;
And rais'd the patient's drooping fpirits,
By praifing up the plaifter's merits.—

Quoth he, " The roots now fcarcely ftick—
" I'll fetch her out like crab or tick;
" And make it rendezvous, next trial,
" With fix more plagues, in my old vial."
Then purg'd him pale with jalap draftic,
And next applies th' infernal cauftic.
But yet, this femblance bright of hell
Serv'd but to make the patient yell;
And, gnawing on with fiery pace,
Devour'd one broadfide of his face—
' Courage, 'tis done,' the doctor cried,
And quick th' incifion knife applied:
That with three cuts made fuch a hole,
Out flew the patient's tortur'd foul!

Go, readers, gentle, eke and fimple,
If you have wart, or corn, or pimple;
To quack infallible apply;
Here's room enough for you to lie.
His fkill triumphant ftill-prevails,
For DEATH's a cure that never fails.

* * *

THE HYPOCRITE's HOPE.

BY THE SAME.

BLEST is the man, who from the womb,
    To faintfhip him betakes,
And when too foon his child fhall come,
    A long confeffion makes.

When next in Broad Church-alley, he
    Shall take his former place,
Relates his past iniquity,
    And consequential grace.

Declares how long by Satan vex'd,
    From truth he did depart,
And tells the time, and tells the text,
    That smote his flinty heart.

He stands in half-way-cov'nant sure ;
    Full five long years or more,
One foot in church's pale secure,
    The other out of door.

Then riper grown in gifts and grace,
    With ev'ry rite complies,
And deeper lengthens down his face,
    And higher rolls his eyes.

He tones like Pharisee sublime,
    Two lengthy prayers a day,
The same that he from early prime,
    Had heard his father say.

Each Sunday perch'd on bench of pew,
    To passing priest he bows,
Then loudly 'mid the quav'ring crew,
    Attunes his vocal nose.

With awful look then rises slow,
    And pray'rful visage sour,
More fit to fright the apostate foe,
    Then seek a pard'ning power.

Then nodding hears the fermon next,
 From prieſt haranguing loud;
And doubles down each quoted text,
 From Geneſis to Jude.

And when the prieſt holds forth addreſs,
 To old ones born anew,
With holy pride and wrinkled face,
 He riſes in his pew.

Good works he careth nought about,
 But *faith* alone will ſeek,
While Sunday's pieties blot out
 The knaveries of the week.

He makes the poor his daily pray'r,
 Yet drives them from his board:
And though to his own good he ſwear,
 Thro' habit breaks his word.

This man advancing freſh and fair,
 Shall all his race complete;
And wave at laſt his hoary hair,
 Arrived in Deacon's ſeat.

There ſhall he all church honours have,
 By joyous brethren given—
Till prieſt in fun'ral ſermon grave,
 Shall ſend him ſtraight to heaven.

ON GENERAL ETHAN ALLEN.

BY THE SAME.

LO Allen 'ſcaped from Britiſh jails,
   His tuſhes broke by biting nails.
Appears in hyperborean ſkies,
To tell the world the bible lies.
See him on green hills north afar
Glow like a ſelf-enkindled ſtar,
Prepar'd (with mob-collecting club
Black from the forge of Belzebub,
And grim with metaphyſic ſcowl,
With quill juſt pluck'd from wing of owl)
As rage or reaſon riſe or ſink
To ſhed his blood, or ſhed his ink.
Behold inſpired from Vermont dens,
The ſeer of Antichriſt deſcends,
To feed new mobs with Hell-born manna
In Gentile lands of Suſquehanna;
And teach the Pennſylvania quaker
High blaſphemies againſt his maker.
Behold him move ye ſtaunch divines!
His tall head buſtling through the pines;
All front he ſeems like wall of braſs,
And brays tremendous as an aſs;
One hand is clench'd to batter noſes,
While t'other ſcrawls 'gainſt Paul and Moſes,

AN ORATION,

Which might have been delivered to the Students in Anatomy, on the late Rupture between the two Schools in this city.*

THE ARGUMENT.

ADDRESS—the folly and danger of diffention—the Orator enumerates the enemies of the fraternity—reminds them of a late unfeafonable interruption—a night fcene in the Potter's Field---he laments the want of true zeal in the brotherhood --and boafts of his own---the force of a ruling paffion---the earth confidered as a great animal---the paffion of love not the fame in a true fon of Efculapius as in other men---his own amour---a picture of his miftrefs in high tafte---fhews his learning in the defcription of her mouth, arm and hand---his miftrefs dies---his grief---and extraordinary confolation---his unparallel'd fidelity----he apologizes for giving this hiftory of his amour---the great difficulties Anatomifts have to encounter in the prefent times, arifing from falfe delicacy, prejudice and ignorance---a ftrong inftance in proof that it was not fo formerly---curious argument to prove the inconfiftency of the prefent opinions refpecting the practice---he mentions many obftacles in the road to fcience---and reproaches them for their inteftine broils, at a time when not only popular clamour is loud, but even the powers of government are exerted againft them---he then encourages his brethren with hopes of better times, founded on the eftablifhment of the College of Phyficians---is infpired with the idea of the future glory of that inftitution---and prophefies great things.

FRIENDS and affociates! lend a patient ear,
    Sufpend inteftine broils and reafon hear.
Ye followers of F—— your wrath forbear—
Ye fons of S—— your invectives fpare;

---

* This Poem is afcribed to the late Hon. Francis Hopkinfon, Efq. L. L. D. Federal Judge for the Diftrict of Penn-

The fierce diffention your high minds purfue
Is fport for others—ruinous to you.

   Surely fome fatal influenza reigns,
Some epidemic *rabies* turns your brains—
Is this a time for brethren to engage
In public conteft and in party rage?
Fell difcord triumphs in your doubtful ftrife
And, fmiling, whets her anatomic knife;
Prepar'd to cut our precious limbs away
And leave the bleeding body to decay.—

   Seek ye for foes!—alas, my friends, look round,
In ev'ry ftreet, fee num'rous foes abound!
Methinks I hear them cry, in varied tones,
" Give us our father's,—brother's,—fifter's bones."
Methinks I fee a mob of failor's rife—
Revenge!—Revenge! they cry—and damn their eyes—

NOTE,---*continued.*

fylvania, &c. &c.—The occafion of its being written, was
this : A Difpute arofe between the Medical Students who
had attached themfelves to two Anatomical Profeffors, in
the city of Philadelphia. This Difpute was carried on for
a confiderable time, and with great violence. Refolutions
of Committees,—Journals of Meetings,—&c. &c. were
printed ; and the town was threatened with a deluge of un-
interefting publications. In this fituation of affairs, Dr.
Hopkinfon took up the pen ; and by the well-tim'd raillery
of the following Poem, filenced the contending parties, re-
ftored peace to the Schools, and agreeably entertained the
Lovers of Poetry and Humour.—This Poem is reprinted
from the 4to edition, publifhed by T. Dobfon and T. Lang,
February 1789.

Revenge for comrade Jack, whose flesh, they say,
You minc'd to morsels and then threw away.
Methinks I see a black infernal train—
The genuine offspring of accursed *Cain*—
Fiercely on you their angry looks are bent,
They grin and gibber dangerous discontent,
And seem to say,—" Is there not meat enough ?
" Ah ! massa cannibal, why eat poor CUFF ?"
Ev'n hostile watchmen stand in strong array
And o'er our heads their threat'ning staves display,
Howl hideous discord thro' the noon of night,
And shake their dreadful lanthorns in our sight.

 Say, are not these sufficient to engage
Your high wrought souls eternal war to wage ?
Combine your strength these monsters to subdue
No friends of science, and sworn foes to you ;
On these,—on these your wordy vengeance pour,
And strive our fading glory to restore.

 Ah ! think how, late, our mutilated rites
And midnight orgies, were by sudden frights
And loud alarms profan'd—the sacrifice,
Stretch'd on a board before our eager eyes,
All naked lay—ev'n when our chieftain stood
Like a high priest, prepar'd for shedding blood ;
Prepar'd, with wondrous skill, to cut or slash
The gentle sliver or the deep drawn gash ;
Prepar'd to plunge ev'n elbow deep in gore
Nature and nature's secrets to explore——
Then a tumultuous cry—a sudden fear—
Proclaim'd the foe—the enraged foe is near—

     W

In some dark hole the hard got corse was laid,
And we, in wild confusion, fled dismay'd.

Think how, like brethren, we have shar'd the toil,
When in the Potter's Field* we sought for spoil;
Did midnight ghosts, and death, and horror, brave,
To delve for science in the dreary grave.
Shall I remind you of that awful night
When our compacted band maintain'd the fight
Against an armed host?—fierce was the fray,
And yet we bore our sheeted prize away.
Firm on a horse's back the corse was laid,
High blowing winds the winding sheet display'd;
Swift flew the steed—but still his burthen bore—
Fear made him fleet, who ne'er was fleet before;
O'er tombs and sunken graves he cours'd around,
Nor ought respected consecrated ground.
Mean time the battle rag'd—so loud the strife,
The dead were almost frighten'd into life;
Tho' not victorious, yet we scorn'd to yield,
Retook our prize, and left the doubtful field.

In this degen'rate age, alas! how few
The paths of science with true zeal pursue?
Some trifling contest, some delusive joy,
Too oft the unsteady minds of youth employ.
For me—whom ESCULAPIUS hath inspir'd—
I boast a soul with love of science fir'd;
By one great object is my heart possest;
One ruling passion quite absorbs the rest.

---

* The Negro burial ground.

In this bright point my hopes and fears unite,
And one pursuit alone can give delight.

To me things are not as to vulgar eyes,
I would all nature's works anatomize :
This world a living monster seems, to me,
Rolling and sporting in the aerial sea ;
The soil encompasses her rocks and stones
As flesh in animals encircles bones.
I see vast ocean, like a heart in play,
Pant *systole* and *diastole* ev'ry day,
And by unnumber'd *venus* streams supply'd
Up her broad rivers force the *arterial* tide.
The world's great lungs, monsoons and trade-winds shew
From east to west, from west to east they blow
Alternate respiration——
The hills are pimples which earth's face defile,
And burning *Ætna*, an eruptive boil :
On her high mountains *hairy* forests grow,
And *downy* grass o'erspreads the vales below ;
From her vast body perspirations rise,
Condense in clouds and float beneath the skies.
Thus fancy, faithful servant of the heart,
Transforms all nature by her magic art.

Ev'n mighty LOVE, whose power all power controuls,
Is not, in me, like love in other souls ;
Yet I have lov'd---and CUPID's subtle dart
Hath thro' my *pericardium* pierc'd my heart.
Brown CADAVERA did my soul ensnare,
Was all my thought by night, and daily care ;
I long'd to clasp, in her transcendent charms,
A living skeleton within my arms.

Long, lank and lean, my CADAVERA ſtood,
Like the tall pine, the glory of the wood;
Ofttimes I gaz'd, with learned ſkill to trace
The ſharp edg'd beauties of her bony face:
There roſe *Os frontis* prominent and bold,
In deep ſunk *orbits* two large eye-balls roll'd,
Beneath thoſe eye-balls, two arch'd bones were ſeen
Whereon two flabby cheeks hung looſe and lean;
Between thoſe cheeks, protuberant aroſe,
In form triangular, her lovely noſe,
Like EGYPT's pyramid it ſeem'd to riſe,
Scorn earth, and bid defiance to the ſkies;
Thin were her lips, and of a ſallow hue,
Her open mouth expos'd her teeth to view;
Projecting ſtrong, protuberant and wide
Stood *inciſores*---and on either ſide
The *canine* rang'd, with many a beauteous flaw,
And laſt the *grinders*, to fill up the jaw;
All in their *alveoli* fix'd ſecure,
Articulated by *gomphoſis* ſure.
Around her mouth perpetual ſmiles had made
Wrinkles wherein the loves and graces play'd;
There, ſtretch'd and rigid by continual ſtrain,
Appear'd the *zygomatic* muſcles plain,
And broad *montanus* o'er her peeked chin
Extended, to ſupport the heavenly grin.
In amorous dalliance oft I ſtroak'd her arm,
Each riſing muſcle was a riſing charm.
O'er the *flexores* my fond fingers play'd,
I found inſtruction with delight convey'd;

There *carpus*, *cubitus* and *radius* too
Were plainly felt and manifest to view.
No muscles on her lovely hand were seen,
But only bones envelop'd by a skin.
Long were her fingers and her knuckles bare,
Much like the claw-foot of a walnut chair.
So plain was complex *matacarpus* shewn,
It might be fairly counted bone by bone.
Her slender *phalanxes* were well defin'd,
And each with each by *ginglymus* combin'd.
Such were the charms that did my fancy fire,
And love---chaste scientific love inspire.

At length my CADAVERA fell beneath
The fatal stroke of all subduing death :
Three days in grief---three nights in tears I spent,
And sighs incessant gave my sorrows vent.

Few are the examples of a love so true---
Ev'n from her death I consolation drew,
And in a secret hour approach'd her grave,
Resolv'd her precious corse from worms to save ;
With active haste remov'd the incumbent clay,
Seiz'd the rich prize and bore my love away.

Her naked charms now lay before my sight,
I gaz'd with rapture and supreme delight,
Nor could forbear, in extasy, to cry---
Beneath that shrivell'd skin what treasures lie!
Then feasted to the full my amorous soul,
And skinn'd, and cut, and slash'd without controul.

'Twas then I saw, what long I'd wish d to see,
That heart which panted oft for love and me---

In detail view'd the form I once ador'd,
And nature's hidden mysteries explor'd.

    Alas! too truly did the wise man say
That flesh is grass, and subject to decay:
Not so the bones; of substance firm and hard,
Long they remain the Anatomist's reward.
Wise nature, in her providential care,
Did, kindly, bones from vile corruption spare,
That sons their fathers' skeletons might have,
And heaven-born science triumph o'er the grave.

    My true love's bones I boil'd---from fat and lean
These hands industrious scrap'd them fair and clean,
And ev'ry bone did to its place restore,
As Nature's hand had plac'd them long before:
These fingers twisted ev'ry pliant wire
With patient skill, urg'd on by strong desire.
Now what remains of CADAVERA's mine,
Securely hanging in a case of pine.

    Ofttimes I sit and contemplate her charms,
Her nodding skull and her long dangling arms,
'Till quite inflam'd with passion for the dead,
I take her beauteous skeleton to bed;
There stretch'd, at length, close to my faithful side
She lies all night,---a lovely, grinning bride.———

    Excuse, my friends, this detail of my love,
You must the intent, if not the tale, approve;
By facts exemplary I meant to shew
To what extent a genuine zeal will go,

A mind, fo fix'd, will not be drawn afide
By vain diffentions or a partial pride ;
But ev'ry hoftile fentiment fubdue,
And keep the ruling paffion ftill in view.

Falfe delicacy---prejudices ftrong,
Which no diftinctions know 'twixt right and wrong,
Againft our noble fcience fpend their rage,
And mark the ignorance of this vulgar age.

Time was, when men their living flefh would fpare,
And to the knife their quiv'ring *nates* bare,
That fkilful furgeons† nofes might obtain
For nofes loft---and cut and come again ;---
But now the *living* churlifhly refufe
To give their dead relations to our ufe ;
Talk of decorum---and a thoufand whims---
Whene'er we hack their wives' or daughters' limbs ;
And yet their tables daily they fupply
With the rich fruits of fad mortality ;
Will pick, and gut, and cook a chicken's corfe,
Diffect and eat it up, without remorfe ;
Devouring fifh, flefh, fowl, whatever comes,
Nor fear the ghofts of murder'd hecatombs.

Now where's the difference ?---to the impartial eye
A leg of mutton and a human thigh
Are juft the fame : for furely all muft own
Flefh is but flefh, and bone is only bone ;
And tho' indeed, fome flefh and bone may grow
To make a monkey---fome to make a beau,
Still the materials are the fame, we know.

---

* TALIACOTIUS.

Nor can our anatomic knowledge trace
Internal marks diſtinctive of our race.----

Whence, then, theſe loud complaints---theſe hoſts of foes
Combin'd, our uſeful labours to oppoſe?
How long ſhall fooliſh prejudices reign?
And when ſhall reaſon her juſt empire gain?

Ah! full of danger is the up-hill road,
That leads the youth to learning's high abode:
His way thick miſts of vulgar errors blind,
And ſneering ſatire follows cloſe behind;
Sour envy ſtrews the rugged path with thorns,
And lazy ignorance his labour ſcorns.

Is this a time, ye brethren of the knife,
For civil conteſt and internal ſtrife?
When loud againſt us gen'ral clamours cry,
And perſecution lifts her laſh on high?
When government---that many headed beaſt---
Againſt our practice rears her horrid creſt,
And, our nocturnal acceſs to oppoſe,
Around the dead a penal barrier* throws?
To cruſh our ſchools her awful pow'r applies,
And ev'n forbids the gibbet's juſt ſupplies.†

Yet in this night of darkneſs, ſtorms and fears,
Behold one bright benignant ſtar‡ appears---

----

* A Law paſt at New-York, making it penal to ſteal
bodies from the burial ground.
† The wheel-barrow law of Pennſylvania.
‡ The Medical College.

Long may it shine, and, e'er it's course is run,
Increase, in size and splendour, to a sun!---
Methinks I see this sun of future days,
Spread far abroad his *diplomatic* rays---
See life and health submit to his controul,
And, like a planet, *death* around him roll.

Methinks I see a stately fabric rise,
Rear'd on the skulls of these our enemies;
I see the bones of our invet'rate foes
Hang round it's walls in scientific rows.
There solemn sit the learned of the day
Dispensing death with uncontrouled sway,
And by *prescription* regulate with ease
The sudden crisis or the slow disease.

Then shall physicians their millennium find,
And reign the real sov'reigns of mankind :
Then shall the face of this vile world be chang'd,
And nature's healthful laws all new arrang'd---
In min'ral powders all her dust shall rise,
And all her insects shall be Spanish flies :
In medicated potions streams shall flow,
Pills fall in hail-storms, and sharp salts in snow;
In ev'ry quagmire bolusses be found,
And slimy cataplasms spread the ground---
Nature herself assume the chymist's part,
And furnish poisons unsublim'd by art.

Then to our schools shall wealth in currents flow,
Our theatres no want of subjects know ;
Nor laws nor mobs th' Anatomist shall dread,
For graves shall freely render up their dead.

X

PHILOSOPHIC SOLITUDE.

BY WILLIAM LIVINGSTON, ESQ.
Late Governor of the State of New-Jerfey, &c. &c.

LET ardent heroes feek renown in arms,
   Pant after fame, and rufh to war's alarms;
To fhining palaces let fools refort,
And dunces cringe, to be efteem'd at court:
Mine be the pleafure of a rural life,
From noife remote, and ignorant of ftrife;
Far from the painted belle, and white-glov'd beau,
The lawlefs mafquerade, and midnight fhow:
From ladies, lap-dogs, courtiers, garters, ftars,
Fops, fidlers, tyrants, emperors, and czars.

   Full in the centre of fome fhady grove,
By nature form'd for folitude and love;
On banks array'd with ever-blooming flowers,
Near beauteous landfcapes, or by rofeate bowers,
My neat, but fimple manfion I would raife,
Unlike the fumptuous domes of modern days;
Devoid of pomp, with rural plainnefs form'd,
With favage game, and gloffy fhells adorn'd.

   No coftly furniture fhould grace my hall;
But curling vines afcend againft the wall,
Where pliant branches fhould luxuriant twine,
While purple clufters fwell'd with future wine:
To flake my thirft a liquid lapfe diftil
From craggy rocks, and fpread a limpid rill.

Along my manſion, ſpiry firs ſhould grow,
And gloomy yews extend the ſhady row :
The cedars flouriſh, and the poplars riſe,
Sublimely tall, and ſhoot into the ſkies :
Among the leaves, refreſhing zephyrs play,
And crouding trees exclude the noon-tide ray ;
Whereon the birds their downy neſts ſhould form,
Securely ſhelter'd from the battering ſtorm ;
And to melodious notes their choir apply,
Soon as Aurora bluſh'd along the ſky :
While all around th' enchanting muſic rings,
And ev'ry vocal grove reſponſive ſings.

Me to ſequeſter'd ſcenes ye muſes guide,
Where nature wantons in her virgin pride ;
To moſſy banks, edg'd round with op'ning flowers,
Elyſian fields and amaranthine bowers,
To ambroſial founts, and ſleep-inſpiring rills,
To herbag'd vales, gay lawns, and ſunny hills.

Welcome, ye ſhades ! all hail, ye vernal blooms !
Ye bow'ry thickets, and prophetic glooms !
Ye foreſts, hail ! ye ſolitary woods !
Love-whiſpering groves, and ſilver-ſtreaming floods !
Ye meads, that aromatic ſweets exhale !
Ye birds, and all ye ſylvan beauties, hail !
Oh how I long with you to ſpend my days,
Invoke the muſe, and try the rural lays !

No trumpets there with martial clangor ſound,
No proſtrate heroes ſtrew the crimſon ground ;
No groves of lances glitter in the air,
Nor thund'ring drums provoke the ſanguine war :

But white-rob'd Peace, and universal Love
Smile in the field, and brighten ev'ry grove:
There all the beauties of the circling year,
In native ornamental pride appear.
Gay, rosy-bosom'd Spring, and April show'rs,
Wake, from the womb of earth, the rising flow'rs;
In deeper verdure, Summer clothes the plain,
And Autumn bends beneath the golden grain;
The trees weep amber; and the whispering gales
Breeze o'er the lawn, or murmur through the vales:
The flow'ry tribes in gay confusion bloom,
Profuse with sweets, and fragrant with perfume;
On blossoms blossoms, fruits on fruits arise,
And varied prospects glad the wand'ring eyes.
In these fair seats, I'd pass the joyous day,
Where meadows flourish, and where fields look gay;
From bliss to bliss with endless pleasure rove,
Seek crystal streams, or haunt the vernal grove,
Woods, fountains, lakes, the fertile fields, or shades,
Aerial mountains, or subjacent glades.
There from the polish'd fetters of the great,
Triumphal piles, and gilded rooms of state.--
Prime ministers, and sycophantic knaves,
Illustrious villains, and illustrious slaves,
From all the vain formality of fools,
And odious task of arbitrary rules;
The ruffling cares, which the vex'd soul annoy,
The wealth the rich possess, but not enjoy,
The visionary bliss the world can lend,
Th' insidious foe, and false, designing friend,
The seven-fold fury of Xantippe's soul,
And S——'s rage, that burns without controul;

I'd live retir'd, contented, and ferene,
Forgot, unknown, unenvied, and unfeen.

Yet not a real hermitage I'd choofe,
Nor wifh to live from all the world reclufe;
But with a friend fometimes unbend the foul,
In focial converfe, o'er the fprightly bowl.
With cheerful W——, ferene and wifely gay,
I'd often pafs the dancing hours away:
He, fkill'd alike to profit and to pleafe,
Politely talks with unaffected eafe;
Sage in debate, and faithful to his truft,
Mature in fcience, and feverely juft;
Of foul diffufive, vaft and unconfin'd,
Breathing benevolence to all mankind;
Cautious to cenfure, ready to commend,
A firm, unfhaken, uncorrupted friend;
In early youth, fair wifdom's paths he trod,
In early youth, a minifter of God,
Each pupil lov'd him, when at Yale he fhone,
And ev'ry bleeding bofom weeps him gone.
Dear A—— too, fhould grace my rural feat,
Forever welcome to the green retreat:
Heav'n for the caufe of righteoufnefs defign'd
His florid genius, and capacious mind:
Oft have I heard, amidft th' adorning throng,
Celeftial truths devolving from his tongue:
High o'er the lift'ning audience feen him ftand,
Divinely fpeak, and graceful ftretch his hand;
With fuch becoming grace and pompous found,
With long rob'd fenators encircled round,

Before the Roman bar, while Rome was free,
Nor bow'd to Cæfar's throne the fervile knee,
Immortal Tulley plead the patriot caufe,
While ev'ry tongue refounded his applaufe.
Next round my board fhould candid S—— appear,
Of manners gentle, and a friend fincere,
Averfe to difcord, party-rage and ftrife,
He fails ferenely down the ftream of life.
With thefe three friends, beneath a fpreading fhade,
Where filver fountains murmur thro' the glade;
Or in cool grots, perfum'd with native flow'rs,
In harmlefs mirth, I'd fpend the circling hours;
Or gravely talk, or innocently fing,
Or, in harmonious concert, ftrike the trembling ftring.

Amid fequefter'd bow'rs, near gliding ftreams,
Druids and bards enjoy'd fereneft dreams.
Such was the feat where courtly Horace fung,
And his bold harp immortal Maro ftrung:
Where tuneful Orpheus' unrefifted lay
Made rapid tigers bear their rage away:
While groves, attentive to th' extatic found,
Burft from their roots, and, raptur'd, danc'd around.
Such feats the venerable feers of old
(When blifsful years in golden circles roll'd)
Chofe and admir'd: e'en goddeffes and gods
(As poets feign) were fond of fuch abodes:
Th' imperial confort of fictitious Jove
For fount-full Ide forfook the realms above.
Oft to Idalia, on a golden cloud,
Veil'd in a mift of fragrance, Venus rode:

There num'rous altars to the queen were rear'd,
And love-fick youths their am'rous vows prefer'd,
While fair-hair'd damfels (a lafcivious train)
With wanton rites ador'd her gentle reign.
The filver-fhaft:d huntrefs of the woods,
Sought pendant fhades, and bath'd in cooling floods.
In palmy Delos by Scamander's fide,
Or where Cajifter roll'd his filver tide,
Melodious Phœbus fang; the mufes round
Alternate warbling to the heavenly found.
E'en the feign'd monarch of heav'n's bright abode,
High thron'd in gold, of gods the fov'reign god,
Oft' time prefer'd the fhade of Ida's grove
To all th' ambrofial feafts, and nectar'd cups above.

Behold, the rofy-finger'd morning dawn,
In faffron rob'd, and blufhing o'er the lawn !
Reflected from the clouds, a radiant ftream
Tips with etherial dew the mountain's brim.
Th' unfolding rofes, and the op'ning flow'rs
Imbibe the dew, and ftrew the varied bow'rs,
Diffufe nectareous fweets around, and glow
With all the colours of the fhow'ry bow.
Th' induftrious bees their balmy toil renew,
Buz o'er the field, and fip the rofy dew.
But yonder comes th' il'uftrious god of day,
Invefts the eaft, and gilds th' etherial way ;
The groves rejoice, the feather'd nations fing,
Echo the mountains, and the vallies ring.

Hail, orb ! array'd with majefty and fire,
That bids each fable fhade of night retire !

Fountain of light! with burning glory crown'd,
Darting a deluge of effulgence round!
Wak'd by thy genial and prolific ray,
Nature refumes her verdure, and looks gay:
Fresh blooms the rose, the drooping plants revive,
The groves reflourish, and the forests live.
Deep in the teeming earth, the rip'ning ore
Confesses thy confolidating pow'r;
Hence Labour draws her tools, and artifts mould
The fufile filver and the ductile gold;
Hence war is furnish'd; and the regal shield
Like light'ning flashes o'er th' illumin'd field.
If thou so fair with delegated light,
That all heav'n's splendors vanish at thy fight;
With what effulgence must the ocean glow,
From which thy borrow'd beams inceffant flow!
Th' exhauftless fource whofe fingle smile supplies
Th' unnumber'd orbs that gild the fpangled skies!

Oft' would I view, in admiration loft,
Heav'n's fumptuous canopy, and ftarry hoft;
With level d tube, and aftronomic eye,
Purfue the planets whirling thro' the sky:
Immeafurable vault! where thunders roll,
And forky lightnings flash from pole to pole.
Say, railing infidel! canft thou furvey
Yon globe of fire, that gives the golden day,
The harmonious ftructure of this vaft machine,
And not confefs its architect divine!
Then go, vain wretch! tho' deathlefs be thy foul,
Go, fwell the riot, and exhauft the bowl;

Plunge into vice—humanity refign—
Go fill the ftie—and briftle into fwine !

None but a pow'r omnipotent and wife
Could frame this earth, or fpread the boundlefs fkies ;
He made the whole ; at his omnific call,
From formlefs chaos rofe this fpacious ball,
And one Almighty God is feen in all.
By him our cup is crown'd, our table fpread
With lufcious wine, and life-fuftaining bread.
What countlefs wonders doth the earth contain !
What countlefs wonders the unfathom'd main !
Bedrop'd with gold, there fcaly nations fhine,
Haunt coral groves, or lafh the foaming brine·
Jehovah's glories blaze all nature round,
In heaven, on earth, and in the deeps profound ;
Ambitious of his name, the warblers fing,
And praife their maker, while they hail the fpring ;
The zephyrs breathe it ; and the thunders roar,
While furge to furge, and fhore refounds to fhore,
But man, endu'd with an immortal mind,
His Maker's image, and for heaven defign'd,
To loftier notes his raptur'd voice fhould raife,
And chaunt fublimer hymns to his Creator's praife.

When rifing Phœbus ufhers in the morn,
And golden beams th' impurpled fkies. adorn ;
Wak'd by the gentle murmur of the floods,
Or the foft mufic of the waving woods ;
Rifing from fleep with the melodious quire,
To folemn founds I'd tune the hallow'd lyre.

Y

Thy name, O God! fhould tremble on my tongue,
Till ev'ry grove prov'd vocal to my fong :
(Delightful tafk! with dawning light to fing
Triumphant hymns to heav'n's eternal king.)
Some courteous angel fhould my breaft infpire,
Attune my lips, and guide the warbled wire,
While fportive echoes catch the facred found,
Swell ev'ry note, and bear the mufic round;
While mazy ftreams meand'ring to the main,
Hang in fufpence to hear the heav'nly ftrain,
And, hufh'd to filence, all the feather'd throng
Attentive liften to the tuneful fong.

Father of light! exahuftlefs fource of good!
Supreme, eternal, felf-exiftent God!
Before the beamy fun difpens'd a ray,
Flam'd in the azure vault, and gave the day;
Before the glimm'ring moon, with borrow'd light,
Shone queen amid the filver hoft of night;
High in the heav'ns, thou reign'dft fuperior Lord,
By fuppliant angels worfhip'd and ador'd.
With the celeftial choir then let me join
In cheerful praifes to the pow'r divine.
To fing thy praife, do thou, O God! infpire
A mortal breaft with more than mortal fire :
In dreadful majefty thou fit'ft enthron'd,
With light encircled, and with glory crown'd ;
Thro' all infinitude extends thy reign,
For thee, nor heav'n, nor heav'n of heav'ns contain ;
But tho' thy throne is fix'd above the fky,
Thy omniprefence fills immenfity.

Saints, rob'd in white, to thee their anthems bring,
And radiant martyrs hallelujahs fing:
Heaven's univerfal hoft their voices raife
In one eternal chorus, to thy praife;
And, round thy awful throne, with one accord,
Sing, holy, holy, holy is the Lord.
At thy creative voice, from ancient night,
Sprang fmiling beauty, and yon worlds of light:
Thou fpak'ft—the planetary chorus roll'd,
And all th' expanfe was ftarr'd with beamy gold;
Let there be light, faid God—light inftant fhone,
And from the orient, burft the golden fun;
Heav'n's gazing hierarchs, with glad furprife,
Saw the firft morn inveft the recent fkies,
And ftrait th' exulting troops thy throne furround
With thoufand thoufand harps of heav'nly found:
Thrones, powers, dominions, (ever fhining trains!)
Shouted thy praifes in triumphant ftrains:
Great are thy works, they fing; and, all around,
Great are thy works, the echoing heav'ns refound.
The effulgent fun, infufferably bright,
Is but a beam of thy o'erflowing light;
The tempeft is thy breath: the thunder hurl'd,
Tremendous roars thy vengeance o'er the world;
Thou bow'ft the heav'ns, the fmoking mountains nod,
Rocks fall to duft, and nature owns her God;
Pale tyrants fhrink, the atheift ftands aghaft,
And impious kings in horror breathe their laft.
To this great God alternately I'd pay
The ev'ning anthem, and the morning lay.

For fov'reign gold I never would repine,
Nor with the glitt'ring duft of monarchs mine.
What tho' high columns heave into the fkies,
Gay cielings fhine, and vaulted arches rife?
Tho' fretted gold the fculptur'd roof adorn,
The rubies redden, and the jafpers burn!
O what, alas! avails the gay attire
To wretched man, who breathes but to expire!
Oft' on the vileft, riches are beftow'd,
To fhow their meannefs in the fight of God.
High from a dunghill, see a Dives rife,
And, Titan-like, infult th' avenging fkies:
The crowd, in adulation, calls him Lord,
By thoufands courted, flatter'd and ador'd:
In riot plung'd, and drunk with earthly joys,
No higher thought his grov'ling foul employs:
The poor he fcourges with an iron rod,
And from his bofom banifhes his God.
But oft' in height of wealth and beauty's bloom,
Deluded man is fated to the tomb!
For, lo! he fickens; fwift his colour flies,
And rifing mifts obfcure his fwimming eyes:
Around his bed his weeping friends bemoan,
Extort the unwilling tear, and wifh him gone;
His forrowing heir augments the tender fhow'r,
Deplores his death—yet hails the dying hour.
Ah bitter comfort! Sad relief! to die,
Tho' funk in down, beneath the canopy!
His eyes no more fhall fee the cheerful light,
Weigh'd down by death in everlafting night,
And now the great, the rich, the proud, the gay,
Lie breathlefs, cold—unanimated clay!

He, that juſt now was flatter'd by the crowd
With high applauſe, and acclamations loud—
That ſteel'd his boſom to the orphan's cries,
And drew down torrents from the widow's eyes—
Whom, like a God, the rabble did adore—
Regard him now—and, lo! he is no more.

My eyes no dazzling veſtments ſhould behold,
With gems inſtarr'd, and ſtiff with woven gold;
But the tall ram his downy fleece afford,
To clothe, in modeſt garb, his frugal lord.
Thus the great Father of mankind was dreſt,
When ſhaggy hides compos'd his flowing veſt;
Doom'd to the cumb'rous load, for his offence,
When clothes ſupply'd the want of innocence:
But now his ſons (forgetful whence they came)
Glitter in gems, and glory in their ſhame.

Oft' would I wander-thro' the dewy field,
Where cluſt'ring roſes balmy fragrance yield:
Or in lone grots, for contemplation made,
Converſe with angels and the mighty dead;
For all around unnumber'd ſpirits fly,
Waft on the breeze, or walk the liquid ſky,
Inſpire the poet with repeated dreams,
Who gives his hallow'd muſe to ſacred themes,
Protect the juſt, ſerene their gloomy hours,
Becalm their ſlumbers, and refreſh their pow'rs.
Methinks I ſee th' immortal beings fly,
And ſwiftly ſhoot athwart the ſtreaming ſky:
Hark! a melodious voice I ſeem to hear,
And heav'nly ſounds invade my liſt'ning ear!

" Be not afraid of us, innoxious band,
" Thy cell furrounding by divine command;
" Ere while, like thee, we led our lives below,
" (Sad lives of pain, of mifery, and woe!)
" Long by affliction's boift'rous tempefts toft,
" We reach'd at length the ever blifsful coaft :
" Now in th' embow'ring groves, and lawns above,
" We tafte the raptures of immortal love,
" Attune the golden harp in rofeate bow'rs,
" Or bind our temples with unfading flow'rs.
" Oft' on kind errands bent, we cut the air,
" To guard the righteous, heav'n's peculiar care !
" Avert impending harms, their minds compofe,
" Infpire gay dreams, and prompt their foft repofe.
" When from thy tongue divine hofannas roll,
" And facred raptures fwell thy rifing foul,
" To heav'n we bear thy pray'rs, like rich perfumes;
" Where, by the throne, the golden cenfer fumes;
" And when with age thy head is filver'd o'er,
" And, cold in death, thy bofom beats no more,
" Thy foul, exulting, fhall defert its clay,
" And mount, triumphant, to eternal day."

But to improve the intellectual mind,
Reading fhould be to contemplation join'd.
Firft I'd collect from the Parnaffian fpring,
What mufes dictate, and what poets fing.——
Virgil, as prince, fhou'd wear the laurel'd crown,
And other bards pay homage to his throne;
The blood of heroes now effus'd fo long,
Will run forever purple thro' his fong,

See ! how he mounts toward the bleft abodes,
On planets rides, and talks with demigods !
How do our ravifh'd fpirits melt away,
When in his fong Sicilian fhepherds play !
But what a fplendor ftrikes the dazzled eye,
When Dido fhines in awful majefty !
Embroidered purple clad the Tyrian queen,
Her motion graceful, and auguft her mien ?
A golden zone her royal limbs embrac'd,
A golden quiver rattled by her waift.
See her proud fteed majeftically prance,
Contemn the trumpet, and deride the launce !
In crimfon trappings, glorious to behold,
Confus'dly gay with interwoven gold !
He champs the bit, and throws the foam around,
Impatient paws, and tears the folid ground.
How ftern Æneas thunders thro' the field !
With tow'ring helmet, and refulgent fhield !
Courfers o'erturn'd, and mighty warriors flain,
Deform'd with gore, lie welt'ring on the plain,
Struck through with wounds, ill-fated chieftains lie,
Frown e'en in death, and threaten as they die.
Thro' the thick fquadrons fee the hero bound !
(His helmet flafhes, and his arms refound !)
All grim with rage, he frowns o'er Turnus' head
(Re-kindled ire ! for blooming Pallas dead)
Then in his bofom plung'd the fhining blade—
The foul indignant fought the Stygian fhade !

    The far-fam'd bards that grac'd Britannia's ifle,
Should next compofe the venerable pile.

Great Milton firſt, for tow'ring thought renown'd,
Parent of ſong, and fam'd the world around!
His glowing breaſt divine Urania fir'd,
Or God himſelf th' immortal bard inſpir'd,
Borne on triumphant wings he takes his flight,
Explores all heaven, and treads the realms of light:
In martial pomp he clothes th' angelic train,
While warring myriads ſhake the etherial plain.
Firſt Michael ſtalks, high tow'ring o'er the reſt,
With heav'nly plumage nodding on his creſt:
Impenetrable arms his limbs infold,
Eternal adamant, and burning gold!
Sparkling in fiery mail, with dire delight,
Rebellious Satan animates the fight:
Armipotent they ſink in rolling ſmoke,
All heav'n reſounding, to its centre ſhook.
To cruſh his foes, and quell the dire alarms,
Meſſiah ſparkled in refulgent arms:
In radiant panoply divinely bright,
His limbs incas'd, he flaſh'd devouring light:
On burning wheels, o'er heav'n's cryſtalline road
Thunder'd the chariot of the filial God;
The burning wheels on golden axles turn'd,
With flaming gems the golden axles burn'd.
Lo! the apoſtate hoſt, with terror ſtruck,
Roll back by millions! Th' empyrean ſhook!
Sceptres, and orbed ſhields, and crowns of gold,
Cherubs and ſeraphs in confuſion roll'd;
Till from his hand the triple thunder hurl'd,
Compell'd them, head-long, to th' infernal world.

Then tuneful Pope, whom all the nine infpire,
With fapphic fweetnefs, and pindaric fire,
Father of verfe! melodious and divine!
Next peerlefs Milton fhould diftinguifh'd fhine.
Smooth flow his numbers, when he paints the grove,
Th' enraptur'd virgins lift'ning into love.
But when the night, and hoarfe-refounding ftorm
Rufh on the deep, and Neptune's face deform,
Rough runs the verfe, the fon'rous numbers roar,
Like the hoarfe furge that thunders on the fhore.
But when he fings th' exhilirated fwains,
Th' embow'ring groves, and Windfor's blifsful plains,
Our eyes are ravifh'd with the fylvan fcene,
Embroider'd fields, and groves in living green:
His lays the verdure of the meads prolong,
And wither'd forefts bloffom in his fong.
Thames' filver ftreams his flowing verfe admire,
And ceafe to murmur while he tunes his lyre.

Next fhould appear great Dryden's lofty mufe,
For who would Dryden's polifh'd verfe refufe?
His lips were moiften'd in Parnaffus' fpring,
And Phœbus taught his laureat fon to fing.
How long did Virgil untranflated moan,
His beauties fading, and his flights unknown;
Till Dryden rofe, and, in exalted ftrain,
Re-fang the fortune of the god-like man!
Again the Trojan prince, with dire delight,
Dreadful in arms, demands the ling'ring fight:
Again Camilla glows with martial fire,
Drives armies back, and makes all Troy retire.

Z

With more than native luſtre, Virgil ſhines,
And gains ſublimer heights in Dryden's lines.

The gentle Watts, who ſtrings his ſilver lyre
To ſacred odes, and heav'n's all-ruling Sire ;
Who ſcorns th' applauſe of the licentious ſtage,
And mounts yon ſparkling worlds with hallow'd rage,
Compels my thoughts to wing th' heav'nly road,
And wafts my ſoul, exulting, to my God :
No fabled nine, harmonious bard ! inſpire
Thy raptur'd breaſt with ſuch ſeraphic fire ;
But prompting angels warm thy boundleſs rage,
Direct thy thoughts, and animate thy page.
Bleſt man ! for ſpotleſs ſanctity rever'd,
Lov'd by the good, and by the guilty fear'd :
Bleſt man ! from gay, deluſive ſcenes remov'd,
Thy Maker loving, by thy Maker lov'd,
To God thou tun'ſt thy conſecrated lays,
Nor meanly bluſh to ſing Jehovah's praiſe.
Oh ! did, like thee, each laurel'd bard delight
To paint Religion in her native light,
Not then with plays the lab'ring preſs would groan,
Nor Vice defy the pulpit and the throne ;
No impious rhymers charm a vicious age,
Nor proſtrate Virtue groan beneath their rage :
But themes divine in lofty numbers riſe,
Fill the wide earth, and echo thro' the ſkies.

These for delight. For profit I would read
The labour'd volumes of the learned dead.
Sagacious Locke, by Providence deſign'd,
To exalt, inſtruct, and rectify the mind.

The unconquerable fage* whom virtue fir'd,
And from the tyrant's lawlefs rage retir'd,
When victor Cæfar freed unhappy Rome
From Pompey's chains, to fubftitute his own.
Longinus, Livy, fam'd Thucydides,
Quintilian, Plato, and Demofthenes,
Perfuafive Tully, and Corduba's fage,†
Who fell by Nero's unrelenting rage ;
Him‡ whom ungrateful Athens doom'd to bleed,
Defpis'd when living, and deplor'd when dead.
Raleigh I'd read with ever frefh delight,
While ages paft rife prefent to my fight :
Ah man unbleft ! he foreign realms explor'd,
Then fell a victim to his country's fword !
Nor fhould great Derham pafs neglected by,
Obfervant fage ! to whofe deep-piercing eye,
Nature's ftupendous works expanded lie.
Nor he, Britannia, thy unmatch'd renown !
(Adjudg'd to wear the philofophic crown)
Who on the folar orb uplifted rode,
And fcann'd the unfathomable works of God !
Who bound the filver planets to their fpheres,
And trac'd the elliptic curve of blazing ftars !
Immortal Newton ; whofe illuftrious name
Will fhine on records of eternal fame.

By love directed, I would choofe a wife,
To improve my blifs, and eafe the load of life.

---

* Cato.   † Seneca.   ‡ Socrates.

Hail, wedlock! hail, inviolable tye!
Perpetual fountain of domestic joy!
Love, friendship, honour, truth, and pure delight
Harmonious mingle in the nuptial rite.
In Eden, first the holy state began,
When perfect innocence distinguish'd man;
The human pair, the Almighty pontiff led,
Gay as the morning, to the bridal bed;
A dread solemnity the espousals grac'd,
Angels the witnesses, and God the priest!
All earth exulted on the nuptial hour,
And voluntary roses deck'd the bow'r;
The joyous birds on every blossom'd spray,
Sung hymeneans to the important day,
While Philomela swell'd the spousal song,
And Paradise with gratulation rung.

Relate, inspiring muse! where shall I find
A blooming virgin with an angel mind?
Unblemish'd as the white-rob'd virgin quire
That fed, O Rome! thy consecrated fire?
By reason aw'd, ambitious to be good,
Averse to vice, and zealous for her God?
Relate, in what blest region can I find
Such bright perfections in a female mind?
What phœnix-woman breathes the vital air
So greatly good, and so divinely fair?
Sure not the gay and fashionable train,
Licentious, proud, immoral, and profane;
Who spend their golden hours in antic dress,
Malicious whispers, and inglorious ease.

Lo ! round the board a fhining train appears
In rofy beauty, and in prime of years !
This hates a flounce, and this a flounce approves,
This fhows the trophies of her former loves ;
Polly avers, that Sylvia dreft in green,
When laft at church the gaudy nymph was feen ;
Chloe condemns her optics ; and will lay
'Twas azure fattin, interftreak'd with grey ;
Lucy, invefted with judicial power,
Awards 'twas neither,—and the ftrife is o'er.
Then parrots, lap dogs, monkeys, fquirrels, **beaux,**
Fans, ribands, tuckers, patches, furbeloes,
In quick fucceffion, thro' their fancies run,
And dance inceffant, on the flippant tongue.
And when, fatigu'd with ev'ry other fport,
The belles prepare to grace the facred court,
They marfhal all their forces in array,
To kill with glances, and deftroy in play.
Two fkilful maids with reverential fear,
In wanton wreaths collect their filken hair ;
Two paint their cheeks, and round their temples pour
The fragrant unguent, and the ambrofial fhower ;
One pulls the fhape-creating ftays ; and one
Encircles round her waift the golden zone ;
Not with more toil to improve immortal charms,
Strove Juno, Venus, and the queen of arms,
When Priam's fon adjudg'd the golden prize,
To the refiftlefs beauty of the fkies.
At length, equip'd in Love's enticing arms,
With all that glitters, and with all that charms,

The ideal goddesses to church repair,
Peep thro' the fan, and mutter o'er a pray'r,
Or listen to the organ's pompous sound,
Or eye the gilded images around;
Or, deeply studied in coquettish rules,
Aim wily glances at unthinking fools;
Or show the lily hand with graceful air,
Or wound the fopling with a lock of hair :*
And when the hated discipline is o'er,
And misses tortur'd with repent, no more,
They mount the pictur'd coach; and, to the play,
The celebrated idols hie away.

Not so the lass that should my joys improve,
With solid friendship, and connubial love :
A native bloom, with intermingled white,
Should set her features in a pleasing light;
Like Helen flushing with unrival'd charms,
When raptur'd Paris darted in her arms.
But what, alas! avails a ruby cheek,
A downy bosom, or a snowy neck!
Charms ill supply the want of innocence,
Nor beauty forms intrinsic excellence :
But in her breast let moral beauties shine,
Supernal grace and purity divine :
Sublime her reason, and her native wit
Unstrain'd with pedantry, and low conceit;
Her fancy lively, and her judgment free
From female prejudice and bigotry :
Averse to idol pomp, and outward show,
The flatt'ring coxcomb, and fantastic beau.

The fop's impertinence she should despise,
Tho' sorely wounded by her radiant eyes;
But pay due rev'rence to the exalted mind,
By learning polish d, and by wit refin'd,
Who all her virtues, without guile, commends,
And all her faults as freely reprehends.
Soft Hymen's rites her passion should approve,
And in her bosom glow the flames of love:
To me her soul, by sacred friendship, turn,
And I, for her, with equal friendship burn:
In ev'ry stage of life afford relief,
Partake my joys, and sympathize my grief;
Unshaken, walk in Virtue's peaceful road,
Nor bribe her Reason to pursue the mode;
Mild as the saint whose errors are forgiv'n,
Calm as a vestal, and compos'd as heaven.
This be the partner, this the lovely wife,
That should embellish and prolong my life,
A nymph! who might a second fall inspire,
And fill a glowing cherub with desire!
With her I'd spend the pleasurable day,
While fleeting minutes gayly danc'd away:
With her I'd walk, delighted, o er the green,
Thro' ev'ry blooming mead, and rural scene;
Or sit in open fields damask'd with flow'rs,
Or where cool shades imbrown the noon-tide bow'rs.
Imparadis'd within my eager arms,
I'd reign the happy monarch of her charms;
Oft on her panting bosom would I lay,
And, in dissolving raptures melt away;

Then lull'd, by nightingales, to balmy reſt,
My blooming fair ſhould ſlumber at my breaſt.

And when decrepid age (frail mortals' doom)
Should bend my wither'd body to the tomb,
No warbling ſyrens ſhould retard my flight
To heavenly manſions of unclouded light.
Tho Death, with his imperial horrors crown'd,
Terrific grinn'd, and formidably frown'd,
Offences pardon'd and remitted ſin,
Should form a calm ſerenity within:
Bleſſing my natal and my mortal hour,
(My ſoul commited to the eternal pow'r)
Inexorable Death ſhould ſmile, for I
Who knew to live, would never fear to die.

DESCRIPTIVE LINES,

*Written at the requeſt of a Friend, upon the ſurrrounding
Proſpect from* BEACON-HILL *in* BOSTON.

BY PHILENIA, A LADY OF BOSTON.

FAR from this ſpot let ſportive FICTION hie,
  While rapt ATTENTION lifts her ſearching eye,
O'er CHARLESTOWN's *field* each hallow'd view explores,
Sees the *twin* rivers lave the purple ſhores,
Where the high ſoil diſdain'd the trembling flood,
And ſtain'd the white wave with *Britannia's* blood,

While the fierce blaze* its wafting vengeance pours,
Wraps the wide domes, and climbs the afcending towers,
The crimfon eye of frantic SLAUGHTER turn'd,
Where *valour* perifh'd, and where *vict'ry* mourn'd,
And kindred worth unboafting forrow fhed,
As deathlefs WARREN bow'd his patriot head.

Thy Temple, *Charles!* a new-rais'd Phœnix fhines,
Thy far fam'd bridge the fifter-city joins,
Whofe flame-tipt fpires reflect the folar ray,
And ftrew with ftars the azure robe of day;
Here varied MARTS one full EMPORIUM boaft,
Rich with the wealth of ev'ry foreign coaft;
How chang'd the fcene, fince round the dreary glade
The frowning foreft bent its murky fhade!
E'en on this fpot, with green favannas fpread,
Adorn'd by GENIUS, and by PLENTY fed,
The hungry *Savage* dafh'd the foaming flood,
Trac'd the blue rock, and fwept the weedy wood;
Our patient Sires the wild'ring region gain,
Bend the hard oak, the wat'ry valley drain,
'Till down the tide the moving foreft flows,
And where the *defart* howl'd, the polifh'd *City* rofe,
Whofe *crefcent* haven's lib'ral furface fmiles,
Clad in the verdure of unnumber'd ifles,
Where fcepter'd WILLIAM's maffy bulwarks ftand,
The *guard* and *glory* of the fceneful land.

A a

---

* Alluding to the burning of Charleftown by the Brit-
in 1775.

Yon orient heights† their rifted foreheads raife,
And claim the triumph of the VICTOR's praife ;
Still lives the morn, when from thofe armed brows
The SONS OF FREEDOM brav'd their *prifon'd* foes ;
While o'er the deep the giant *Terror* bends,
Death's lifted arm his fable dart extends,
The *Dance*‡ no more its graceful charm fupplies,
No more the fcenes of *mimic nature* rife,
Thro' bleeding ranks the deathful dangers roll,
And peals of ruin fhake the foldier's foul ;
For him no beauty decks the vernal fields,
But ev'ry breeze a more than winter yields,
Flight all his *hope*, and honor all his *care*,
The warlike Briton learns for once *to fear*,
To the bleak wave refigns his murm'ring hoft,
And quits the fullen fanguinary coaft.
So in the climes, where changeful feafons roll,
Ere threat'ning winter gains his full control,
While ruftling leaves in crumbling ruin lie,
Ting'd with the rainbow's variegated dye,
The *feather'd race* the howling ftorm forefee,
The barren meadow, and the naked tree ;
Late to thofe fhores were all their joys confin'd,
Now death and hunger float in ev'ry wind,
With outftretch'd wing they fkim along the main,
And quit the Terrors of an hoftile plain.

----

† Dorchefter heights, the fortifying of which by General WASHINGTON in March 1776, compelled the Britifh
to evacuate the town.

‡ The Ball and the Drama formed the amufements of
the Garrifon, during the fiege.

Let yon VAST FANE rear its ionic fide,
The boaft of art, the *great defigner's*‖ pride ;
There refts in filent cells the holy dead,
There weeping SCIENCE droops her widow'd head,
Since BOWDOIN fleeps, deaf to his country's praife,
Deaf to the heavenly poet's living lays.

What varied charms adorn the circling main,
The peopled ifthmus, and the velvet plain !
Here ruddy HEALTH the grateful foil divides,
There gen'rous COMMERCE cleaves the freighted tides.
How fweet the fragrance of the fylvan fcene,
The rofy arbor, and the bow'ry green !
At eve to climb the mountain's pendent brow,
While at its bafe the boiling waters flow,
See the low fun his rubied globe difplay,
And lean collected on the edge of day !
From cultur'd dales behold the high hills rife
With piny fummits, curtain'd by the fkies !
Down whofe green flopes, in all their pearly pride,
Thro' mantling flowers the glaffy riv'lets glide,
While the flocks whiten thro' the cottag'd vale,
And notes of mufic fill the fcented gale.

Like a new planet mid the vaft ferene,
Lo ! rifing HARVARD fwells the extended fcene,
O'er diftant regions fpreads a ray divine,
Bids " other BOWDOINS other WINTHROPS fhine"!
Such QUEEN OF CITIES ! are thy rich domains,
And fuch the realm, where GODLIKE FREEDOM reigns !

‖ The celebrated Architect, Mr. Harrifon.

ODE

To the President,

On his visiting the Northern States.

BY THE SAME.

THE Season sheds its mildest ray,
  O'er the blue waves the sun-beams play,
The bending harvest gilds the plain,
The tow'ring vessels press the main,
The ruddy ploughman quits his toil,
The pallid miser leaves his spoil,
And grateful pæans hail the festive year,
Which bids *Columbia's* guardian God appear.

Hence! DISAPPOINTMENT'S anxious eye,
And pale AFFLICTION's ling'ring sigh;
Let sorrow from the brow be torn,
And ev'ry heart forget to mourn;
Let smiles of peace their charms display
To grace this joy-devoted day,
And, where *that* arm preserv'd the peopled plain,
Shall mild Contentment hold her placid reign.

Let " *white rob'd choirs*" in beauty gay
With lucid flowrets strew the way,
Let Lilachs scent the purpled lawn,
And roses emulate the dawn,
Let domes their circling honors spread,
And wreaths entwine that glorious head;
To thee, GREAT WASHINGTON, each lyre be strung,
Thy matchless deeds by ev'ry bard be sung!

When FREEDOM rais'd her drooping head,
Thy arm her willing heros led,
When all her hopes, to thee refign'd,
Were refting on thy god-like mind,
How did that foul, to fear unknown,
And feeling for *her* fate alone,
O'er Danger's threat'ning form the faulchion wield,
And tread with dauntlefs ftep the crimfon field!

Not DECIUS—patriot dear to fame!
Not CINCINNATUS—deathlefs name!
Not HE,* who led the Athenian band,
The faviour of a bleeding land,
Could fuch exalted worth difplay,
Nor fhine with fuch unclouded ray.
Of *Age* the HOPE, of *Youth* the LEADING STAR,
The *Soul* of PEACE, the CONQUERING ARM OF WAR.

---

* THEMISTOCLES.

INVOCATION to HOPE.

BY THE SAME.

SOOTHER of Life! by whofe delufive charm
   This feeling heart refifts the pointed woe,
Whofe magic power, with fancied joys can warm,
   And wipe the tear which Anguifh taught to flow;

If, thro' the varied griefs my Youth has known,
   No charm but thefe could raife my votive eye;
O leave me not, now every blefling's flown,
   Whilft my fad bofom heaves the lengthen'd figh.

The grated prifon, and the lov'd-form'd bower,
   The wretch, whom Difappointment waftes away,
The frugal hut, the gilded dome of power,
   Joy in thy fmiles and court thy equal fway.

By thee, the friendlefs fufferer learns to bear;
   By thee, the patient heart forgets its woe;
Thou mak'ft Misfortune's iron afpect fair,
   And e'en the frozen cheek of Mifery glow.

Leave me no more, as on that fated morn
   When my rafh foul the impious deed defign'd,
And when, unconfcious of thy bleft return,
   The foe Defpair ufurp'd my tortur'd mind.

But yet, bright Goddefs! with deceptive fmile,
   Come, and a hoft of Fictions in thy train,
With dreams of peace my wearied heart beguile,
   And fink in fancied blifs the real pain.

PRAYER to PATIENCE.

BY THE SAME.

GODDESS of the steady eye !
　　All thy Apathy impart,
From a world of woe I fly,
　　Take, oh take me to thy heart !

Lend me all thy healing power,
　　Teach me to suppress the groan,
Let me while affliction's lower,
　　Turn like NIOBE *to stone.*

Let me to the *sneer* of scorn,
　　Still return the placid *smile,*
Calm,—when angry passions frown,
　　Silent,—when the rude revile.

Check the Tyrant of the mind,
　　Source of *sorrow,* *Foe* to *thee*;
Who can peace, or solace find,
　　Rack'd by *Sensibility !*

Snatch me from her wasting sway,
　　Shield me with thy firmer aid,
Let me still thy voice obey,
　　Gentle, peace-preserving maid !

If greater pangs this bosom rend,
　　Than ever bosom felt before ;
Further may thy sway extend,
　　Greater, deeper be thy power.

Be every *wrong* difarm'd by thee,
   Rob ftern *Oppreffion* of his pride,
Bid *Malice* at thy prefence flee,
   Turn *Envy's* venom'd dart afide.

Let hard *Reproach* foft kindnefs feel,
   To cold *Difdain* be pity lent,
From *Anger* wreft his lifted fteel,
   From black *Revenge* his difcontent.

Goddefs of the tearlefs eye!
   Yet give me thy pacific charms;
To thy calm bofom let me fly,
   And find a refuge in thy arms!

L I N E S,

Addreffed to the inimitable Author *of the* Poems *under the
fignature of* Della Crufca.

BY THE SAME.

A CROSS the vaft Atlantic tide,
   Down *Apalachia's* graffy fide,
What echoing founds the foul beguile,
And lend *the lip of grief* a fmile!
'Tis DELLA CRUSCA's heavenly fong,
Which floats the weftern fhores along,

Breathing as sweet, as soft a strain,
As kindness to the ear of pain ;
Splendid as noon, as morning clear,
And chaste as evening's pearly tear ;
Where *cold despair* in music flows,
While all the FIRE OF GENIUS glows.

Still thy enchanting powers display,
Still charm me with the magic lay !
The Muses all thy soul inspire,
Apollo tunes thy matchless lyre !
O strike the lustral string again,
And o'er Columbia waft the strain.

Ah ! would to light my clouded days,
One ray from thy unequall'd blaze,
Might thro my dark'ning fortunes shine,
And grace me with a note like thine !
But no, BRIGHT BARD, for thee alone
The Muses weave the *laurel crown :*
Ne'er can the *timid, plaintive dove,*
Soar with the DAUNTLESS BIRD OF JOVE;
Nor *silv'ry Hesper's* dewy ray
Beam like the *Golden Orb of Day.*

Bb

ALFRED to PHILENIA.*

MY morn of life was bright and fair,
    The diftant mifts of gloomy *Care*,
By *Joy's* light breeze, which daily blew,
Were fcatter'd far beyond the view.
Then bleffings crown'd the happy hours—
Then *Pleafure* ftrew'd my path with flowers;
Then *Virtue* oped an eafy way,
And led my footfteps up to day.
If e'er the *Child* of *Sorrow* mourn'd
My fympathetic bofom burn'd ;
The higheft blifs my foul could know,
Was, to relieve the pang of woe.

   Such fcenes my fondeft feelings warm'd—
Such fcenes my earlieft habits form'd ;
This dangerous race thro' youth I ran,
And, ruin'd, reach'd the verge of man.

   Alas ! fad wretch !—I've wept, and run
At *Pity's* call——to be undone ;
Beneath the flowers which ftrew'd my way,
The thorn of keeneft anguifh lay ;
Even in the bofs of *Virtue's* fhield,
The fting of torture lay conceal'd.

   Ah, fatal *Love !*——
   Now *Hope* has clof'd her fun-bright eye,
And midnight glooms my midday fky ;

---

* This, and the three next fucceeding Poems, are extracted from the Columbian Centinel of 1791.

Despair now heaves his horrid form,
And frowns terrific in the storm;
No ray of blifs now meets my fight,
And my whole foul is wrap'd in night.

    Ah, fweeteft *Poetefs*! thy lay
  Can charm the weightieft woes away;
The foft compaffion of thy feeling breaft,
Can fhed a drop of balm, and lull my foul to reft.

PHILENIA TO ALFRED.

ALFRED! the heaven lent mufe is thine,
    Then bid impetuous forrow ceafe;
And at the bright *Apollo's* fhrine,
  Recal thy exil'd heart to peace.

  Vain is the tear in anguifh fhed,
And vain the pang by paffion fed,
Then to the mufe thy moments give,
And for her deathlefs laurel *live*.

  Ne'er hope in carelefs crouds to find
A refuge for thy *lonely* mind,
Think not the fympathetick figh,
The language of the moving eye,
    Will o'er thy with'ring forrows flow;
Envy will fneer, and *rancour* frown,
Or *ignorant malice* drag thee down,
    And fcorn to folace what it cannot know.

Yet there are *some* to mercy true;
 And such *my griefs* have found,
 Who o'er each life-destroying wound,
Shed pity's healing dew.

Such be thy favour'd lot, for they
Will live beyond the summer day,
Will mid'st the weeping autumn smile,
And e'en the wintry waste beguile;
Will thy sad breast from anguish free,
The friends of gentleness and thee.

But, if the slave of love thou art
 Still languish and *endure*,
For when that strikes *the feeling heart*,
 Like death, it has no cure.

ALFRED TO PHILENIA.

AND does the heart, by love distress'd,
 " Like death, admit no cure?"
Must *Alfred's* deeply-tortur'd breast,
 " Still languish, and endure?"

Ah! for a moment stay thy doom,
Nor drive him frantic to the tomb.
Thy sweet, thy all-subduing lay,
The tempests of the soul obey—
At thy command its ragings cease—
Thou speak'st and ev'ry heart is peace;
While thron'd sublime above the storm,
Thou wear'st a radiant Seraph's form,

And, smiling o'er the solemn scene,
Thy aspect speaks a mind serene.

Know then—o'er *Alfred's* sinking soul,
The waves of ceaseless anguish roll—
Love has assail'd his yielding heart,
And pierc'd it with his sharpest dart;
Time's lenient hand its healing aid denies,
And every hour a heavier pang supplies.

When life's quick eddies warm'd his youthful heart,
He fell a prey to soft deceptive art—
To DELIA every real charm was given,
And ALFRED lov'd her next to Truth and Heaven.
Unus'd to guile, in love with truth,
And glowing with the fire of youth,
His mind the future prospect view'd,
Where fancy every blessing shew'd—
The path of bliss expanded lay,
And flowers EDENIAN strew'd the way,
While all around the alluring scene,
Transported Friendship smil'd serene,
And Nature with endearing smile,
Spread out each gay enchanting wile,
And from the landscape scene refin'd,
Brought sweetest rapture to the mind.

But when this gay delusion flew,
A dreary desart oped to view;
Where nought but thorns the cheerless heath supplied,
Where Hope swift fled, and Expectation died.

But ALFRED lives amid a world of night,
Each hour beguiles him of a fresh delight;

" Chill Penury's" fiends, with angry afpect lour
Round his fad path, and wither every flower,
No gleams of joy pierce thro' the encreafing gloom,
And Peace eludes his grafp, and flies beyond the tomb.

Muft ALFRED then, "the flave of Love,"
   " Still languifh and endure ?"
Can nought the torturing pangs remove
   Is death the only cure ?

The world has "friends to mercy true"—
   " Such ALFRED's griefs have found,"
Who in his breaft " fhed pity's healing dew"—
But Friendfhip's pity cannot heal the wound.

P H I L E N I A TO A L F R E D.

"PEN'RY," no ALFRED ! 'tis not thine,
   In thy rich Soul's exhauftlefs Mine
Abounds more Wealth, than GANGES golden Shores
   E'er on the tawny Chiefs beftow'd,
   When parting from the facred Flood,
   The falfly, glitt'ring, yellow Sand,
   Spreads Treafure thro' the torrid Land,
   Or tho' from out the burning Soil,
   Drawn by the harden'd Hand of Toil,
   The precious fparkling Drops are plac'd
   Round the flim Zone of Beauty's Waift,
And add new Splendour to fome Monarch's Stores.
   Does not the vernal Morning rife
   With Radiance to thy grateful Eyes?

Does not the breezy Flow of Eve
A Tranſport to thy Boſom give?
And ev'ry life-diſſolving Sigh,
Fill thy rapt Soul with Extacy,
When thy loſt Charmer on thy Viſion beams,
And feeds wild Fancy with deluſive Dreams?

Ah! ALFRED, I of Griefs could ſpeak,
'Till at ſoft Pity's call
The iron Tears would fall
In burning Streams down hard Oppreſſion's Cheek.
But no! I quit the heartleſs Lay,
And caſt the unavailing Theme away.

When wand'ring o'er the fragrant Vale,
Soft Warblings wafting thro' the Gale,
Does not thy Soul a Pardon find
For Words unjuſt, and Deeds unkind?
Do not the cruel Herd inſpire
Compaſſion or Diſdain?
Can Scorn's cold Eye thy boſom fire.
To yield one Wrong again?
No! ALFRED, no! the MUSE is thine!
And where her Bounties flow,
All the bright beaming Virtues ſhine,
The warm Affections glow.
Then can that Duſt poor Miſers hoard,
Enrich thy wealthy Soul?
Can ſordid Ore one Bliſs afford?
One tyrant Pang controul?

The friendlefs Flatt'rer's fmile to prove,
　To purchafe venal Beauty's Eye,
　To fwell mad Envy's frantic Sigh,
And lofe each Sympathy of Love;
Such are the Joys which Gold can give,
And fuch e'en Mifers may receive,
　　But fuch can ne'er be thine.—
The MUSE extends her open Arms,
She courts thee with unbounded Charms,
Her Pencil paints each glowing Scene,
Her Mufick floats along the Green,
By her the laurel'd Virtues live,
She bids degraded Vice, the Blufh of Confcience give.
　　Science is her's, and ev'ry Art divine.
　Then like PHILENIA quit the Herd,
　　Where Mercy is unknown:
　And be thy votive Prayer preferr'd,
　　At great APOLLO's Throne.

Sweet Solitude, kind Nurfe of Song,
Allures me from the joylefs Throng,
Spreads her repofing Breaft to me,　　　　[to thee.
And bids my tunelefs Harp waft long Adieus to cities and

POEM,

Written in Boston, at the commencement of the late Revolution.

BY JAMES ALLEN, OF BOSTON.

FROM realms of bondage and a tyrant's reign,
   Our godlike fathers bore no slavish chain;
To Pharaoh's face the inspired patriarchs stood,
To seal their virtue, with a martyr's blood:
But lives so precious, such a sacred seed,
The source of empires, heaven's high will decreed:
He snatch'd the saints from Pharaoh's impious hand,
And bade his chosen seek this distant land:
Then to these climes the illustrious exiles sped,
'Twas freedom prompted, and the Godhead led.
Eternal woods the virgin soil defac'd,
A dreary desert, and an howling waste;
A haunt of tribes no pity taught to spare,
And they oppos'd them with remorseless war,
But heaven's right arm led forth the faithful train,
The guardian Godhead swept the insidious plain,
Till the scour'd thicket amicable stood,
Nor dastard ambush trench'd the dusky wood:
Our sires then earn'd, no more, precarious bread,
Nor midst alarms their frugal meals were spread;
Fair boding hopes inur'd their hands to toil,
And patriot virtue nurs'd the thriving soil;

Nor scarce two ages have their periods run,
Since o'er their culture smil'd the genial sun;
And now what states extend their fair domains
O'er fleecy mountains and luxuriant plains!
Where happy millions their own fields possess,
No tyrant awes them, and no lords oppress;
The hand of rule, divine discretion guides,
And white-robed virtue o'er her paths presides,
Each polic'd order venerates the laws,
And each, ingenuous, speaks in freedom's cause;
The Spartan spirit, nor the Roman name,
The patriot's pride, shall rival these in fame;
Here all the sweets that social life can know,
From the full font of civil sapience flow;
Here golden Ceres clothes the autumnal plain,
And art's fair empress holds her new domain;
Here angel science spreads her lucid wing,
And hark, how sweet the new-born Muses sing!
Here generous commerce spreads her liberal hand,
And scatters foreign blessings round the land.
Shall meagre Mammon, or proud lust of sway,
Reverse these scenes? Will heaven permit the day?
Shall in this era all our hopes expire,
And weeping freedom from her fanes retire?
Here, shall the tyrant still our peace pursue,
From the pain'd eye-brow drink the vital dew?
Nor nature's barrier wards, our fathers' foe,
Seas roll in vain, and boundless oceans flow?

　　Stay, Pharaoh,* stay : that impious hand forbear,
Nor tempt the genius of our souls too far;

------

* The King of Great-Britain.

How oft, ungracious, in thy thanklefs ftead,
Mid fcenes of death, our generous youth have bled!
When the proud Gaul thy mightieft powers repell'd,
And drove thy legions, trembling, from the field,
We rent the laurel from the victor's brow,
And round thy temples taught the wreath to grow.†
Say, when thy flaughter'd bands the defart dy'd,
Where lone Ohio rolls her gloomy tide,
Whofe dreary banks their wafting bones infhrine,
What arm aveng'd them? thanklefs! was it thine?‡
But generous valor fcorns a boafting word,
And confcious virtue reaps her own reward:
Yet confcious virtue bids thee now to fpeak,
Tho' guilty blufhes kindle o'er thy cheek;
If wafting wars and painful toils at length,
Had drain'd our veins, and wither'd all our ftrength,
How could ft thou, cruel, form the vile defign,
And round our neck the wreath of bondage twine?
And if fome lingering fpirit rous'd to ftrife,
Bid ruffian murder drink the dregs of life?
Shall future ages e'er forget the deed?
And fhan't, for this, impious Britain bleed?

----

† The taking of Louifbourg in the year 1755, by General Pepperell.

‡ The fame year the King's troops were furprized near the banks of the Ohio; when our illuftrious General Wafhington covered the retreat, and faved the deftruction of the whole army. A body of the French was repulfed at an affault of the provincial lines at the weftward, their General taken prifoner, and their whole army compelled to fly back to Canada.

When comes the period, heaven predeſtines muſt,
When Europe's glories ſhall be whelm'd in duſt,
When our proud fleets the naval wreath ſhall wear,
And o' r her empires hurl the bolts of war,
Unnerv'd by fate, the boldeſt heart ſhall fail,
And, mid their guards, auxiliar kings grow pale ;
In vain ſhall Britain lift her ſuppliant eye,
An alien'd offspring feels no filial tye,
Her tears in vain ſhall bathe the ſoldiers' feet,
Remember, ingrate, Boſton's crimſon'd ſtreet ;§
Whole hecatombs of lives the deed ſhall pay,
And purge the murders of that guilty day.‖

But why to future periods look ſo far,
What force e'er fac'd us, that we fear'd to dare?
Then can'ſt thou think, e'en on this early day,
Proud force ſhall bend us to a tyrant's ſway?
A foreign foe oppos'd our ſword in vain,*
And thine own troops we've rallied on the plain.†
If then our lives your lawleſs ſword invade,
Think'ſt thou, enſlav'd, we'll kiſs the pointed blade?
Nay, let experience ſpeak, be this the teſt,—
Tis from experience that we reaſon beſt,—

----

§ The Maſſacre of the 5th of March 1770.

‖ The Poet ſeems to have been very prophetic in this
beautiful paſſage.

* The extirpation of the Neutrals from Nova-Scotia.

† The Provincials covered the retreat from the French
lines at Ticonderoga, when the Britiſh General, Aber-
crombie, was defeated by the Marquis Montcalm, in 1758.

When first the mandate fhew'd the fhameless plan,
To rank our race beneath the clafs of man,
Low as the brute to fink the human line,
Our toil our portion, and the harvest thine,
Modeft but firm, we plead the facred caufe,
On nature bal'd, and fanction'd by the laws;
But your deaf ear the confcious plea denied,
Some demon counfel'd, and the fword reply'd;
Your navy then our haven cover'd o'er,
And arm'd battalions trefpafs'd on our fhore,
Thro the prime ftreets, they march'd in war's array:
At noon's full blaze, and in the face of day:
With dumb contempt we pafs'd the fervile fhow,
While fcorn's proud fpirit fcowl'd on every brow;
Day after day fucceffive wrongs we bore,
Till patience, wearied, could fupport no more,
Till flaughter'd lives our native ftreets prophan'd,
And thy flaves' hand our hallow'd crimfon ftain'd;
No fudden rage the ruffian foldier tore,
Or drench'd the pavements with his vital gore,
Deliberate thought did all our fouls compofe,
Till, veil'd in glooms, the lowery morning rofe;
No mob then furious urg'd the impaffion'd fray,
Nor clamorous tumults dinn'd the folemn day;
In full convene the city‡ fenate fat,
Our fathers' fpirit rul'd the firm debate:
The freeborn foul no reptile tyrant checks,
Tis heaven that dictates when the people fpeaks;

---

‡ Town-meeting at Faneuil-Hall.

Loud from their tongues the awful mandate broke,
And thus, infpir'd, the facred fenate fpoke ;
Ye mifcreant troops, be gone! our prefence fly ;
S ay, if ye dare, but if ye dare, ye die!
Ah, too fevere, the fearful chief § replies,
Permit one half, the other, inftant, flies.
No parle, avaunt, or by our fathers' fhades,
Your reeking lives fhall glut our vengeful blades.
Ere morning's light, begone,—or elfe we fwear,
Each flaughter'd corfe fhall feed the birds of air!
Ere morning's light had ftreak'd the fkies with red,
The chieftain yielded, and the foldier fled.
Tis thus experience fpeaks—the teft forbear,
Nor fhew thefe ftates your feeble front of war.
But ftill your navies lord it o'er the main,—
Their keels are natives of our oaken plain ;
  E'en the proud maft that bears your flag on high,
  ” Grew on our foil, and ripen'd in our fky :
  “ Know then thyfelf, prefume not us to fcan,
Your power precarious, and your ifle a fpan.

  Yet could our wrongs in juft oblivion fleep,
And on each neck reviv'd affection weep,
The brave are generous, and the good forgive,
Then fay you've wrong'd us, and our parent live ;‖
But face not fate, oppofe not heaven's decree,
Let not that curfe our mother light on thee.

_____

  § The infamous Governor Hutchinfon.

  ‖ Her tyrants were too felf-conceited, and too obftinate,
to take the advice of men of the beft fenfe and underftand-
ing. The confequence has been the eftablifhment of liberty and univerfal commerce in America.

AN INTENDED INSCRIPTION

Written for the Monument on Beacon-Hill, in Boston, and addressed to the Passenger.

BY THE SAME.

WHERE stretch'd your sail, beneath what foreign sky
 Did lovlier landscapes ever charm your eye?
Could fancy's fairy pencil, Stranger! say,
E'en dipt in dreams, a nobler scene portray?

   Behold yon vales, whose skirts elude your view,
And mountains fading to ærial blue!
Along their bow'ry shades how healthy toil
Alternate sports, or tends the mellow soil.
See rural towns mid groves and gardens rise,
And eastward,—where the stretching ocean lies,
Lo! our fair capital sublimes the scene,
New *Albion's* pride, and ocean's future queen;
How o'er the tradeful port august she smiles,
Her sea-like haven boasts an hundred isles,
Whence hardy commerce swells the lofty sails
O'er arctic seas, and mocks the polar gales,
Thence tides of wealth the wafting breezes bring,
And hence e'en culture feels its vital spring.

   These scenes our Sires from rugged nature wrought,
Since—what dire wars their patriot race have fought!
Witness yon tracts, where first the Briton bled,
Driv'n by our youth redoubted PIERCY fled:

There BREED afcends, and BUNKER's bleeding fteeps,
Still o'er whofe brow abortive Vict'ry weeps;
What Trophies fince! the gaze of after times,
Rear'd *Freedom's* empire o'er our happy climes!

But hence, fond Stranger, take a nobler view,
See yon fhorn elm,* whence all thefe glories grew.
Here, where the armed foe prefumptious trod,
Trampled our fhrines, and even mouth'd our GOD,
His vengeful hand, deep as the parent-root,
Lopt each grown branch, and ev'ry fuckling fhoot;
Becaufe beneath her confecrated fhade
Our earlieft vows to LIBERTY were paid.
High from *her Altar* blew the heaven-caught fire,
While all our wealth o'erhung the kindling pyre.
How at the deed the Nations ftood aghaft,
As on the pile our plighted lives we caft!

O! if an alien from our fair domains,
The blood of *Britain*, haplefs, taint your veins,
Pace o'er that hallow'd ground with awful tread,
And tears, atoning, o'er yon relick fhed;
But if, American! your lineage fprings,
From Sires, who fcorn the pedigree of kings,
A Georgian born you breathe the tepid air,
Or on the breezy banks of *Delaware*,
Or hardy *Hampfhire* claim your haughty birth,
Revere yon root and kifs its nurt'ring earth:
O be its fibre fed by flowing fprings,
Whence rofe our empire o'er the thrones of kings:

❦ The ftump of Liberty-Tree.❧

E'en now defcend, adore the dear remain,
Where firft rear'd Liberty's illumin'd fane,
There all her race, while time's revolve fhall come,
As pilgrims flock to MECCA's idol'd tomb.

ELEGIAC ODE,

Sacred to the Memory of General GREENE.

BY GEORGE RICHARDS, OF BOSTON.

SAY, fhall the bards of ancient Greece and Rome,
    In all the pathos of impaffion'd woe,
Mourn with their country, at the hero's tomb,
    And fire a world to emulation's glow?
Shall weeping mufes quit Pierian groves,
    To deck the fod, where reft the good, the brave;
And fhall the warrior, whom an empire loves
    Repofe, unfung, unhonor'd in the grave?

Forbid it, heaven! Columbia claims the fong:
    Touch'd with her griefs, I fweep the plaintive lyre:
To her, to Greene, immortal ftrains belong:
    An angel's pencil, and a feraph's fire.
Whilft facred Truth, from realms of light divine,
    Shall pour the tide of intellectual day,
And lead my footfteps to the hero's fhrine,
    Where patriots guard, and freemen watch the clay.

D d

When firſt Britannia bath'd her ſword in gore,
  His ſoul, indignant, ſpurn'd the peaceſul ſhade;
Inſtant he arm'd, to brave the Lion's roar,
  And the keen terrors of the Highland blade.
Prompt at his call, to hoſtile fields he led
  The hardy yeomen of his native iſle;*
True ſons of liberty; whom virtue bred,
  Strong for the labors of Herculean toil.

Mild of acceſs, in him, no little pride
  Obſcur'd the greatneſs of a noble mind;
He felt for all; the ſoldier at his ſide
  Brought down the ſweeteſt " milk of human kind."
For council honor'd, in the camp belov'd,
  Sagacious, cool, amid the ſtorm ſerene;
Heroes rever'd, applauding States approv'd,
  And Albion trembled at the name of GREENE.

Oft have his limbs the frozen earth compreſs'd,
  Whilſt round his head the watery torrent pour'd;
Thick clouds the curtains to his couch of reſt,
  Where the bleak wind and midnight hail-ſtorm roar'd.
And oft, advancing with the ſolar ray,
  His banners flam'd to meet the lightning's glare,
In torrid realms of more than burning day;
  Sad haunts of death, and plagues, and putrid air.

There hallow'd truths, inſcrib'd on glory's roll,
  Written in blood on honor's purple veſt,
Shall gallant warriors, born of kindred ſoul,
  With conſcious pride, and martial zeal atteſt.

---

  * General GREENE commanded the troops raiſed by the
State of Rhode-Iſland, the firſt campaign of the late war.

Illustrious men! ye nerv'd his mighty hand,
  To crush the savage on the warlike plain;
When to the south he wheel'd his conquering band,
  And broke the iron of oppression's chain.

Around the shores which Hudson's billows lave,
  His laurel wreaths shall ever verdant bloom;
And Trenton's cypress shade the hero's grave,
  Whilst pensive Princeton mourns his early tomb.
August abodes! ye heard the trumpet's sound;
  Which bade his columns range, his squadrons form;
Ye saw his coursers snuff the embattled ground,
  And Greene, triumphant, rule the vengeful storm.

Array'd in tears and garb of sable hue,
  See Brandywine the chieftain's hearse attend;
And Germantown † lament—and Monmouth, rob'd in
  And Ashley's waters wail their god-like friend. [yew,
Immortal grounds! the theme of every age,
  Your meanest dust shall speak the hero's praise;
Here bolted vengeance burst with tenfold rage,
  And there he drove the lightning's rapid blaze.

Nor less illustrious are the banks of Dan,
  Or Guilford's fields, where feats of bold emprise,
Proclaim the genius of the matchless man:
  Though all the regions, mark'd by azure skies,
Ye saw his arms the vollied thunders deal,
  Which check'd Cornwallis in his mid career;
With Tarleton's sword, and Rawdon's murderous steel,
  And savage Balfour pal'd with guilty fear.

---

† At Germantown, Monmouth, and in South-Caroli-
na, Gen. GREENE was honored with distinguished command.

Illustrious spots of earth's high favor'd mould!
  What, tho no clarions swell to dire alarms,
And no proud chief, in pomp of burnish'd gold,
  Leads on his troops in the bright glow of arms;
Yet shall the veteran there recount the tale
  Of armies rais'd, uncloth'd, unfed, unpaid,
Who stood the summer's heat, the winter's gale,
  Nor turn'd their bosoms from the tyrant's blade.

Such were the men, who own'd the power of GREENE,
  When the shrill music, lengthening down the line,
Urg'd rank on rank, to try the dubious scene,
  And combat hosts, by despots thought divine.
Thrice honor'd chief! the work of death is past,
  Thy task completed, smiling peace descends,
Hush'd is the din, and mute the trumpet's blast,
  And ardent warrior's greet as ancient friends.

Mature in life, with endless honor crown'd,
  Too bright for earth, and fit for purer skies,
Celestial bards his mighty deeds resound,
  Whilst thus, aloud, a prince of angels cries.
" At God's decree, by heaven's high throne, I swear,
  " Tis done! tis done! his time shall be no more!
" Thou king of death descend, on wings of air,
  " And waft the hero to his native shore."

The obedient monarch cleft the etherial way,‡
  His golden darts were tipp'd with sacred fire,
He rode the chariot of eternal day,
  And, fleet as lightning, pass'd the applauding choir.

---

‡ General GREENE died of the *Coup de Soleil*, or Stroke of the Sun.

His radiant form the hero kenn'd afar,
 Refolv'd in death to boaft fupernal fame,
He mounted fwift, lafh'd on the burning car,
 And tower'd fublime in robes of folar flame.

According fpirits tun'd the fong of love,
 From heavenly harps was heard triumphant praife,
Which breath'd thrice welcome to the climes above,
 In the mild mufic of harmonious lays.
A paufe enfued ; the melting lyre was ftill,
 And this the voice which trumpets roll'd around.
" Go, fix the hero's throne on glory's hill,
 " And be the chief by mightieft warriors crown'd."

The laurel wreath was borne in Warren's hand,
 The great Montgomery thron'd the immortal GREENE,
The gentle Mercer join'd the feftive band,
 And gallant Laurens graced the glorious fcene.
Uncounted veterans throng'd the bleft abodes ;
 Loud fwell'd the notes to extacy divine ;
And Spartan heroes, next in rank to Gods,
 Proclaim'd, with Wolfe, the palm of merit thine.

THE COUNTRY SCHOOL.†

PUT to the door—the school's begun—
  Stand in your places every one,—
Attend ———

  •   •   •   •   •   •   •   •   •   •

Read in the bible,—tell the place,—
" *Job twentieth and the seventeenth varse*—
Caleb, begin. *And—he—shall—suck—*
Sir,—Moses got a pin and stuck———
Silence,—stop Caleb—Moses! here!
What's this complaint? *I didn't, Sir,—*
Hold up your hand,—What is't a pin?
O dear, I won't do so agin.
Read on. *The increase of his h--h--horse—*
Hold: H, O, U, S, E, spells house.
Sir, what's this word? for I can't tell it.
Can't you indeed! Why spell it. *Spell it.*
Begin yourself, I say. *Who, I?*
Yes, try. Sure you can spell it. *Try.*
Go, take your seats and primers, go,
You sha'n't abuse the bible so.

———

† This Poem is extracted from the New-Hampshire Spy,
where it is introduced by the following note: ——" Mr.
Osborne, The following may fill a corner of your Spy, if
there is any thing original, natural or just, in thus sketching
out a picture of a common Town School, where there are
frequently such vast numbers of every age, size and sex
sent together, as to create perpetual confusion, distract an
illiterate master, and frustrate the noble design of sending
them."

Will pray Sir Master mend my pen?
Say, Master, that s enough.—Here Ben,
Is this your copy? Can't you tell?
Set all your letters parallel.
I've done my sum—'tis just a groat—
Let's see it.—*Master, m' I g' out?*
Yes,—bring some wood in—What's that noise?
It isn't I, Sir, it's them boys.——

Come Billy, read—What's that? *That's A—*
Sir, Jim has snatch'd my rule away——
Return it, James.—Here, rule with this—
Billy, read on,—*That's crooked S.*
Read in the spelling-book—Begin—
The boys are out— Then call them in—
My nose bleeds, mayn't I get some ice,
And hold it in my breeches?—Yes.
John, keep your seat. *My sum is more—*
Then do't again—Divide by four,
By twelve, and twenty—Mind the rule.
Now speak, Manassah, and spell tool.
I can't—Well try---*T, W, L.*
Not wash'd your hands yet, boody, ha?
You had your orders yesterday.
Give me the ferrule, hold your hand.
Oh! Oh! There,---mind my next command.

The grammar read. Tell where the place is.
C sounds like K in cat and cases.
My book is torn. The next----*Here not---*
E final makes it long---say note.
What are the stops and marks, Susannah?
Small points, Sir.——And how many, Hannah?

Four, Sir. How many, George? You look :
Here's more than fifty in my book.
How's this? Juſt come, Sam? *Why I've been---*
Who knocks? *I don't know, Sir.* Come in.
" Your moſt obedient, Sir ?" And yours.
Sit down, Sir. Sam, put to the doors.
What do you bring to tell that's new !
" Nothing, that s either ſtrange or true.
" What a prodigious ſchool ! I'm ſure
" You've got a hundred here, or more.
" A word, Sir, if you pleaſe." I will---
You girls, till I come in be ſtill.

" Come, we can dance to night---ſo you
" Diſmiſs your brain diſtracting crew,
" And come---For all the girls are there.
" We'll have a fiddle and a player."
Well, mind and have the ſleigh-bells ſent,
I'll ſoon diſmiſs my regiment.

Silence ! The ſecond claſs muſt read.
As quick as poſſible---proceed.
Not found your book yet? Stand---be fix'd—
The next read, ſtop---the next---the next.
You need not read again, tis well.
Come Tom and Dick, chuſe ſides to ſpell.
Will this word do? Yes, Tom ſpell dunce.
Sit ſtill there all you little ones.
I've got a word, Well, name it. *Gizzard.*
You ſpe'l it Sampſon.---*G, I, Z.*
Spell conſcience, Jack. *K, O, N,*
S, H, U, N, T, S.---Well done !

Put out the next---*Mine is folks.*
Tim, spell it.---*P, H, O, U, X.*
O shocking! 'Have you all try'd? *No.*
Say Matter, but no matter, go---
Lay by your books---and you, Josiah,
Help Jed to make the morning fire.

THE SPEECH OF HESPER.†

YE sires of nations, call'd in high debate,
  From kindred realms, to save the sinking state,
A boundless sway on one broad base to rear——
My voice paternal claims your listening ear;
O er the wide clime my fostering cares extend,
Your guardian genius and your deathless friend.

  When splendid victory on her trophy'd car,
Swept from these shores the last remains of war,

E e

---

† This Poem forms part of a series of publications, in the Connecticut Magazine, for the years 1786 and 1787, under the title of " American Antiquities;" of which it makes the tenth number, and is call d an " Extract from the Anarchiad, book xxiv,"—being prefaced by the following lines, viz.———' At the op ning of this book, and previous to the great and final conflict, which, by what is legible at the close of the Poem, appears to establish the Anarch in his dominion of the new world, Hesper, with a solicitude and energy becoming his high station, and the importance of the subject, makes his last solemn address to his principal counsellors and sages, whom he had convened at Philadelphia."

Bade each glad ftate, that boafts Columbia's name,
Exult in freedom and afcend to fame,
To blifs unbounded ftretch their ardent eyes,
And wealth and empire from their labour rife,
My raptur'd fons beheld the difcord ceafe,
And footh'd their forrows in the fongs of peace.

 Shall thefe bright fcenes, with happieft omens born,
Fade like the fleeting vifions of the morn?
Shall this fair fabric from its bafe be hurl'd
And whelm in duft the glories of the world?
Will ye, who faw the heavens tempeftuous lower,
Who felt the arm of irritated power,
Whofe fouls diftending with the wafting flood,
Prepar'd the firm foundations, built in blood,
By difcord fiez'd, will ye defert the plan?
The unfinifh'd Babel of the blifs of man?

 Go fearch the field of death, where heroes, loft
In graves obfcure, can tell what freedom coft.
Tho' conqueft fmil'd; there flain amid the croud,
And plung'd promifcuous with no winding fhroud,
No friendly hand their gory wounds to lave,
The thoufands moulder in a common grave.
Not fo thy fon, oh Laurens! gafping lies,
Too daring youth, war's lateft facrifice;
His fnow-white bofom heaves with writhing pain,
The purple drops his fnow-white bofom ftain;
His cheek of rofe is wan, a deadly hue
Sits on his face, that chills with lucid dew.——
There Warren, glorious with expiring breath,
A comely corfe, that fmiles in ghaftly death:

See Mercer bleed——and o'er yon wintry wall,
Mid heaps of flain, fee great Montgomery fall!

Behold thofe veterans worn with want and care,
Their finews ftiffen'd, filver'd o'er their hair,
Weak in their fteps of age, they move forlorn,
Their toils forgotten by the fons of fcorn;
This hateful truth ftill aggravates their pain,
In vain they conquer'd and they bled in vain.
Go then, ye remnants of inglorious wars,
Difown your marks of merit, hide your fcars,
Of luft, of power, of titled pride accuf'd,
Steal to your graves difhonor'd and abuf'd.

For fee proud Faction waves her flaming brand,
And difcord riots o'er the ungrateful land;
Lo, to the north a wild adventurous crew
In defperate mobs the favage ftate renew;
Each felon chief his maddening thoufands draws,
And claims bold licence from the bond of laws;
In other States the chofen fires of fhame,
Stamp their vile knaveries with a legal name;
In honor's feat the fons of meannefs fwarm,
And fenates bafe the work of mobs perform,
To wealth, to power the foes of union rife,
While foes deride you and while friends defpife.

Stand forth, ye traitors, at your country's bar,
Inglorious authors of inteftine war;
What countlefs mifchiefs from their labours rife!
Pens dipp'd in gall and lips infpir'd with lies!
Ye fires of ruin, prime detefted caufe
Of bankrupt faith, annihilated laws,

Of felfish fyftems, jealous, local fchemes,
And union'd empire loft in empty dreams,
Your names expanding with your growing crime
Shall float difguftful down the ftream of time,
Each future age applaud the avenging fong,
And outrag d nature vindicate the wrong.

    Yes there are men, who, touch'd with heavenly fire,
Beyond the confines of thefe climes afpire,
Beyond the praifes of a tranfient age,
To live immortal in the patriot page;
Who greatly dare, though warring worlds oppofe,
To pour juft vengeance on their country's foes.

    And lo! the etherial worlds affert your caufe,
Celeftial aid the voice of virtue draws;
The curtains blue of yon expanfion rend,
From opening fkies heroic fhades defcend.
See, rob'd in light, the forms of heaven appear,
The warrior fpirits of your friends are near;
Each on his fteed of fire (his quiver ftor'd
With fhafts of vengeance) grafps his flaming fword,
The burning blade waves high, and, dipt in blood,
Hurls plagues and death on difcord's faithlefs brood.

    Yet what the hope? the dreams of Congrefs fade,
The federal union finks in endlefs fhade,
Each feeble call, that warns the realms around,
Seems the faint echo of a dying found,
Each requifition wafts in fleeting air,
And not one ftate regards the powerlefs prayer.

    Ye wanton States, by heaven's beft bleffings curft,
Long on the lap of foftening luxury nurft,

What fickle frenzy raves, what visions strange?
Inspire your bosoms with the lust of change?
And frames the wish to fly from fancy'd ill,
And yield your freedom to a monarch's will?

Go, view the lands to lawless power a prey,
Where tyrants govern with unbounded sway;
See the long pomp in gorgeous state display'd,
The tinsel'd guards, the squadron'd horse parade;
See heralds gay with emblems on their vest,
In tissued robes tall beauteous pages drest;
Where moves the pageant, throng unnumber'd slaves,
Lords, Dukes, and Princes, titulary knaves
Consus'dly shine, the purple gemm'd with stars,
Sceptres, and globes, and crowns, and ruby'd cars,
On gilded orbs the thundering chariots roll'd,
Steeds snorting fire, and champing bitts of gold,
Prance to the trumpet's voice—while each assumes
A loftier gait, and lifts his neck of plumes.
High on the moving throne, and near the van,
The tyrant rides, the chosen scourge of man;
Clarions, and flutes, and drums, his way prepare,
And shouting millions rend the conscious air;
Millions whose ceaseless toils the pomp sustain,
Whose hour of stupid joy repays an age of pain.

From years of darkness springs the regal line,
Hereditary kings by right divine;
'Tis theirs to riot on all nature's spoils,
For them with pangs unblest the peasant toils,
For them the earth prolific teems with grain,
Theirs, the dread labours of the devious main,

Annual for them the wafted land renews
The gifts oppreffive, and extorted dues,
For them, when flaughter fpreads the gory plains,
The life-blood gufhes from a thoufand veins,
While the dull herd, of earth-born pomp afraid,
Adore the power that coward meannefs made.

Let Poland tell what woe returning fprings,
Where right elective yields the crown to kings !
War guides the choice—each candidate abhorr'd
Founds his firm title on the wafting fword,
Wades to the throne amid the fanguine flood,
And dips his purple in a nation's blood.

Behold, where Venice rears her fea-girt towers,
O'er the vile croud proud oligarchy lowers ;
While each Ariftocrate affects a throne,
Beneath a thoufand kings the poor plebeians groan.

Nor lefs abhor'd the certain woe that waits
The giddy rage of democratic ftates ;
Whofe pop'lar breath, high-blown in reftlefs tide,
No laws can temper and no reafon guide ;
An equal fway their mind indignant fpurns,
To wanton change the blifs of freedom turns,
Led by wild demagogues the factious croud,
Mean, fierce, imperious, infolent and loud,
Nor fame nor wealth nor power nor fyftem draws,
They fee no object and perceive no caufe,
But feel by turns, in one difafterous hour,
The extremes of licence and the extremes of power.

What madnefs prompts, or what ill-omen'd fates,
Your realm to parcel into petty ftates?

Shall lordly Hudſon part contending powers?
And broad Potowmac lave two hoſtile ſhores?
Muſt Allegany's ſacred ſummits bear
The impious bulwarks of perpetual war?
His hundred ſtreams receive your heroes ſlain?
And bear your ſons inglorious to the main?
Will ſtates cement by feebler bonds allied?
Or join more cloſely as they more divide?
Will this vain ſcheme bid reſtleſs factions ceaſe?
Check foreign wars or fix internal peace?
Call public credit from her grave to riſe?
Or gain in grandeur what they looſe in ſize?
In this weak realm can countleſs kingdoms ſtart
Strong with new force in each divided part?
While empire's head diſſected into four
Gains life by ſeverance of diminiſh'd power?
So when the philoſophic hand divides
The full grown polypus in genial tides,
Each ſever'd part, inform'd with latent life,
Acquires new vigour from the friendly knife,
O'er peopled ſands the puny inſects creep,
Till the next wave abſorbs them in the deep.

What then remains? muſt pilgrim Freedom fly
From theſe lov'd regions to her native ſky?
When the fair fugitive the orient chaced,
She fixt her ſeat beyond the watry waſte;
Her docile ſons (enough of power reſign'd,
And natural rights in ſocial leagues combin'd)
In virtue firm, tho' jealous in her cauſe,
Gave ſenates force and energy to laws,

From ancient habit local powers obey,
Yet feel no reverence for one general fway,
For breach of faith no keen compulfion feel,
And find no interest in the fœderal weal.
But know, ye avour'd race, one potent head,
Muft rule your ftates; and ftrike your foes with dread,
The finance regulate, the trade controul,
Live thro' the empire, and accord the whole.

   Ere death invades, and night's deep curtain falls,
Thro ruin'd realms the voice of Union calls;
Loud as the trump of heaven thro' darknefs roars,
When gyral gufts entomb Caribbean towers,
When nature trembles thro' the deeps convulft,
And ocean foams from craggy cliffs repulft,
On you fhe calls! attend the warning cry,
" YE LIVE UNITED, OR DIVIDED DIE."

From the New-Haven Gazette, and Connecticut Magazine,
for 1788. *

TO THE PRINTER.

THE diſtreſs which the inhabitants of Guinea experience
at the loſs of their children, which are ſtolen from them
by the perſons employed in the barbarous traffic of human fleſh, is, perhaps, more thoroughly felt than de-
ſcribed.   But, as it is a ſubject to which every perſon
has not attended, the Author of the following lines hopes
that, poſſibly, he may excite ſome attention, (while he
obtains indulgence) to an attempt to repreſent the anguiſh of a mother, whoſe ſon and daughter were taken
from her by a Ship's Crew, belonging to a Country
where the GOD of Juſtice and Mercy is owned and wor-
ſhipped.

" HELP! oh, help! thou GOD of Chriſtians!
　　　" Save a mother from deſpair!
" Cruel white-men ſteal my children!
　" GOD of Chriſtians, hear my prayer!

" From my arms by force they're rended,
　" Sailors drag them to the ſea;
" Yonder ſhip, at anchor riding,
　" Swift will carry them away.
　　　　　F f

---

* This Poem was originally printed in the above-men-
tioned Paper, February 21ſt, 1788, in rather an incorrect
manner.   It is now offered to the public, with the amend-
ment of the errors reprehenſible at its firſt appearance.

" There my son lies, stripp'd, and bleeding;
  " Fast, with thongs, his hands are bound.
" See, the tyrants, how they scourge him!
  " See his sides a reeking wound!

" See his little sister by him;
  " Quaking, trembling, how she lies!
" Drops of blood her face besprinkle;
  " Tears of anguish fill her eyes.

" Now they tear her brother from her;
  " Down, below the deck, he's thrown;
" Stiff with beating, thro' fear silent,
  " Save a single, death-like, groan.

" Hear the little creature begging!"—
  ' Take me, white-men, for your own!
' Spare! oh, spare my darling brother!
  ' He's my mother's only son.

' See, upon the shore she's raving:
  ' Down she falls upon the sands:
' Now, she tears her flesh with madness;
  ' Now, she prays with lifted hands.

' I am young, and strong, and hardy;
  ' He's a sick, and feeble boy;
' Take me, whip me, chain me, starve me,
  ' All my life I'll toil with joy.

' Christians! who's the GOD you worship?
  " Is he cruel, fierce, or good?
' Does he take delight in mercy?
  ' Or in spilling human blood?

' Ah! my poor diftracted mother!
  ' Hear her fcream upon the fhore.'—
Down the favage Captain ftruck her,
  Lifelefs on the veffel's floor.

Up his fails he quickly hoifted,
  To the ocean bent his way;
Headlong plunged the raving mother,
  From a high rock, in the fea.

NEW YEAR's WISH.*

By Dr. ————.

TO you, my young friends, while I write,
  Kind wifhes fpontaneous arife;
And does ought my rude paffions excite,
  They are hufh'd by benevolent fighs.
A mufe, in the form of a Dove,
  Hovers round, and difpels every fear;
She bids me each talent improve
  To hail you a HAPPY NEW YEAR!

Her mandates I cheerful obey,
  As her fmiles I would ftrive to procure;
For the lines that my wifhes convey,
  May her favors in future fecure.

---

* Firft publifhed in No. 85, of the Gazette of the United States; and originally addreffed, by the author, to a circle of his female friends.

On you, my young friends, may she smile,
    That yonr verse may with melody flow ;
And may joy all your forrows beguile,
    Nor an hour be reserved for woe.

When WINTER shall sternly appear,
    And Nature in gloom be array'd ;
When the Mariner shudders thro' fear,
    Left his bark should by winds be betray'd ;
Then, in safety, well shelter'd from snow,
    May you all, putting forrow aside,
In domestic tranquility know
    All the joys of a social fire-side.

When SPRING in young beauty shall smile,
    And charm following charm shall unfold ;
In rapture beholding the while,
    May your portion be pleasures untold.
May each songster that chirps on the spray,
    May each floweret that blows in the field,
For you be more cheerful and gay,
    For you its choice fragrances yield.

When SUMMER shall sultry advance,
    And flocks from their sports shall retire ;
May each youth, who declines the light dance,
    Your charms, and your virtues admire.
May the grape-vine form Arbors of ease,
    While the eglantine skirts them around ;
And then may the fresh balmy breeze
    Waft perfumes from each neighboring ground.

When AUTUMN his treasures shall bring,
  When each fruit tree shall bend with its load;
May your hearts ever gratefully sing,
  The hand that such blessings bestow'd.
Thus sweetly shall time roll away,
  Nor shall you once wish it in haste;
And the YEAR that commences to-day,
  Far happier shall be than the past.

Then, when WINTERS and SPRINGS shall decay,
  When SUMMERS and AUTUMNS are o'er,
And PHOEBUS, the Prince of the day,
  Shall wake the glad Seasons no more:
To you, each forgeting her mirth,
  May beauty immortal be given;
May you change the faint joys of this earth,
  For transports uncloying in heaven.

From a Gentleman, to a Lady, who had presented him with a
CAKE HEART.

BY THE SAME.

WITH eager haste I homeward flew
  My precious gift to unfold;
I saw, and at the flattering view,
  My transports thus I told.

Thou beauteous semblance of the heart
  That warms Lucinda's breast,
Come, and each gentle joy impart
  As to my soul thou'rt press'd.

But ſtill, tho chaſte delight full oft
   To my fond heart you give,
Yet thou, ſay what I will, no ſoft
   Impreſſion canſt receive.

O had Lucinda, lovely fair,
   Deign'd but her own to have given,
The gift I'd cheriſh with that care
   As if 'twere ſent from heaven.

In my own boſom it ſhould lie,
   By no rude paſſion toſs'd ;
And, huſh'd to love, it ſhould ſupply
   The place of mine that's loſt.

From the American Magazine, for May 1788.

UTRUM HORUM MAVIS, ELIGE.

LET ſage diſcretion the gay world deſpiſe ;
   Let dull philoſophers o'er lamps grow wiſe,
Like bees their ſummer providently waſte,
And hoard that treaſure which they ne'er ſhall taſte ;
Let ſtateſmen court the bubble of applauſe,
And ſtaring cry for ſumptuary laws ;
Let peeviſh prelates in devotion kneel,
And curſe that pleaſure which they try to feel ;
Life is a bleſſing, uſe it as you can,
And the beſt purpoſe of that bleſſing ſcan.
All human reaſon is no more than this,
To guide our footſteps in the realms of bliſs ;
While, as in drinking, ſo in life, the will
Muſt bound our joy, and dictate what to fill.—

Live freely then ; for if thy life offend
'Tis ne'er too late to alter and amend :
But fhould you hefitate the feafon's loft,
As backward fruits are fubject to the froft.
Then, if true fpirit every hope inflame,
Mark well the leffon of my proffer'd fame.

Firft trace the limits of thy deftin'd fphere :
Here reft thy wifdom, thine ambition here.
'Tis not each clown that triumphs, tho' he dare
Afpire to charm and captivate the fair ;
'Tis not each witling, who the ape difplays,
That ftrikes our fancy, or provokes our praife :
But would you fin, be finful with a grace—
Inaptitude can even vice debafe.
Search then your genius, every bent furvey,
And where fhe prompts be ready to obey.
See thro' this crowd where brilliant profpects rife
The chace how luring, and how rare the prize !
The paths of pleafure to no bounds confin'd,
As in their fhape, are various in their kind.
Fix then thy province, make thy talents good,
And be a fop, a gentleman, or blood.

Happy the *firft*, who ftudious to difpenfe
With all the cumberous pedantry of fenfe,
Knows no ambition but the pride of drefs,
And for that toy can every wifh fupprefs :
Whofe natal bounties, like the fly's, confift
In two fhort words, to flutter and exift.
If to fuch fame thine emulation turn,
Hear his purfuits, and from example learn.

—'Till ten the morn is fquander'd in his bed ;
One precious hour's devoted to his head ;
Another's finifh'd ere, his drefs complete
From top to toe be critically neat ;
Then he ftruts forth to greet his kindred beaux,
And urge fome tardy tradefman for his clothes ;
Or mid the town to faunter and to ftare,
And kill an hour or two he knows not where.
In the noon's buftle, vacant and ferene,
He deals in bows, his bufinefs to be feen :
Perhaps united to fome fair he meets,
From fhop to fhop purfues her thro' the ftreets ;
For the laft fafhions ftimulate her pride,
And on the modes he's zealous to decide.
Next his foil'd charms he haftens to repair,
To give a finer polifh to his hair,
His every grace with every art entwine,
And form his looks more ftrikingly divine ;
Till the laft, nobleft paftime of the day,
To his bright zenith fummons him away.
There, in the circle of fome coterie,
Rous'd by the exhilirating fumes of tea,
View him, triumphant, with unrivall'd fame,
Attract each ogle, and each breaft inflame ;
To every fenfe a magic thrill impart,
And fteal thro' all the mazes of the heart.

Next let us view the Gentleman at eafe,
Too rich to toil, too indolent to pleafe ;
Whofe days, unharrafs'd by defire or woe,
In one fmooth ftream uninterrupted flow ;

Born to no end, for no one purpofe fit,
A load of vanity, a grain of wit,
Who, far remov'd from every wordly ftrife,
Lives for himfelf, and fleeps away his life.

If to the *third* thy happier choice incline,
And thy warm genius as a Blood would fhine,
Be the firft caution, in thy bold career,
To fhun low comrades, and a vulgar fphere :—
The great unpunifh'd, from their rank, offend ;
But humbler culprits with the laws contend.—
Then if fome revel, or a midnight joke,
Infult our flumbers, or the watch provoke,
Thy looks can wreft ftern juftice from the fcale,
Sufpend her frowns, and fnatch thee from a jail.
Let dauntlefs fpirit animate thy foul,
No fears reftrain thee, and no threats controul ;
Whether, in hunting, at an arm's expence,
You dafh a furious courfer o'er a fence ;
Or, at the bottle, be thy matchlefs boaft,
To fit the longeft, and to drink the moft :
So fhall thy fame to wonderous heights afcend ;
And every rake fhall hail thee as a friend.

But, if thy foul fuch bafe ambition fpurn,
And in thy breaft a purer fpirit burn,
Leave fuch poor laurels to the brows of Youth ;
And place thy zeal in wifdom and in truth.
Then, in thy way, tho mean temptation rife,
The tafk difcourage, or the world defpife,
Proceed ——

G g

Until the triumph of thy worth record
That virtue is the fureſt, beſt reward.
The Fop, whofe merits on his charms depend,
May gain a miſtrefs, but will lofe a friend;
The Blood will tell thee, ere he quit the ſtage,
That joy of youth's the mifery of age;
And the deluded Idler, with remorfe,
Will own a *bleſſing* what he fear'd a *curfe*;
But he whofe wifdom, fuch defires withſtood,
Unites his pleafure with his greateſt good,
Knows not misfortune, tho a fair one frown,
His wealth efcape him, and his friends difown;
But, firm in what he is, in what he *may* be, bleſt,
Feels an unvaried fun-fhine in his breaſt.

E L L A.   A NORWEGIAN TALE.

BY WILLIAM DUNLAP.

Hiſtory fays that SIVARD, King of Sweden, entered Norway
with a numerous army, and committed the greateſt en-
ormities, but was at laſt overthrown, his Army routed,
and himſelf ſlain by one of thofe women whom he had
brutally abufed.

BETWEEN Norwegian hills, wide fpreads a plain,
    By Nature form'd for fport;
The vet'ran warrior here, and hardy fwain,
    To annual games refort.

High o'er their heads was hung the hoary brow,
    Which caſt an ample ſhade ;
From thence theſe words majeſtic ſeem'd to flow—
    " Fierce foes your ſports invade !"

They upward gaze—a warrior ſtruck their ſight ;
    He bore aloft his lance,
All ſheath'd in arms, inſufferably bright,
    Where beamy ſplendours dance.

The weſtern ſun beam round his helmet flies,
    He more than man appears ;
And more than mortal ſeem'd to ſound the voice
    That rang upon their ears.

" Ye ſons of Norway ! hearken to my tale,
    " Your rural games oh ceaſe ;
" Sivard is marching through Dulvellon's vale,
    " Break off the ſports of peace !

" The bloody Sivard leads his conqu'ring Swedes,
    " He riots in our ſhame ;
" The man, the matron, and the infant bleeds—
    " Norway is but a name !

" The huſband ſees—curſe on the tyrant's luſt—
    " He ſees his beauteous bride—
" Her virtue, worth and honour in the duſt—
    " Oh where is Norway's pride !

" Rouſe ! rouſe Norwegians ! ſeize your arms amain,
    " Let helms o'erſhade the brow ;
" Let's meet theſe Swediſh demons on the plain,
    " And lay their triumphs low.

" Oh had you feen what thefe poor eyes have feen !
  'Twas Sivard did the deed—

" Our hoary monarch, and our helplefs queen,
  " I—yes, I faw them bleed.

" Their daughter Ella—no, I will not tell !
  " Norwegians ne'er enquire—

" Ne'er hear it—what the royal maid befel ;
  " I fee your fouls on fire.

" Oh feize your fwords, your fpears, your helms and fhields !
  " Oh vindicate your fame !

" Sivard and Sweden glare on Norway's fields ;
  " Remember Norway's name."

He faid, tears flow apace---fierce glow the fwains,
  Rage fills each honeft breaft ;
In Swedifh blood, to wipe away their ftains
  Was ev'ry thought addrefs'd.

Then red hair'd Rollo, fierce advancing cried
  " Whoe'er thou art, come down !

" We live on hills, to ev'ry toil we're tried,
  " And war is all our own.

" Let Sivard come, we'll meet the tyrant here.
  " But Stranger come thou down."
He came ; old Athold gaz'd with look fevere ;--
  He gaz'd---but ceas'd to frown.

" Or Athold has forgot his monarch's face,
  " Or fure thou art his fon !

" Eric, of mighty Norway's royal race !"———
  Full quick the tidings run

With ſhouts they preſs to ſee the beauteous chief;
  The aged kiſs his hand!
On either ſide faſt roll'd the marks of grief,
  Then Athold ſpoke the band——

" Ye ſons of Norway, to your homes repair,
  " There ſeize the ſword and ſhield,
" And ere the morning's purple ſtreaks the air,
  " Meet Eric in the field.

" Oh Prince! do you with aged Athold go,
  " And take refreſhing ſleep;
" Athold will ſing, and ſooth the riſing woe,
  " Or,---break his harp and weep."——

'Twas night---in Athold's hall each took his place;
  Of other times he ſung;
Faſt ſtream'd the tears adown the hero's face
  And groans reſponſive rung.

Bright came the morn! and bright in batter'd arms
  The ruſtic vet'rans came;
And many a youth, untried in rough alarms,
  Now hop'd a patriot's name.

They hear'd from far the hum of Sivard's hoſt;
  Young Eric ſtruck his ſhield;
Then high in air his heavy ſpear he toſt,
  And blaz'd along the field.

Next aged Athold follow'd; Rollo ſtrong;
  Black Calmar lifts his mace;
Culullin, Marco, Streno, ruſh along,
  And all the rugged race.

Fierce came the Swede, in ſtrength of numbers proud,
    He ſcorn'd his feeble foe ;
But ſoon the voice of battle roar'd aloud,
    And many a Swede lay low.

Strong Rollo ſtruck the towering Olaus dead,
    Full fifteen bled beſide.
Old Athold cleft the brave Adolphus' head,
    In all his youthful pride.

But Eric ! Eric ! rang'd the field around,
    On Sivard ſtill he cried :
The gaſping Swedes lay heap'd upon the ground---
    Sivard ! the hills reply'd.

In fury Sivard ſeiz'd his ſhining ſhield,
    His mail, his helm and ſpear ;
He mounts his car, he thunders o'er the field ;
    And Norway knows to fear.

Great Rollo falls beneath his dreadful arm,
    His ſteeds are ſtain'd with blood ;
Young Eric ſmil'd to hear the loud alarm,
    And flew to ſtop the flood.

He rag'd, he foam'd,---fierce flew the thirſty ſpear,
    Down fell the foremoſt ſteed :
Aſtoniſh'd Sivard felt unuſual fear——
    " Tyrant, thou'rt doom'd to bleed !"

Up ſprung the youth---deep griding fell the ſword
    Sunk in the Tyrant's brow ;
Faſt fly the Swedes, and leave their hated lord,
    His tow'ring pride laid low.

Now Norway's fons their great deliverer hail,
 But lo! he bleeds! he falls!
Old Athold ftrips the helm and beamy mail,
 And on his Gods he calls.

He lifts the helm, and down the fnowy neck
 Faft falls the filky hair—
" And could thofe limbs, the conquering Sivard check
 Oh Pow'r of great defpair!——"

Life ebbs apace---fhe lifts her languid head,
 She ftrives her hand to wave,
Confefs'd to all, the beauteous Ella faid——
 " Thanks, thanks companions brave."

" Freedom rewards you---naught can Ella give
 " Low, low, poor Ella lies;
" Sivard is dead! and Ella would not live."
 She bleeds, fhe faints, fhe dies.

EULOGIUM ON RUM.

BY J. SMITH.

ARISE! ye pimpled, tipling race, arife!
 From ev'ry town and village tavern, come!
Shew your red nofes, and o'erflowing eyes
 And help your poet chant the praife of Rum.
The cordial drop, the morning dram, I fing,
The mid-day toddy, and the evening fling.

Hail, mighty Rum! and by this general name
 I call each fpecies—whifky, gin, or brandy:
(The kinds are various—but the effects the fame;
 And fo I choofe a name that's fhort and handy;
For, reader, know, it takes a deal of time,
To make a crooked word lie fmooth in rhyme.)

Hail, mighty Rum! thy fong-infpiring merit
 Is known to many a bard in thefe our days:
Apollo's drink, they find, is void of fpirit—
 Mere chicken-broth—infipid as their lays:
And, pleas'd, they'd give a riv'let—aye a fea
Of tuneful water, for one quart of thee!

Hail, mighty Rum! how wond'rous is thy pow'r!
 Unwarm'd by thee, how would our fpirits fail,
When dark December comes, with afpect four,
 And, fharp as razor, blows the northern gale!
And yet thour't grateful in that fultry day,
When raging Sirius darts his fervid ray.

Hail, mighty Rum! to thee the wretched fly:
 And find a fweet oblivion of their woes;
Lock'd in thy arms, as in the grave, they lie—
 Forget their kindred—and forgive their foes.
And Lethe's ftream, (fo much extoll'd by fome,
In ancient times) I fhrewdly guefs, was Rum.

Hail, mighty Rum! what can thy pow'r withftand!
 E'en lordly Reafon flies thy dreadful face:
And Health, and Joy, and all the lovely band
 Of focial Virtues, fhun thy dwelling place:
(For in whatever breaft it rears its throne,
Like Turkifh monarchs, Rum muft rule alone.)

When our bold fathers crofs'd the Atlantic wave,
　And here arriv'd—a weak defencelefs band—
Pray, what became of all the tribes fo brave—
　The favage owners of this happy land?
Were they fent headlong to the realms below,
" By doom of battle?" friend, * I anfwer no.

Our fathers were too wife to think of war;
　They knew the woodlands were not quickly paft:
They might have met with many an ugly fcar—
　Loft many a foretop—and been beat at laft.
But Rum, affifted by his fon, Difeafe,
Perform'd the bufinefs with furprifing eafe.

And would our weftern brethren be lefs proud, or,
　In other words, throw by their gun and drum—
For ducks and fquirrels, fave their lead and powder,
　And fend the tawny rogues fome pipes of rum—
I dare predict, they all would gladly fuck it;
And ev'ry mother's fon foon *kick the bucket.*

But lo! the ingratitude of Adam's race!
　Tho' all thefe clever things to Rum we owe—
Gallons of ink are fquirted in his face;
　And his bruis'd back is bang'd with many a blow;
Some hounds of note have rung his funeral knell,
And ev'ry puppy joins the gen'ral yell.

So have I feen (the fimile is fine—
　And wonderfully pat—tho' rather old)
When rifing Phœbus fhot his rays benign,
　A flock of fheep come fkipping from the fold;

H h

* This alludes only to Jerfey, Pennfylvania, &c.

Some reftlefs fheep cries baa : and all the throng,
Ewes, rams, lambs, wethers, bellowing pour along,

But fear not, Rum, tho' fiercely they affail,
　And none but I, the bard, thy caufe defend,
Think not thy foes—tho' num'rous—fhall prevail,
　Thy pow'r diminifh, or thy being end :
Tho' fpurn'd from table, and the public eye,
In the fnug clofet fafely fhalt thou lie.

And oft, when Sol's proud chariot quits the fky,
　And humbler Cynthia mounts her one-horfe chair,
To that fnug clofet fhall thy vot'ry fly ;
　And, rapt in darknefs, keep his orgies there ;
Lift the full bottle, joyous, to his head,
Then, great as Cæfar, reel fublime to bed.

Burlington, Dec. 7th, 1789.

THE COUNTRY MEETING.*

BY T. C. JAMES.

OF war's tremendous deeds, the din of arms,
　And acts by Fame renown'd, fain would I fing,
But that ambition ne'er my bofom warms,
　Nor would Calliope her fuccour bring
　To bard that foars with too advent'rous wing.

---

* Or friends' place of worfhip.

O 'Shenftone! fweeteft child of fancy fair,
    Dart one fond ray, and guide the weakeft quill,
That ever rafhly claim'd thy guardian care,
    To point the high path up the flipp'ry hill,
    Where thou thy lyre doft touch with ftill improving fkill.

Themes that have ne'er been polifh'd into rhyme,
    Would a faint pencil in this verfe pourtray,
If in the fond attempt to gain on time,
    No taunting critic meet me on my way,
    And with thefe accents rude my heart difmay:
' Vain youth, forbear, by defp'rate folly mov'd,
    ' Of poetafters the mean herd to fwell;
' But mark his ftrain whom laurell'd Phœbus lov'd,
    ' What Horace, tuneful bard, has fung fo well,
    ' How Dædalus's fon, bold artift, headlong fell.'

View yonder ancient dome with trees befet,
    From which no lofty fpire doth proudly rife,
Nor hence each week, when congregation's met,
    Are ftudied hymns e'er wing'd unto the fkies,
    Nor doth amen from parifh clerk arife.
E'en mufic's lulling charms befeemeth wrong
    To thofe who did this modeft temple rear;
For all, who to thofe lonely confines throng,
    Worfhip in guife of folemn filent prayer;
    Nor can they think that words their finful deeds repair.

No pulpit here doth grace the naked wall,
    Nor doth the fculptor his gay art exprefs:
For thus they teach: ' Religion does not call
    ' For the vain ornaments of fplendid drefs,
    ' Nor will meek heaven fuperfluous grandeur blefs.'

And wrong they hold it, that the flock fhould pay
  For truths which ought to flow without controul,
Free as the filver dew, or light of day,
  To beam mild virtue on the expanding foul,
  And fpread celeftial fparks,-free gift, from pole to pole.

But fee, o'er yonder field, the elder train
  Of village dames their little infants-bring,
Who elfe might loiter on the graffy plain,
  And wet their new clothes in yon bubbling fpring,
  Which would their parents' minds with forrow fting.
The fportive urchins oft will fkip away,
  To chafe the partridge from the neighb'ring bufh :
And oft, with balls of well-attemper'd clay,
  Will from its covert fright the trembling thrufh, [hufh.
  Nor mind the matron's careful voice, which would them

Down the flop'd hill the gayer tribe defcend,
  On neighing fteeds, that champ the fteeled bit,
Strait to the fane their pompous way they tend ;
  There 'midft their peers in goodly order fit,
  Young fwains for ftrength renown'd, and maids for wit :
Such ftrength as at the mill-door oft is feen
  When Colin lifts the fack of mighty weight ;
Such wit as fports in gambols o'er the green,
  And would the ear of nicer townfman grate :
  He'd call it fhocking ftuff, and rude, unfeemly prate.

Yet Humour her abode will deign to fix
  Amidft the lively ruftics of the place,
And with the village hinds will often mix,
  Giving to ev'ry feat a feftive grace,
  And fpreading chearfulnefs o'er ev'ry face.

Let the polite, the polifh'd, blame their joys,
   Whom Nature, unconftrain'd, can never charm:
This is the life which ennui never cloys,
   Nor e'er can fell Ambition work it harm,
    Blowing with hideous blaft its poifonous alarm.

See yonder youth on prancing bay fteed ride,
   While fatisfaction on his broad front beams;
And view his gentle charmer by his fide,
   For whom he wifhes, and of whom he dreams;
    Of heavenly form and mind to him fhe feems.
For her each ev'ning anxioufly he culls,
   Of wild flow'rs fair, a nofegay fcented fweet:
For her the chefnut drops its prickly hulls,
   And the wood pigeon yields its fav'ry meat,
    With thoufand tempting gifts which verfe cannot repeat.

And now thro' folding doors, full wide difplay'd,
   The affembly's grave and pious numbers throng,
While well each noify buzzing murmur's ftay'd,
   With the loofe prattling of each infant tongue;
    For oft confufion has from childhood fprung.
See the wife elder's venerable grace,
   Mark with what flow-pac'd dignity he moves;
See ev'ry little eye hangs on his face,
   And over all his features fondly roves,
    For he the junior train affectionately loves.

The village teacher fits with looks profound,
   And marks the ent'ring throng, with eye afkance;
If, as he careful views the dome around,
   He fhould on carelefs pupil's vifage chance,
    He fends him ftraight a play-forbidding glance.

Of looks like thefe he hath a plenteous ftore,
    To fright his ftudents from each frolic mood :
And well they watch to fee his afpect lour,
    Trying each art to avert the baleful wood,
      By fitting wond'rous ftill, and feeming e'en as good.

Silence with Sleep his empire now divides,
    While fome on this, and fome on that fide nod ;
The ploughman ftill his fteers and ploughfhare guides,
    And breaks in pleafing dreams the fancied fod ;
      While the fchool-miftrefs wields the birchen rod.
Others, more wakeful, plan their future deeds,
    While on increafe of wealth their wifhes ftray :
The farmer thus in rapture counts his fteeds,
    And deals to each his part of winter's hay,
      Till fpring renews the grafs, and gives returning May.

Where will not thirft of treach'rous gold approach,
    Since here, e'en here, it holds its wide domain !
From the warm cit who rolls in gilded coach,
    To the dull carter, whiftling o'er the plain,
      Does Plutus, god of fhining lucre, reign.
Happy, thrice happy are th' inftructed few,
    On whom fell Want ne'er lays her harpy claws,
But, far retir'd from 'midft the toiling crew,
    Live in obfervance of wife Nature's laws,
      And learn from her to trace the great Eternal Caufe.

WRITTEN AT SEA, IN A HEAVY GALE.

By CAPT. PHILIP FRENEAU.

HAPPY the man who, fafe on fhore,
 Now trims, at home, his evening fire;
Unmov'd he hears the tempeſt roar,
 That on the tufted groves expire;
  Alas! on us they doubly fall,
  Our feeble bark muſt bear them all.

Now to their haunts the birds retreat,
 The fquirrel feeks his hollow tree,
Wolves in their fhaded caverns meet,
 All, all are bleſt but wretched we—
  For, doom'd a ſtranger to repofe,
  No reſt the unfettled ocean knows.

Whilſt o'er the dark abyfs we roam,
 Perhaps whate'er the pilots fay,
We faw the fun's defcending gloom,
 No more to fee the rifing ray;
  But buried low, by far too deep,
  On coral beds unpitied fleep!

But what a ſtrange uncoafted ſtrand
 Is that where death permits no day,
No charts we have to mark that land,
 No compafs to direct the way!
  What pilot fhall explore that realm,
  What new Columbus take the helm!

While death and darkneſs both ſurround,
   And tempeſts rage with lawleſs power,
Of friendſhip's voice I hear no ſound,
   No comfort in this dreadful hour——
     What friendſhip can in tempeſts be,
     What comforts on this angry ſea !

The barque accuſtom'd to obey,
   No more the trembling pilots guide,
Alone ſhe gropes her trackleſs way,
   While mountains burſt on every ſide.
     Thus ſkill and ſcience both muſt fall,
     And ruin is the lot of all.

TO ELLA.†

AH ! vainly Ella, do I hear
   Thy lute complain, in note ſo clear,
As would ſeduce an angel's ear ;
That bids me check the ſong of praiſe,
And give to *other themes*, my lays.

To fierce diſeaſe and grief a prey,
In pain I paſs the lingering day.

---

* This, and the ſucceeding Poems, ſigned BIRTHA, are
extracted from the Gazette of the United States; where
they form part of a poetical Correſpondence, carried on under the ſignatures of ELLA and BIRTHA. We have ſe-
lected the following Poems as being moſt correct, and moſt
worthy of preſervation ; eſpecially as they are now offered
to the public with the author's corrections.

No more I raife the fprightly ftrain,
  Or warble the melodious fong,
That fill'd the breaft with envied pain,
  And could the joys of life prolong.

Now, when the *glowing orb* of day,
  Hath funk beneath the weftern wave;
With melancholy heart I ftray
  To hear the ftream his border lave.

Or like fome pilgrim prefs the yielding grafs,
  And wet my fandals with the nightly dew,
A fprig of laurel breaking as I pafs,
  To *thee* I fay the *honoring branch* is due.

My dangerous courfe along the vale I take,
  Beneath the hanging rock, that feems to fhake
With ev'ry blaft, and threatens on my head
  Its crufhing weight to roll;
  But my undaunted foul,
Enjoys the fcene, nor feels the chill of terror fpread.

Now, near a cavern dark, and wild,
  With folded arms I ftand,
Like melancholy's gloomy child;
  I heave the fwelling figh;
  Upon the paffing gale;
  While from my ever-ftreaming eye;
    Adown my cheeks, fo wan and pale,
The tears inceffant drop upon my hand.
There I hear the moping owl,
His difmal whoopings roll,

Upon the heavy ear of night,
In founds that would thy foul affright.

But oh! my burfting heart!
So tortur'd by the fang of grief,
In other fcenes would feek relief:
On fancy's rapid wing I'd dart
Where Horror with his ftaring eye,
And upright hair,
Sits gazing on the fiery fky,
When fulphurous lightnings fly,
And fwell the foul to wild defpair.

Where the vex'd wave with mad'ning roar,
Rolls thundering on the craggy fhore,
And aims with ev'ry dreadful fhock,
To burft apart the flinty rock;
When ftill like wretched man! in vain
He ftrives his purpofe to obtain;
Mad to defpair, he flies again
And clamours to his parent main.

BIRTHA.

MAY 21, 1791.

TO ELLA.

HARK! while I found my trembling fhell,
And bid the nymph, fweet Echo tell;
Where on her velvet couch fhe lies,
Hid from the gairifh burning fkies;
How the foul-enlivening found
Of thy enchanting lyre,
Was borne on Ether's waves around,
From each foft-fpeaking wire.

'Twas when befide the wizard ftream,
I faw the fun's laft golden beam,
With yellow tip the afpiring heads,
Of time-contending oaks, the king of fhadés!
I faw the night flies buzzing round,
I heard the beetle's humming found:
My foul to fober thought inclin'd,
Thus ran the current of my mind.

No longer now my cheeks difclofe,
The beauty of the budding rofe;
No longer, as in former days,
I joy, the fprightly laugh to raife.
O! then each lovely, fummer's night,
'Twas my enraptured foul's delight,
To tread the lonely filent vale,
And " drink the fpirit of the gale :"

Or when the cloudlefs moon on high,
Beam'd forth her radiance from the fky:
To wander o'er the airy hill,
Where pattering falls the lucid rill;
And fee the wild flow'rs fhining bright,
Crown'd with the *tears of weeping night*.

But O! the wondrous change!
Now, it delights me not to range,
The fields and vallies, bright and gay,
With beauties of the *laughing May*.

When the fhrill fpirits of the coming ftorm,
    Their fhrieks of terror pour along the wind;
And fiercer raging all the grove deform,
    The branches tear, and fhatter down the rind:

When heaven's bright fires defcending from on high,
Flafh awful day along the gloomy fky ;
And from their dwellings the hoarfe thunders roar,
And dufky torrents down the vallies pour :
'Tis then my foul enjoys the dreadful hour,
And bows, my God ! in rev'rence to thy power.
,Twas thus I mus'd, when borne along the air,
Thy heavenly notes came trembling on my ear ;
Sweet as the gentleft fhowers
Of fpring, defcending on the flowers,
When murmuring Zephyr finks to reft,
Soft-fighing on the lily's breaft.

Ah ! wouldft thou with thy arm fuftain
My wearied form, and foothe my pain ?
And wouldft thou all the lingering Eve,
With thy foft founds my foul relieve ?
And haft thou learn'd the healing charm,
    The power to bid the tyrant Sicknefs fly ?
O ! hither come, extend thy potent arm,
    And bid the *beam of Hope* ftand fparkling in my eye !

Ah ! now, ev'n now, this very hour,
I confefs thy magic power !
Charm'd with thy notes divine,
No more my troubled foul,
O'er fcenes of horror loves to brood,
No more my freezing blood,
In lazy tides doth roll,
Bright in my eye the tears of rapture fhine,
Thro' all my nerves I feel a tremor run,
Now cold as Zembla's fnow, now fervid as the fun.

O! may thy generous fympathifing heart,
Ne'er feel the anguifh of affliction's dart;
May ftreams of earthly treafure on thee flow,
That thou, the pure celeftial joy may'ft know,
To bid the beggar fmile, and cheer his *houfe of woe.*

BIRTHA.

JUNE 4, 1791.

TO ELLA.

AGAIN thy fweetly warbled ftrain,
  Thou leader of the choral train;
Again thy fweeping harp I hear,
That long has charmed my ravifhed ear.

New vigour to my foul thy words impart,
With fofter pleafures touch thy wounded heart:
The moral lore that flows along thy line,
Might well befit a PLINY to rehearfe;
The bold defcriptive beauties of thy Verfe,
Would bright on TITIAN's glowing canvas fhine.

When clofed the blazing eye of day,
And on my downy couch I lay,
Deep mufing on thy moral lore;
The God of Sleep around me threw
His mantle dipt in flumbrous dew;
And thus arofe my fervent pray'r—

O! thou from whom creation fprung!
O! fend from thy bright realms above,
Some faint to cheer me with thy love,
And bid me raife the rapturous fong—

For I have heard thy spirits ~~who~~ on high
Possess the plains of yon cerulean sky;
Have oft, in pity to the mortal race,
Descending closed them in their pure embrace;
And whispering soothing music to their breast,
Charm'd all the tempests of the soul to rest—
Scarce had the words escaped my moving tongue,
Yet on my lips the trembling accents hung;
When lo! a form descending from on high,
On silver plumes thro' yonder orient sky:
Wide flows in circling-locks her golden hair,
And plays with every eddying of the air.
Her robes of filmy texture white as snow,
Around her form in graceful foldings flow.
Her bright blue eyes beam forth a gentle light,
And fix and charm at once the gazer's sight.
When near she moved I saw bewitching grace,
And heavenly beauty lighten up her face.
Now by my side upon the earth she stood,
Her quickened glance warm'd all my chilly blood.
High waving in the air a sky-blue wand,
She bade me follow to yon lofty land;
The path she led, with joyous heart I flew,
'Till near the high and verdant hill I drew;
Then turning round she took my trembling hand,
And waved again her bright cerulean wand:
Soft as the sound of some angelic lute,
Sweet as the breath of Orpheus' mellow flute.
Her words in rapt'rous warblings pour'd along,
And thrill'd my trembling soul with heavenly song.
Behold! she said, that lovely country round,
With nature's richest gifts and beauty crown'd;

There pureſt joy flows thro the circling year,
The happy people know no pain, nor fear ;
Their queen I am, from realms of light I came,
Fair virtue's offspring, *blue-eyed Hope* my name."
She ceaſed ; then roſe before my raviſh'd ſight,
Enchanting ſcenes in nature's beauty bright ;
Here ſpreads a wide and ever verdant plain,
And waves the yellow life-ſupporting grain :
There grandly riſe the proud aſpiring hills,
Between whoſe rocky chinks ſlide down the rills.
Here in majeſtic beauty towering high,
Shoot verdant groves toward the cloudleſs ſky ;
The feathered warblers hop from ſpray to ſpray,
And hold their tuneful ſtrife till cloſing day ;
Then pours the plaintive Nightingale her notes,
And all night long her melting muſic floats—
Along the walks of thoſe e'er blooming bowers,
Forever ſpring new crops of fragrant flowers.
The priſtine colors of the ſun are ſeen
With countleſs changes waving o'er the green—
Rich ſculptur'd figures form'd of blazing gold,
Attract the eye, and firm the ſenſes hold—
Here *Dove-like Innocence*, engaged in play,
With frolic lambs prolongs the happy day ;
There *Charity* throws forth her copious ſtore,
Till the glad ſuppliants ceaſe to aſk for more :
Here, with celeſtial glory in her eye,
Mild Faith with firmneſs gazes on the ſky,
And *Adoration* pours her ſong of praiſe,
While tears of rapture wander down her face.
There o'er white curling lakes the nodding trees,
Wave ſlowly to the gentle paſſing breeze ;

And wildly-grand around deep rocky caves,
Return the Echo of the dashing waves.
Here chrystal mountains shooting to the sky,
With the bright sun in splendor seem to vie ;
Where rise the rugged rocks an awful height !
The sheeting torrent holds my wandering sight :
From steep to steep down dash with thundering roar
The mad'ning waves, and foam along the shore.
" Lo said the maid there bursting from the ground,
A bubbling fountain casts its waters round ;
And see behind, where opens yonder bower,
The virtuous souls enjoy the rapturous hour :
There many a harp, and many a breathing flute
Is heard ; responding sounds the silver lute ;
Whilst ravish'd with the melody of sound
The vocal chorus pour their songs around.
Thus all the blest their happy days employ,
And each contributes to the other's joy ;
Their grateful incense rises up to heaven,
And for their praise a double joy is given :
Know thou, she said, whoe'er pursues the path
That leads to *Virtue* and unwavering *Faith*,
Shall hail me Queen ! and where they dwell shall rise
A scene like this, enchanting to their eyes ;
The spheres shall warble music in their ear,
And all creation harmony appear."
Now ceased her voice, she clap'd her silver wings,
And rising to the sky thro Ether sings.

BIRTHA.

July 2, 1791.

THE *Lord of light* has journey'd down the ſky,
　　And bath'd his courſers in the foaming wave;
　　The twinkling ſtar of Even too, haſtes to lave
Her ſilver form, and vaniſh from my eye.
　Now duſky twilight flings her ſombre ſhade,
　　O'er the bright beauties of the ſilent vale;
　The aſpin trembles not, the verdant blade
　　No longer nodding anſwers to the gale.
Come ſweet Reflection! hither penſive maid!
　　Direct thy wandering ſteps, and on this ſtone,
Worn by no traveller's feet, with moſs o'ergrown,
　　Repoſe with me in ſolitude's deep ſhade.
　　Then ſhall I know the height of human bliſs,
　　And taſte the joy of *other worlds* in this.

BIRTHA.

MAY 25th, 1791.

Kk

END OF SELECTED POETRY.

ORIGINAL POETRY.

AN ELEGY,

WRITTEN IN FEBRUARY 1791.

BY MR. RICHARD ALSOP.

DARK is the hour and lone, o'er icy plains
 The wandering meteors gleam a deadly light;
Wild howls the blaft amid defcending rains,
 And forms funereal flit along the night.

Retir'd from fcenes where Pleafure's airy wand
 Gilds the light moments with delufive joy,
Where Mirth exulting leads her feftive band,
 Far other fcenes my penfive foul employ.

The clouds of death that gloom the baleful year,
 The days of joy, alas, fo lately fled!
While Friendfhip bids its fympathetic tear
 Stream in remembrance of the much-lov'd dead.

My friend, but now, of every blifs poffeft
 That love connubial can on man beftow,
When mutual wifhes warm the mutual breaft;
 Behold the prey of life-confuming woe.

Of late, how fair the beauteous profpect fhow'd,
 How lovely glittering in the morning's eye;
But long ere noon, like April's painted cloud,
 Or hues that tinge the fummer's evening fky,

The fairy hopes that raptur'd Fancy drew,
　　The dream of future blifs that fhone fo bright,
On Fate's fwift pinions vanifh'd from the view,
　　And funk in fhadows of eternal night.——

What notes of woe in mournful cadence fwell
　　Along the Weftern breeze from climes afar,
Mix'd with the dying groan, the favage yell,
　　And all the horrid diffonance of war!

And lo! mid gliding fpectres dimly feen,
　　Pale as the mifts that Autumn's car furround,
A form fuperior lifts his penfive mien,
　　While on his bofom glares the fhadowy wound.

" Behold," he cries, " the band who lately bled,
　　" Mid weftern wilds in glorious conflict flain;
" While recreant troops in pale confufion fled,
　　" Ignobly left unburied on the plain."——

Far opes the view, fublime in favage pride
　　A wild unbounded frowns on Fancy's eye;
Tall rife the trees, and o'er favannahs wide
　　The rank grafs trembles to the breeze on high.

With torrent fweep, amid a night of woods
　　Where fcarce the fun a livid glimmering lends,
A blood-ftain'd river rolls his foaming floods,
　　And o'er the plains in wild meanders bends.

Lo! this the fcene where War, with bloody hand,
　　Wav'd his red ftandard o'er the carnag'd ground;
Where wild-eyed Horror led the tawny band,
　　And fell the brave with dear-bought laurels crown'd.

Here, grim with gore, beneath the inclement ſky,
  Smote by the parching ray and driving rain,
The mangled forms of breathleſs warriors lie,
  All pale extended on the lonely plain.

In ſlaughter'd heaps, around promiſcuous caſt,
  Mid ſavage chiefs Columbia's ſons are ſpread,
While, breath'd from polar ſnows, the northern blaſt
  Shakes its cold pinions o'er the unburied dead.

For them no more ſhall morning gild the ſky,
  No more ſhall May unveil her radiant charms,
No more ſhall Joy illume the ſparkling eye,
  Or Glory's voice excite the ſoul to arms.

Near yon grey rock by withering leaves conceal'd,
  Amyntor lies, benevolent and brave ;
Whoſe duteous hand a father's age upheld,
  And ſmooth'd his dreary paſſage to the grave.

Not far, a corſe diſtinguiſh'd o'er the reſt,
  Of noble ſtature and heroic mien ;
Deep opes the wound that gor'd his manly breaſt,
  And his pale features wear a ſmile ſerene.

Too well alas ! that much-lov'd form I know,
  Thoſe features pale with gory duſt o'erſpread,
O'er whom has Friendſhip mourn'd in bittereſt woe,
  For whom Affection's tendereſt tears are ſhed.

Still, ſtill in Fancy's view recurs the day
  When war's black demons pour'd their hideous yell,
When left expos'd to ſavage rage a prey,
  Thy gallant band beſide their leader fell.

Oppreſt with toil, while countleſs foes ſurround,
 Thy arm, thy voice, the fainting troop inſpir'd ;
And e'en when ſinking with the deadly wound,
 Thy lateſt breath their martial ardor fir'd.

Lamented Hero, far from weeping friends !
 No funeral honours to thy corſe were paid,
And no memorial o'er thy grave extends
 To mark the lonely ſpot where low thou'rt laid.

Yet what avails to pleaſe the ſenſeleſs clay,
 " The trophied tomb," the monumental buſt,
Or recks the ſpirit mid the realms of day,
 The empty rites attendant on its duſt.

A fairer wreath ſhall friendſhip's hand beſtow,
 A fairer tribute ſhall thy ſhade receive,
Than all the idle pageantry of woe,
 Than all its pompous monuments can give.

Long, long ſhall Memory's ardent eye recall
 Thy worth, thy milder virtues to her view ;
Thy Country long lament her hero's fall,
 And o'er thee Fame her brighteſt laurels ſtrew.

O'er the lone ſpot where reſts thy mouldering form,
 Shall opening ſpring her mildeſt breezes wave ;
And Flora's hand with every fragrant charm
 Deck the ſoft turf that forms thy verdant grove.

There the Wild-Roſe in earlieſt pride ſhall bloom,
 There the Magnolia's gorgeous flowers unfold,
The purple Violet ſhed its ſweet perfume,
 And beauteous Meadia wave her plumes of gold.

Reſt much-lov'd Chief with thy Jer——a bleſt,
  Amid yon realms of light, yon ſeats of joy,
Where huſh'd is ſorrow in perpetual reſt,
  And pleaſure ſmiles unconſcious of alloy.

From that calm ſhore with pitying eye ſurvey
  The varying ſchemes of man, the buſy ſtrife,
The vain purſuits that fill his " little day,"
  And toſs with ceaſeleſs ſtorms the ſea of life.

While ſeraphs, bending from their thrones of gold,
  With ſongs of triumph hymn thy ſoul to peace ;
And to thy raptur'd eye, with ſmiles, unfold
  The happy manſions of eternal bliſs.

VERSIFICATION

OF A PASSAGE FROM THE FIFTH BOOK OF OSSIAN'S
TEMORA.

BY THE SAME.

THE hoſts like two black ridges ſtood,
  On either ſide wild Lubar's ſtream ;
Here Foldath frown'd a darken'd cloud,
  There Fillan ſhone a brightening beam.

Their long ſpears glittering in the wave,
  Each hero pour'd his voice afar ;
Gaul ſtruck the ſhield, the ſignal gave,
  At once both armies plung'd in war.

Steel pour'd its flashing gleam on steel;
 The fields two rushing torrents glow,
That whitening foam, in mingled swell,
 O'er the dark rock's projecting brow.

He comes, with fame immortal crown'd,
 His faulchion lays the heroes low;
Death rides the shadowy blasts around;
 Thy paths O Fillan warriors strew!

Between two rocks in fissures rent,
 Brave Rothmar stood, the warrior's pride;
Two aged oaks, that winds had bent,
 Their branches spread on either side.

Silent he shades his friends in flight,
 While his dark eyes on Fillan roll;
Fingal beheld the approaching fight,
 And all the father fill'd his soul.

As falls the stone of Loda, hurl'd
 From trembling Drumanard's high cliff,
When angry spirits rock the world;
 So Rothmar fell, blue-shielded chief.

Young Culmin's friendly steps are near,
 His eye the bursting tear o'erflows;
Wrathful he cuts the empty air,
 Ere yet with Fillan's mix his blows.

He first with Rothmar bent the bow,
 Along his own blue-winding streams;
And mark'd the dwelling of the roe,
 As shone the fern with morning beams.

" Why Youth would'ft thou provoke the might
 Of that bright beam, that wafting fire?
Unequal were your fires in fight;
 Retire, Culalluins's fon retire!"

Lone in her hall, his mother cafts
 Her eyes o'er Strutha's winding ftreams;
Wrapp'd in a whirlwind's eddying blafts,
 Her fon's thin fpectre faintly gleams.

His dogs ftand howling on the plain,
 Red his fufpended fhield with gore;
" And is my fair-hair'd hero flain?
 Pale does he lie on Ullin's fhore?"

As pierc'd in fecret lies a hind,
 Panting her wonted ftreams befide;
The hunter views her feet of wind;
 Culalluin's fon thus Fillan eyed.

In a fmall ftream his hair is roll'd,
 His blood flow wanders o'er his fhield;
Still grafps his hand, with dying hold,
 The fword that fail'd in danger's field.

" Thou'rt fallen ere thy fame was known,"
 Said Fillan, mufing o'er the flain;
" Elate, in hopes of thy renown,
 Thy father fent thee to the plain.

Perhaps, his ftreams grey bending o'er,
 His dim eyes feek thee on the heath;
In vain,—for ah! returns no more,
 His fon extended pale in death."

Wide o'er the heath, in terror loft,
The flight of Erin Fillan pour'd;
But, man on man, falls Morven's hoft,
Before the rage of Foldath's fword.

Undaunted, Dermid meets his courfe;
The fons of Cona wake the fight;
But cleft his fhield, by Foldath's force,
And far is fpread his people's flight.

The exulting foe with haughty boaft,—
"Go Malthos, go to Erin's lord;
And bid him guard blue ocean's coaft,
Left Morven's king efcape my fword.

For cold muft Fingal lie in gore,
Near fome low fen his tomb fhall rife
Without a fong, while hovering o'er,
Half hid in mift, his fpirit flies."

In darkening doubt ftood Malthos bold,
He knew the boafter's heart of pride;
Around his gloomy eyes he roll'd,
And plung'd in war with fullen ftride.

In Clono's narrow vale, two trees
Dark-bending o'er the rolling flood,
Shook their broad branches to the breeze;
There Duthno's fon in filence ftood.

The blood is ftreaming from his thigh;
A rock fuftains his afhen fpear;
His boffy fhield lies broken nigh;
"Why Dermid, why that burfting tear?"

" I hear the battle roar afar,
   Alone my people on the plain ;
No ſhield is mine to ſtem the war,
   And weak and ſlow my ſteps of pain.

Shall Foldath then prevail in fight?
   Ere that in death ſhall Dermid lie ;
Again ſtern chief I'll prove thy might,
   Again thy fierceſt rage defy."

He ſeiz'd his ſpear the ſtrife to join,
   When Morni's ſon before him ſtood ;
" Stay Dermid ſtay, no ſhield is thine,
   Thy trembling ſteps are mark'd with blood."

" Chief of Strumon give thy ſhield,
   Oft has it ſtemm'd the battle's force ;
This arm may yet ſuſtain the field,
   May yet repel yon boaſter's courſe.

Behold that ſtone, with moſs o'erſpread,
   Where ſpires the waving graſs ſo high ;
There low a kindred chief is laid—
   And there in night let Dermid lie."

Slowly he roſe the hill's tall brow,
   And view'd the troubled field of death ;
The gleaming ranks of fight below,
   Disjoin'd, and broken o'er the heath.

As fires at diſtance, ſeem by night
   Now loſt in ſmoke, in darkneſs drown'd,
Now rear on high their ſtreams of light,
   As ceaſe or blow the winds around ;

So met the battle from afar
  Broad-fhielded Dermid's eager eye.
Amidft the varying fcene of war
  The chief of Morna towers on high;

Like fome black fhip, in lofty pride,
  Dark rider of the billowy plain;
Wide fporting o'er the echoing tide,
  When winter rules the ftormy main.

Dermid with rage beheld his courfe,
  He rufh'd to meet the gloomy foe;
But fails the wounded hero's force,
  And tears of pride his eyes o'erflow.

He founded thrice his boffy fhield,
  And thrice on Foldath call'd aloud;
Foldath with joy the chief beheld,
  And lifted high his fpear of blood.

As fome vaft rock whofe rugged fide
  Is mark'd with ftreams of many a ftorm;
So look'd, with wandering blood bedyed
  The gloomy chief of Morna's form.

Each hoft, appall'd, in terror flies,
  From the contending fierce of Kings.
At once their gleaming points arife,
  With fpeed of lightning Fillan fprings.

The haughty foe, with trembling, view'd,
  That dazzling beam of early fame;
That fwift, as iffuing from a cloud,
  To fave the wounded hero came.

In founding ftrife as on the gale
    Two broad-wing'd eagles fierce contend;
So, on Moilena's far-fpread vale,
    The chiefs in gloomy battle bend.

Low on his fhield is Foldath laid,
    Pierc'd by th youthful hero's fpear;
Nor o'er the fallen Fillan ftaid,
    But onward roll'd the ftorm of war.

Malthos beheld the warrior low,
    Low laid on Lubar's winding fhore;
His bofom melts in generous woe,
    And hatred fills his foul no more.

He feem'd a rock, down whofe grey fides
    The defart waters trickling ftray;
When flow the failing mift divides,
    And gives its blafted trees to day.

Thus to the dying chief he faid,—
    " Say fhall thy moffy ftone afcend,
Where Ullin's dark green hills are fpread,
    Or Morna's woody vales extend?

There, where the fun looks forth ferene,
    On blue Dalrutho's bordering glades;
Fair Dardulena's fteps are feen,
    Thy daughter, pride of Erin's maids."

" Rememberest thou," the chief reply'd,
    " The maid, becaufe no fon is mine,
To roll the battle's deathful tide,
    And in revenge in arms to fhine?

I am reveng'd, for not in vain
  Has fhone the lightning of my fpear.
Amidft the tombs of thofe I've flain
  My narrow houfe, O Malthos! rear.

Oft fhall I leave my airy fold,
  To hail the fpot where low they lie;
When, fpread around me, I behold,
  The rank grafs of their graves on high."

His fpirit rufh'd on eddying winds,
  And came to Dardulena's dream;
As, wearied with the chace of hinds,
  She flept by blue Dulrutho's ftream.

Her bow unftrung is near her placed,
  The breezes fold her raven hair;
Each charm of youthful beauty graced
  The love of chiefs, the blue-eyed fair.

From the dark fkirts of Morna's wood,
  Her father's ghoft, pale bending, gleam'd;
At times his bloody form he fhew'd,
  Then hid in fhrouding vapors feem'd.

She rofe in tears, her foul divin'd
  The chief in death was lowly laid;
To her a beam of light he fhin'd.
  When folded in his darkeft fhade.

HABAKKUK, Chap. III.

BY THE SAME.

THE Lord of Hoſts from Teman came,
    From Paran's mount the Almighty God,—
The heavens his glory wide proclaim,
    And bent the earth beneath his nod.

As light his awful brightneſs ſhow'd,—
    There was the hiding of his power;
On burning coals Jehovah trode,
    Dire mov'd the peſtilence before.

He ſtood, and meaſur'd earth and air,
    He look'd, apart the nations fled,
The eternal mountains ſcatter'd were,
    And hills perpetual bow'd the head.

I ſaw when Midian's curtains ſhook,
    I ſaw pale Cuſhan's tents in woe;
Say, did the ſtreams thy wrath provoke?
    Againſt them did thine anger glow?

Did e'er the deep his God diſpleaſe,
    That on thy horſes thou did'ſt ride?
Thy path was thro' the troubled ſeas,
    In heaps roll'd back the aſtoniſh'd tide.

The mountains ſaw, they trembling ſhook,
    The o'erflowing waters paſſed by,
The mighty deep in horror ſpoke,
    And lifted up his hands on high.

The rolling ftars their courfes ftay'd,
   The fun and moon ftood ftill in fear;
Before thine arrows blaze they fled,
   Before the lightning of thy fpear.

With rivers did ft thou cleave the earth,
   And naked made thy dreadful bow;
Thou march d in indignation forth,
   And laid in duft the heathen low:

Thou wenteft forth on Ifrael's fide,
   To fave from death thy chofen race;
Thy fword has fmote the heathen's pride,
   And everlafting are thy ways.

Altho' the fig-tree fhall not fhoot,
   Nor grape the withering vine fhall yield,
The olive fhall withhold her fruit,
   And blafted be the herbag'd fie'd;

Tho' in the fold the flock fhall die,
   And in the ftall no herd fhall be,
Yet on the Lord will I rely,
   Yet, O my God! will joy in thee.

RUNIC POETRY.

===========

TWILIGHT OF THE GODS;
OR
DESTRUCTION OF THE WORLD
FROM THE EDDA, A SYSTEM OF ANCIENT SCANDINAVIAN
MYTHOLOGY.

————

BY THE SAME.

————

A TIME shall come, a barbarous time,
   Dark shadowed o'er with every crime,
When ties of kin shall cease to bind,
In love's soft bands, the human mind:
When sons their fathers' blood shall pour
And brother blush with brother's gore:
When, lost to every tender care,
Not one his dearest friend shall spare;
And man, oppress'd with bitterest woes,
Wish the sad scene of life to close.

Winter, clad in wild array,
Then shall hold his direst sway;
The sun withdraw his golden light,
And veil the world in darkest night;
The winds with wildest rage contend;
The snow in ceaseless storms descend;
The earth in icy fetters bound;
And desolation glare around.

Mm

Uncherish'd by one genial ray,
Three such winters pass away.
Portents dire shall then succeed;
The Monsters from their chains be freed:
Dreadful, in his fiery car,
Giant Rymer * rush to war;
The Serpent † roll his hideous train
Deep beneath the billowy main,
Whose lifted waters, wildly swell'd,
Wide o'er the earth shall be impell'd;
In thousands men resign their breath,
And throng the gloomy courts of death;
His prey the screaming eagle seek,
And tear the dead with gory beak;
The Earth in dread convulsions heave;
Its wonted course the river leave;
The tottering mountain headlong borne,
From its deep base resistless torn;
Rent from their roots, whole forests fall;
And one vast ruin spread o'er all.
Floating on the whelming tides,
Fate's black Ship ‡ in triumph rides;

---

* Rymer—One of those Giants who, according to the Edda, are in continual enmity with the Gods, and shall, in co-operation with the Evil Genii, eventually overpower them.

† The Great Serpent—or Serpent of Midgard, is said to have been cast by the Gods into the ocean; where he soon became of such an enormous size as to encircle the earth.—Midgard—the Residence, or Fortress of the Deities.—

‡ The Ship of the Gods, or of Fate, in which the Host of the Evil Genii, &c. arrives.

Perfidious Loke § directs her courſe,
Leader of the giant force.
Fenris ‖ burſts his iron chain ;
Nought his fury can reſtrain ;
His noſtrils ſparkling flames expire ;
His eye-balls flaſh terrific fire ;
Urged by rage, by vengeance driven,
He rends the beauteous ſun from heaven :
The Serpent floods of venom pours
O'er the wide ſea and circling ſhores ;
Rocks ruſh on rocks, together hurl'd ;
Deſtruction triumphs o'er the world ;
From the torn concave of the ſky,
The affrighted ſtars confus'dly fly ;
The vaults of heaven in ſunder rend ;
The Evil Genii ſwift aſcend ;
Pour'd from the ſouth, in terrors dire,
Before them moves the Prince of Fire,
Surtur * the Black, in flames array'd—
Shines like the ſun his waving blade,
The ſign of death ; with him their might
The Serpent, Fenris, Loke, unite ;

-----

§ Loke,—the Evil Being : in the higheſt degree malicious and deceitful.

‖ Fenris,—or the Wolf,—of all the others a monſter
moſt dreaded by the Gods ; who by ſtratagem confined him
with a magic chain ; which he breaks at the diſſolution of
nature.

* Surtur,—the deſtroying Principle ; ſuppoſed to reſide
in the South, in the flaming Gulf of Muſpelſheim ; leader
of the Evil Genii, who are to deſtroy the Univerſe by Fire.

Succeeds a death-determined hoft,
The hideous Giants of the Froft.
His crooked trumpet Heimdall†† takes,
With potent breath the blaft awakes ;
Far heard thro heaven's remoteft bound,
Pours the fhrill clangor of the found ;
Loud crows the Cock, the bird divine,
Whofe crefts in golden glory fhine ;
Hoarfe from beneath, with difmal cries,
The Herald black of death replies ;
Trembles the facred Afh ‡‡ with dread,
And groaning fhakes its lofty head ;
All nature's fill'd with wild affright ;
The Gods, convened, prepare for fight.
A mid-day fun is Odin §§ bold,
Far beaming in his arms of gold ;
Againft the Wolf |||| he bends his courfe,
And Frey * encounters Surturf's force.
The enormous ferpent Thor† affails ;
The God's refiftlefs might prevails ;

———

†† Heimdall,—the Centinel of Heaven.

‡‡ The Sacred Afh of Ydrafil, under which the Council of the Deities is held.

§§ Odin, the firft and moft powerful of all the Gods.

|||| Fenris.

* Frey,—a Deity reprefented as clothed in white ; and fuppofed to prefide over the productions of the earth.

† Thor,—the firft of the fons of Odin, and ftrongeft of the Gods ; who prefides over the thunder ; and whofe office it is to protect the injured and oppreffed.

But short his joy, he sinks in death,
From the Monster's venom'd breath.
By each others falchions slain,
Loke and Heimdall press the plain.
The snow-white God §§ resigns his life,
By Surtur slain in furious strife.
Rushing from the dark abodes,
Death denouncing to the Gods,
Hideous howls the Dog of night;
He meets with Tyr ‖‖ in mortal fight;
Long the contest fierce they wage,
And victims fall of mutual rage.
Goddess, * weep! thy cares are vain—
Odin falls, by Fenris slain.
Swift to vengeance Vidar †† flies;
By his hand the monster dies:
Wild Destruction, hovering o'er,
Waves her banner dipt in gore;
O'erpower'd the heavenly legions fall,
And Death's dark billows close on all.
The gloomy Prince, ‡ with conquest crown'd,
Dreadful scatters flames around;
In one wide conflagration driven,
The raging fires ascend to heaven;

---

§§ " The snow-white God,"—Frey.

‖‖ Tyr,—a Deity answering to the Roman Mars.

* The Goddess Friga, or Freya,—the Mother of Odin.

†† Vidar, a Son of Odin.

‡ " The gloomy Prince:"—Surtur.—

Sinks the world to ruin's power,
And time itself exifts no more.

Burfting from exiftence' grave,
O'er the bofom of the wave,
Lo ! a new-born World unroll'd,
Far more beauteous than the old,
Smiles adorn'd with lovelieft green ;
Spring unfading decks the fcene ;
The eagles, foaring mid the breeze,
Their fifhy prey on mountains feize ;
The earth her fruits fpontaneous yields ;
Rich harvefts glad the uncultured fields ;
Unknown to grief, to torturing pain,
There eternal pleafures reign.
Then, from feats of orient light,
In divineft glories bright,
Comes forth the great, the all-powerful One,*
Incommunicate, alone,—
Who was ere Time began his race,
Or being fill'd the vaft of fpace ;
And, unchangable, fupreme,
Thro endlefs ages is the fame.
There a Palace glows, more bright
Than the fun's meridian light,

------

* This Being is entirely diftinct from Odin, and the other Gods of the Scandinavian Mythology ; who had their birth foon after the creation of the World, and who perifh with it.

Where the virtuous fhall refide;
And, as pleafure rolls its tide
Un^debafed by pain's alloy,
Know an eternity of joy.

EXTRACT FROM THE

CONQUEST OF SCANDINAVIA;

BEING THE INTRODUCTION OF THE FOURTH BOOK.

BY THE SAME.

ODIN *having defeated the Scandinavians in feveral*
tles, WOLDOMIR, *the druidical fovereign of Scandinavia,*
reduced to the utmoft diftrefs, obtains the affiftance of
GRYMER, *Prince of the Saraceni,—a Scythian Tribe,—*
the hereditary foe of ODIN; *and having affembled his*
forces on an extenfive plain, near the banks of a river,
prepares to attack the Enemy, who are encamped on the
oppofite fhore.—The prefent Book commences with the Night
preceding the engagement.

NOW Night, in clouds involv'd, her mantle drew,
    And deepeft darknefs veil'd the etherial blue;
Dire heard afar, with wild and hollow roar,
Hoarfe groan'd the woods along the rocky fhore;
Loaded with vapours dank and drizzling rains,
The chill North-eaft fhrill whiftled o'er the plains;
Pale fhone the phantom fires, whofe boding light
In tenfold horror vefts the ftorms of night;

And, wildly yelling thro the dreary shade,
Shriek'd the sad spectres of the unburied dead;
Involv'd in anxious cares, and gloomy thought,
When Mondak's* Son the tent of Ulfo sought.
Ulfo the old, renown d for magic lore,
From Volga's flood to cold Kamschatka's shore;
Amid the gloom of Scythian forests bred,
Where Altai lifts on high his wintry head;
Among a savage race, rapacious, rude,
Wild as the storms that toss the Caspian flood,
As thunder dreadful, bursting from the cloud,
When Night o'er Altai hangs her sable shroud.
Olaf his sire, in fields of death renown'd,
As chief in war, the stern barbarians own'd,
Sprung from that race accurst, whose demon sway
The hoary Giants of the Frost obey,
The same stern soul which mark'd his sires of yore,
The same fell hate to Woden's laws he bore,
The same inspir'd the son, whose rebel pride
The God derided, and his power defied.
In nature vers'd, to him each plant was known
That blooms mid Scythia's snows, or Afric's torrid zone;
Each secret power that earth's dark bosom hides,
That rules in ocean, or in air presides.
To him had Grymer sent, o'er realms afar,
With costly gifts, to win him to the war,
When first imperial Woldomir implor'd,
In Scandinavia's aid, the hero's sword;

---

* Grymer.

Nor lefs impell'd by envious hate, he came,
Of Odin's glory and of Woden's name.

Intent to folve the dark decrees of fate,
In deep enquiry fix'd, the Wizard fate ;
When, Grymer entering, from his feat he preft,
With eager hafte, and thus the Chief addreft.
" Say, at this hour, when o'er the dreary plains,
In all her horrors, Night funereal reigns ;
While fhrieks of terror on the blaft arife,
And the black tempeft howls along the fkies ;
At this untimely hour, what potent caufe
Forth from his tent the Prince of Scythia draws?"

" O Sire of magic !" thus the Prince replied,—
" My Shield in battle, and my counfels' guide,
Full well to thee is known what weight of care
Hangs on the vaft uncertainty of war ;
What anxious fears a leader's peace annoy,
Poffefs his foul, and every thought employ.
The chief who hopes in glory's walks to fhine,
And round his brows the palms of conqueft twine,
When war's dark tempeft fpreads its horrors round,
Not in the bowers of thoughtlefs Eafe is found ;
Not on the lap of Sloth reclines his head,
By proud Prefumption's flattering glare mifled ;—
Which oft the vainly confident betrays,
And lights to ruin with its phantom blaze ;—
But, when the hour of battle hovers near,
Neglects no caution, tho' he knows no fear.
By cares like thefe impell'd, I hither come,
Of reft neglectful, mid the dreary gloom ;

N n

While, wide around, the camp in silence lies,
And slumber seals the wearied soldier's eyes:
For lo! to morrow wakes the rage of fight,
When morning opes the golden gates of light;
To morrow gives my eager arm to dare
This scourge of Scandia's realms, this pest of war;
Gives me, perchance, that first of joys to know,
The joy of vengeance on a hated foe.
For that fell hate, which steel'd our sires of yore,
Which dyed so oft in blood Jaxartes' shore,
That hate my breast with all its rage inspires,
Sublim'd, by rival love, to fiercer fires.
Yes! still revenge has set that day aside,
When, scorn'd my passion, and my suit denied,
Hermanric's daughter gave her heaven of charms,
Detested thought! to Odin's happy arms.
But tho' my soul delights where Danger rears
His awful crest, amid the strife of spears,
And glows with transport in the fierce alarms,
The shock of battles, and the din of arms;
Tho', in comparison, the foe are lost
Mid the vast numbers of our warlike host;
Yet not, in vain security, reclin'd,
The events of battle fill my anxious mind.
Perchance the Gods, too partial to the foe,
Our strength may wither, and our hopes o'erthrow;
For Odin long has prov'd their guardian care,
By Woden shielded in the storms of war;
And still the favoring God his aid affords,
And bears him harmless mid descending swords.
How oft has Scandia mourn'd her heroes' doom,
Swept, by that arm, in thousands, to the tomb!

Before his might her hosts have shrunk away,
Like mountain snows before the vernal ray.
Then let the all-conquering force of spells be tried,
And range the Powers of magic on our side;
Bid panic terror hover o'er their fight,
Chill the pale foe, and turn their steps to flight;
So may thy friend a double triumph prove,
And, with a nation's wrongs, avenge his slighted love."

The monarch ceas'd,—the words the wizard took,
While sarcasm smil'd contemptuous in his look.
" Dread'st thou that feeble race? Can Grymer's soul
Thus bend to phantom terror's vile controul?
Do thoughts like those which little minds debase,
Become the leader of a warlike race?
Thy mighty Woden, and his Gods, at most,
A narrow sway, and power precarious boast.
In time's first day-spring, when as yet the earth
Knew not its place, nor ocean roll'd to birth;
Alone one torpid, vast abyss, was seen,
Uncloth'd with form, undeck'd with cheerful green;
Ere man the breath of first existence drew;
Those sons of Bore the mighty Ymir slew,
By fraud his race confin'd, usurp'd the sway
O'er the blue mansions of unclouded day.
Yet still in fear their ill-got rule they hold,
Still dread the day, when vengeance uncontroll'd
Shall burst its chains, and, in destruction hurl'd,
A fiery deluge wrap the sinking world.
Then go, and Valhall's feeble Gods despise,
For Powers more mighty in thy aid shall rise;—

Thofe Powers who o'er the gloom of night prefide,
Live in the ftorm, and on " the whirlwind ride;"—
Shall whelm in duft the foes prefumptuous boaft,
And roll dark ruin o'er their proftrate hoft."

The Wizard ceas'd—with brightening hopes infpir'd,
The Scythian monarch to his tent retir'd.

Forth from his camp the dire Enchanter ftray'd,
Mid the weird horrors of the midnight fhade,
Till a lone dell his wandering footfteps found,
Fenc'd with rough cliffs, with mournful cyprefs crown'd,
There ftay'd his courfe: with ftern, terrific look,
Thrice wav'd on high, his magic wand he fhook;
And thrice he rais'd the wild funereal yell
That calls the fpirits from the abyfs of hell.
When, fhrilly anfwering to the yell afar.
Borne on the winds, three female forms appear;
Dire as the hag who, mid the dreams of night,
Purfues the fever'd hectic's trembling flight.
With geftures ftrange, approach the haggard band,
And nigh the wizard take their filent ftand.
Near, in a rock, adown whofe rugged fide
The lonely waters of the defart glide,
O'ergrown with brambles, op'd an ample cave,
Drear as the gloomy manfions of the grave.
Within, the fcreech-owl made her mournful home,
And birds obfcene that hover round the tomb;
Dark, from the mofs-grown top, together clung,
Ill-omen'd bats, in torpid clufters, hung;
And o'er the bottom, with dank leaves beftrow'd,
Crept the black adder, and the bloated toad.

Thither the magic throng repair'd, to form
Their ſpells obſcure, and weave the unhallow'd charm.
Muttering dire words, thrice ſtrode the wizard round;
Thrice, with his potent wand, he ſmote the ground;
Deep groans enſued; on wings of circling flame,
Slow-riſing from beneath, a Cauldron came;
Blue gleam'd the fires amid the ſhades of night,
And o'er the cavern ſhot a livid light.

Now op'd a horrid ſcene : all black with blood,
The infernal band, prepar'd for ſlaughter, ſtood.
Two beauteous babes, by griffons borne away,
While lock'd in ſleep the hapleſs mothers lay,
Whoſe ſmiles the frozen breaſt to love might warm,
And e'en the unſparing wolf to pity charm,
The hags unveil'd; and ſportive as they play'd,
Deep in their hearts embrued the murderous blade;
Their dying pangs with ſmile malignant view'd,
And life's laſt ebbings in the ſanguine flood.
Now, mix'd with various herbs of magic power,
In the dark cauldron glows the purple gore :
The Night-ſhade dire, whoſe baleful branches wave,
In glooms of horror, o'er the murderer's grave;
The Manchineel, alluring to the eye,
Where, veil'd in beauty, deadlieſt poiſons lie;
The far-fam'd Indian Herb, of power to move
The foes of nature to unite in love,
The ſerpent race to infant mildneſs charm,
And the fierce tiger of his rage diſarm,—
Known to the tribes that range the trackleſs wood
Where mad Antonio heaves the headlong flood;—

The * Monster plant that blasts Tartaria's heath ;
And Upas fatal as the stroke of death :
Boil'd the black mass, the associate fiends advance,
And round the Cauldron form the magic dance.
Three times around, in mystic maze they trod,
With hideous gesture, and terrific nod ;
While Runic rhymes, and words that freeze the soul,
From their blue lips, in tones of horror, roll.
The wizard rais'd his voice, the cavern round,
Wild-shuddering, trembled at the fearful sound ;
In mute attention stood the haggard throng,
As thus he woke the incantatory song.

> From the dreary realms below,
>   From the dark domains of fear,
> From the ghastly seats of woe,
>   Hear ! tremendous Hela, hear !

I.

> Dreadful Power ! whose awful form
> Blackens in the midnight storm ;
> Glares athwart the lurid skies,
> While the sheeted lightening flies ;
> When the thunder awful roars ;
> When the earthquake rocks the shores ;

---

* BAROMETZ, Tartarian Lamb :——A plant found in
Tartary and the northern parts of China : It-is covered
with a very beautiful kind of furze or wool, of a bright yellow, and in its form has some resemblance to a LAMB, ap-
pearing to stand upon four legs, from so many roots to
which it is attached. It is said to be of a nature so destruc-
tive to every other species of vegetables, that none will live
within its vicinity.

Mounted on the wings of air,
Thou rul'ft the elemental war.
When Famine brings her fickly train;
When Battle ftrews the carnag'd plain;
When Peftilence her venom'd wand
Waves o'er the defolated land;
Rufh the ocean's whelming tides
O'er the foundering veffel's fides;
Then afcends thy voice on high;
Then is heard thy funeral cry;
Then, in horror, doft thou rife
On the expiring wretch's eyes.

From the dreary realms below,
    From the dark domains of fear,
From the ghaftly feats of woe,
    Hear! tremendous Hela, hear!

II.

Goddefs! whofe terrific fway
Naftrande's realms of guilt obey;
Where, amid impervious gloom,
Sullen frowns the ferpent Dome;
Roll'd beneath the envenom'd tide,
Where the fons of forrow 'bide;
Thee, the mighty Demon hoft;
Thee, the Giants of the Froft;
Thee, the Genii tribes adore;
Fenris owns thy fovereign power:
And the imperial Prince of Fire,
Surtur, trembles at thine ire.

Thine, the victor's pride to mar;
Thine, to turn the scale of war;
Chiefs and princes at thy call,
From their spheres of glory fall;
Empires are in ruin hurl'd;
Desolation blasts the world.

From the dreary realms below
   From the dark domains of fear,
From the ghastly seats of woe,
   Hear! tremendous Hela, hear!

III.

Queen of terror, queen of death!
Thee, we summon from beneath.
From the deep infernal shade;
From the mansion of the dead;
Nieslehm's black, funereal dome;
Hither rise, and hither come!
By the potent Runic rhyme,
Awful, mystic, and sublime;
By the streams that roar below;
By the sable fount of woe;
By the burning gulph of pain,
Muspell's home, and Surtur's reign;
By the Day when, o'er the world,
Wild confusion shall be hurl'd,
Rymer mount his fiery car,
Giants, Genii, rush to war,
To vengeance move the Prince of Fire,
And heaven, and earth, in flames expire!

From the dreary realms below,
　　From the dark domains of fear,
　From the ghaſtly ſeats of woe,
　　Hear ! tremendous Hela ! hear.

He ceas'd—the flames withdrew their magic light,
And, cloth'd in deeper horrors, frown'd the night.
At once, an awful ſtillneſs paus'd around,
Huſh'd were the winds, and mute the tempeſt's ſound,
One deep, portentous, calm o'er nature ſpread,
Nor e'en the aſpin's reſtleſs foliage play'd ;—
Such the dire calm that glooms Carribean ſhores
Ere, rous'd to rage, the fell Tornado roars :—
Not long, for lo ! from central earth releas'd,
Shrill through the cavern ſigh'd an hollow blaſt ;
Wild wails of woe, with ſhrieks of terror join'd,
In deathful murmurs groan along the wind ;
Peal following peal, hoarſe burſts the thunder round ;
Redoubling echoes ſwell the dreadful ſound ;
Flaſh the blue lightnings in continual blaze ;
One ſheet of fire the kindling gloom diſplays ;
And o'er the vault, with pale, ſulphureous ray,
Pour all the horrors of infernal day.
Now heav'd the vale around, the cavern'd rock,
The earth, deep trembling, to its center ſhook,
Wide yawn'd the rending floor, and gave to ſight
A chaſm tremendous as the gates of night.
Slow from the gulph, mid lightnings faintly ſeen,
Roſe the dread form of Death's terrific Queen ;
Of wolfiſh aſpect, and with eyes of flame,
Black Jarnvid's Witch, her fell attendant, came ;

O o

Than whom, no monster roams the dark abodes,
More fear'd by friends, more hated by the Gods.

More frightful, more deform'd, than Fancy's power
Pourtrays the demon of the midnight hour,
In hideous majesty, of various hue,
Part sallow pale, and part a livid blue,
A form gigantic, awful Hela frown'd ;
Her towering head with sable serpents crown'd ;
Around her waist, in many a volume roll'd,
A crimson adder wreath'd his poisonous fold ;
And o'er her face, beyond description dread,
A sulphury mist its shrouding mantle spread.
Her voice, the groan of war, the shriek of woe
When sinks the city whelm'd in gulphs below,
In tones of thunder, o'er the cavern broke,
And nature shudder'd as the Demon spoke.

" Presumptuous mortal ! that, with mystic strain,
Dost summon Hela from the realms of pain,
What cause thus prompts thee rashly to invade
The deep repose of death's eternal shade ?
What, from the abodes of never-ending night,
Calls me, reluctant, to the climes of light ?"

" Empress supreme ! whose wide-extended sway
All nature owns, and earth and hell obey ;
The solemn call no trivial wish inspires ;
No common cause thy potent aid requires ;
The dooms of empires on the issue wait,
And doubtful tremble in the scale of fate.
The glow of morn, on yon extended heath,
Will light the nations to the strife of death.

There Saracinia's fons their force unite
With Scandia's monarch, Woldomir, in fight;
By ftrength combin'd, proud Odin to o'erwhelm,
The fierce invader of the Scandian realm;
By Woden favor'd with peculiar grace;
Friend of the gods, and odious to thy race.
Then, in the impending fight, thy fuccour lend,
And o'er our hoft thy arm of ftrength extend;
The hoftile bands, protected by thy foes,
With dangers circle, and with ruin clofe;
With wild difmay their fhrinking ranks pervade;
Whelm their pale numbers in the eternal fhade;
And wing, with certain aim, the miffive dart,
Or point the faulchion, to the leader's heart."

Thus Ulfo fpoke—and Hela thus return'd.
" Know, while in primal night creation mourn'd,
The eternal caufe, the great, all-ruling mind,
The various term of human life affign'd;
Irrevocably firm, the fix'd intent
No power can vary, and no chance prevent.
Mark'd, by the fates, for years of bloody ftrife,
Rolls the long flood of Odin's varied life;
Nor is it ours the ftern decree to thwart
By open violence, or by covert art.
Yet ftill the power is left us to annoy,
Whom rigid heaven denies us to deftroy;
And, tho of life fecure, the hoftile chief,
The wretched victim of fevereft grief,
Shall mourn his arms difgrac'd, on yonder plain,
His laurels blafted, and his heroes flain."

She ceafed ;—in thunder vanifhing from view,
The fiends, the cauldron, and the hags withdrew.
Back to the camp the Inchanter fped his way,
Ere, o'er the eaft, arofe the firft faint glimpfe of day.

ODE TO CONSCIENCE.

BY THEODORE DWIGHT, ESQUIRE.

HAIL Confcience, faithful inmate of the breaft!
    Thy fmiles can charm to fweeteft reft,
Thy frowns can wake the keeneft woe,
Without thy aid even heaven would grow
A cheerlefs void of deep diftrefs,
And angels want the power to blefs.

When great Jehovah's voice creation form'd,
    When worlds unnumber'd fprang to inftant birth;
When morning ftars to ecftacy were warm'd,
    And man ftood ruler of the boundlefs earth,
Thou in the realms of light and love,
Did'ft dwell emboffom'd with the Etherial Dove.
" Where Guilt fhall dare extend her reign,
" And Satan ftretch his dark domain,
" There let the tides of horror roll,
" And torture rend the finking foul."
The GODHEAD fpoke,—Creation round,
Deep trembled to its utmoft bound.

Hail mighty Confcience ! hail'!
    When the black deed of guilt is done,
Thou mak'ft the quivering wretch turn pale,
    And ftartle at the fun.
When Murder fearlefs of thy power,
    Lifts up the fateful knife,
And in the dark and midnight hour,
    Deftroys the guiltlefs life ;
High fwells thy awful voice :
Awaking at the fearful found,
The fiends of vengeance gather round ;
    The villain ftarts at every noife,
His foul, to judgment fummon'd, fhakes,
His frame convuls'd with horror, quakes ;
'Till urg'd to fate by all-refiftlefs fear,
He owns his crime, and dies the victim of defpair.

    When the quick tide of life fwells high,
    And Pleafure hourly wantons nigh,
    The Sceptic braves thy ftern command,
    Nor dreads thy executing hand.
    But when the powers of life decay,
    And fickening nature waftes away,
    When Age brings on a lengthening train
    Of weaknefs, dire difeafe, and pain,
    When Death uplifts its horrid form,
    And Juftice wakes the avenging ftorm ;
    Torn with diftracting doubts and fears,
    Thy terrors thunder in his ears ;
    Pale fpectres haunt the fhades of night,
    Deep blufhes meet the morning light,—

Above he sees the tempest lower,
And floods of wrath around him pour,—
Wide yawns beneath the world of woe,
Where waves of burning vengeance flow.

Impell'd by conscious guilt he strives to fly,
Far from the light of God's all-searching eye,
And plunging headlong in the midnight shade,
Calls rocks and hills to shield his guilty head;
'Till robb'd of Hope,—life's latest stay,—Despair
Breathes the faint wishes of unutter'd prayer:
In dread suspence, his last sad refuge fled,
His schemes all frustrate, his delusions dead,
Heaven shut from view, annihilation vain,
He shrinks from life, and flies to endless pain.

Not such thy lot, O man* divine!
Peace on the bed of death was thine.
Calm with a retrospective view,
Thy mind look'd past existence thro;
In bright, and regular array,
And blazing on the face of day,
    The deeds of virtue stood;
Conscience beheld them as they shone,
Approv'd and hail'd her darling son,
    And God pronounc'd them good.
And when the messenger of death,
Receiv'd thy faint expiring breath,
Soft slumbering on the bed of peace,
Thy voice bade every sorrow cease,

---

* Mr. ADDISON.

While to the world's aſtoniſh'd eye,
Thou ſhew'd'ſt with what repoſe a virtuous man can die.

Hail Conſcience! hail the good man's friend!
Thy ſmiles thro' life his ſteps attend;
And on his dread departing day,
Impart a ſweet, and gladſome ray,
To cheer his ſoul, to ſooth his dying breath,
To light his path-way thro' the vale of death,
And ope his proſpect to awaiting ſkies,
Where Faith looks forward with prophetic eyes,
And ſees unmov'd the moon in blood expire,
The ſun in darkneſs, and the earth on fire,
Stars, planets, ſyſtems, into ruin hurl'd,
And the laſt trumpet rend a guilty world.

COLOLOO,——AN INDIAN TALE,
Thrown into Engliſh Verſe.

BY WILLIAM DUNLAP.

COLWALL! the Women crie;
   Colwall! the dales reſound,
Colwall, the hills reply,
   And hollow caves rebound.

Wild ſhrieks thro thickets ring,
   Faſt flies the dark-brown night:
" Come ye Warriors bring
   The Captive ta'en in fight.

Draw tight the cutting bands!
  Bring matches blazing blue!
Now! now! the victim stands
  To mighty Colwall due."

With scorn the Captive smil'd,
  With scorn he ey'd the throng,
Then thus his pain beguil'd,
  With high exulting song.

SONG.

And are these all the means ye know
  To give a warrior pain?
Oh give your fires a fiercer glow;
  Remember Colwall slain.

My father gloried in his son.
  My warriors came from fight,
None staid behind; the scalps we won
  Declar'd our matchless might.

Who has not heard Cololoo's fame?
  My nation well ye know,——
And dreadful is the Tiger's name,
  And fear'd by every foe.

Pain does not lie so near the skin,
  More burning pine-knots bring!
Cololoo's all at peace within,—
  And Logan's fame he'll sing.

RECITAL.

Then whilst from every limb the red streams gush,
  And round him glows the fire;
Whilst thorns and nails transfix the quivering flesh,
  The death song rises higher.——

SONG.

Aged Logan led the fight,
  Logan's fame is ever new,——
Logan ſeiz'd a treacherous White,
  His murder'd Children ruſh to view:

" Curſes blaſt thee! pale-fac'd Savage,
  Ruin ſeize thy ruthleſs kind,
Train'd to rapine, ſkill'd to ravage,
  Gain, the God that graſps thy mind.

Now ye red men take your fill,
  Give the ſcalping knife its due,
The red right arm is bare to kill,——
  This my children, this to you."

Reeking from the white man's brain,
  Lo! he lifts the ſcalp on high;
" Logan does not wiſh thee pain,
  Fly to death's dark caverns, fly!

See they come! they come to meet us!
  Raiſe the yell that makes them quake,
Say,—ſhall puny white men beat us?
  Men that every blaſt can ſhake?

Men that fear the ruſhing rain,
  Men that fear the clouded ſky,
Men that ſhrink and howl at pain,
  Nor know to triumph when they die.

Now ye Tiger tribe be brave,
  Think that Logan ſees the fight;
Scalps on ſcalps adorn my cave,
  Glad'ning to my children's ſight.

Sulph'rous fmokes obfcure the view,
 War ! the hills and dales reply.
Now ye red men, now be true !
 Ye know to fight ! ye dare to die !"

Hand to hand the Warriors rufh,
 Shouts and yells in echos die;
Tom'hawks cleave, and bay'nets pufh,—
 They fly ! they fly ! the white men fly !

One brave band alone remains,
 One alone of all that band,
Every fhot and blow fuftains,
 Red like ours his heavy hand.

See they fink,—he's left alone,—
 Still our Warriors ftain the fields;
See ! he falls, but fighting on
 Sits, and ftill his fword he wields.

Logan feiz'd the brave man's arm,
 Longing, look'd upon his face;
Logan will not do thee harm,
 Tho' thou art of faithlefs race.

Logan's fons had been like thee,—
 White men fhot them from the bufh;
The brave fhall not be harm'd by me,—
 He's dead,—he's flown,—and all is hufh.

None thy beauteous corfe fhall wound;
 None thy hairy fcalp fhall tear;
Thou fhalt fleep with warriors round,
 Thou the dead-mens, feaft fhall fhare.

Seize the fcalps, and count the flain;
　　White-men, weep your brothers' woes!
Eafe our dying chiefs from pain :—
　　White-men learn to fear your foes!

So, Logan triumph'd o'er the foe;
　　Logan's fame was fairly won :
So, Logan laid the white-men low,—
　　——But fet is Logan's fun.——

Why bring ye not the heated ftone
　　To fear and feam my manly breaft?
Why fure the torture is not done !
　　Such pain Cololoo bears in jeft.

RECITAL.

Round his head Idiego hurl'd
　　His hatchet keen and good;
Whizzing, fierce the weapon whirl'd,
　　And quiver'd in the wood.

Reldor then with fullen ftride,
　　His knife was in his hand,
Advanc'd, and thus aloud he cried,—
　　And cut the twifted band.

Reldor takes thee for his fon,
　　Colwall in battle flain,
In many a fight his fame he won,
　　Nor fhrunk from death or pain.——

Silent now the warrior train
　　Bear the blood-ftain'd chief,—
No more they weep for Colwall flain,—
　　No more is known of grief.——

ODE TO TIME.*

FULL oft the Painter's pencil, oft the Bard,
   On canvas, or on Fancy's airy scene,
Hath shewn thee laughable, with grisly beard
Stiff-staring from a peaked chin;
A few white hairs thin-scatter'd round thy head,
Thine eyes turn'd grey with age;
Thy nose quite shrivell'd, like a pointed hook,
Thy visage bearing all a wrinkled wizard look:
Bent down and crooked was thy form,
And tottering on thy weak, lank legs,
Like some slim weed amid the shaking storm:
Thy blood, poor miserable dregs
Of life, crept thro' each wind-puff'd vein,
Which seem'd as tho' 'twould burst with ev'ry strain:
Thy long and dangling arms a scythe sustain,
To top off men as they cut down their grain:
Most laughable indeed! thus to deform
A God in power first, as first in form!

But look ye painters! hear ye bards this truth!
His face shall ever bloom unfading youth.

---

* This Poem was originally published, in an imperfect
state, in No. 20 of the 3d volume of the Gazette of the
United States, for July 6th, 1791, with its present signa-
ture.   The great alterations which it has since undergone,
and the many important additions now made to it, form a
sufficient excuse for the conduct of the Editors in placing
it among the Original Poems.

Bright golden locks adorn his head,
  Majeſtick beauty ſeems his form;
Where'er he ſteps, his awful tread
  Sounds like the thunder of the ſtorm.

Imperial Rome! once miſtreſs of the world!
Who rear'd her palaces, her towers on high,
Bade her tall obeliſks aſſail the ſky!
In ruin lies, by his ſtrong arm of power hurl'd.
Some broken arch, or nodding tower,
Falls prone to earth each paſſing hour;
And oft the wary traveller hears the ſound
Of ſome lofty column broke,
By TIME's rudely ſhattering ſtroke,
When down it comes loud-craſhing on the ground,
And hills and vales, the horrid roars rebound.

Behold yon figure ſtarting on the ſight!
His awful brow around,
With palm and laurel bound;
His forceful eye with genius bright,
Seems now in Fancy's view to roll,
And ſpeak the bloody Cæſar's warlike ſoul!
But Cæſar! thou art gone!
And TIME ſhall bid thy ſtatue follow ſoon.

The ſpacious Forum where great Tully's voice,
A clear and ſwelling torrent pour'd along,
'Till the tumultuous faction check'd their murmuring noiſe,
And mute—with dumb attention hark—as to the ſong
Of Orpheus, did fierce Cerberus of old,
When he with muſic's tongue his tender ſtory told;
Touch'd by TIME's deſtructive, potent wand,
Lies in ruins mouldering on the land.

From Rome the Mufe now turns her eagle-eye,
To where the fun burns in the weftern fky,
Where Niagara loud and ftrong,
His deep majeftic torrent rolls along :
From many a noble ftream and lake fupplied
The rufhing tide,
With rapid force, moft awful roars;
While echo fwells the folemn found upon his folitary fhores.
But lo ! the boiling flood check'd by a rocky mound,
It madly foams, and whirling round,
In one ftupendous fheet,
From the dizy awful height,
Fierce rufhing, headlong thunders to the ground.
The trembling groves, and caves around,
For many a league the dreadful fhout refound—
And while the bellowing flood midft craggy rocks below
Boils into foam, above the heaven-depicted bow
In rapture holds the wondering traveller's eye,
And all his fenfes thrill with heavenly extacy.
But hold my Mufe ! reprefs thy airy flight,
Nor give thy quick'ned foul to fweet delight ;
For e'en thofe haughty rocks, that rear on high
Their fhaggy heads, and rend the vaulted fky
With their loud-roaring founds fublime,
Shall bow beneath the fhattering hand of TIME.

Yet waft away ! oh ! diffipate thy fears,
For now thro' the deep gloom of future years,
A beauteous fcene beneath the weftern fkies,
Refplendent burfts upon my ravifh'd eyes.
Where thro' uncultur'd wilds Ohio rolls,
And hears the rav'nous wolf's terrific howls ;

Or fees upon his fhores at midnight hour,
The cruel favage exercife his power;
Sees him with a demoniack's joy elate,
Commit the haplefs victim to his fate,
And while with grinning rage, the blazing wood
He quenches in the Prifoner's hiffing blood,
Hears the fhrill fhrieks that pierce the diftant air,
And freeze the heart of pity with defpair :
There TIME's command fhall bid thofe horrors ceafe,
And wild Ohio fmile with fcenes of peace.

Where beafts of prey prowl o'er the defert ground,
Some future youths fhall liften to the found
Of wifdom, flowing from the fage's tongue,
In tones attractive as the voice of fong.
Then fhall fair temples, villas, cities rife,
To beam new fplendor on the natives' eyes;
The heaven-taught Painter, Sculptor, and the Bard
Shall there in future ages feek reward;
The voice of mufic warble thro' the air,
And all the glorious arts of peace appear.

But now again, the Mufe prophetic, fighs,
While fcenes of future defolation rife.
She fees her City, fair Columbia's pride,
A heap of ruins fpreading far and wide :
She fees her ftreets once beauteous to behold,
Partition'd off, the fhepherd flocks to fold ;
The crumbling bricks, and feparated ftone,
By pale-green mofs, and fcattering fern o'ergrown.
The wiley fox from broken arches peeps,
Thro' the deferted dome the weafle creeps,
The owl fits whooping on the temple door,
While hops the fqualid toad along the floor;

The hiffings of the deadly fnake fhe hears,
The warning rattle, trembles in her ears.
Begone delufive fancy! may thy wand
No more deform the beauty of our land!
Be unprophetic all thy gloomy views,
The airy offspring of the weeping Mufe—
But all too true alas! thy words may prove,
When TIME's deftructive power fhall o'er their beauties
                                        [move!

Ere thrice ten times the God of day,
Has drove his flaming, annual Car,
Adown the rofy weft;
My flender frame of clay,'
With TIME and fierce difeafe at war
May moulder into duft:
Thefe grief-ftrung nerves of mine may ceafe to move
In fad vibrations to the voice of Love;
With many a haplefs Bard whofe tender breaft
Now knows no more the goading thruft
Of pride, or penury his nerves of feeling tear.
But hold! ah hold thy lifted hand!
Nor lowly bow,
Beneath thy awful blow
The Father of Columbia's favor'd land:
Oh fpare! the glorious Patriot fpare!
Nor give the ftroke of fate,
Until his equal fhall appear
To fill with equal dignity the lofty chair of ftate.

                                        BIRTHA.

Philadelphia, July 1791.

AN ODE,
ADDRESSED TO MISS ****.

BY THE LATE REV. JOSEPH HOWE, OF BOSTON.

NEVER did parting Youth feel more
  Than I, fair Maid, when from the shore
Thy veffel fail'd away ;
And can not then my prayers prevail,
Nor love, nor vows, nor tears, avail,
  Nor aught procure thy ftay?

Was it for this that I fo long
Liften'd, to Fortune's fyren fong
  Liften'd with rapturous joy?
Did fhe, for this, infpire my heart,
With hopes that we fhould never part,
  And thus thefe hopes deftroy?

Amid the much-admiring crowd,
While thus I figh'd my griefs aloud,
  I fcarce refrain'd to fpeak ;
Shame held my tongue, while from my eye
The pearly drops, full plenteoufly,
  Stole trickling down my cheek.

Thus, near fair Tibur's filver flood,
The Roman Bard, gay Horace, ftood,
  And faw Galatea fail ;
And thrice he warn'd her, o'er, and o'er,
And told the fates Europa bore,
  In hopes he might avail.

Q q

In hopes he might avail to move
The fixed purpose of his love,
   From such a dangerous choice.
But all in vain, like me, he tried,
Galatea still did firm abide,
   Deaf to his moving voice.

" Then go, if naught," the Bard rejoin'd,—
" Can move the purpose of thy mind,
   " Go, and may blessings follow thee ;
" Let every gentle gale attend,
" Let every wave-thy voyage befriend,
   " But think, ah think ! of me."

Nor less to heaven did I prefer,
For thy dear sake, my pious prayer.
   O winds, O waves, agree!
Winds gently blow, waves softly flow,
Ship move with care, for thou dost bear
   The better part of me.

And think, and think, I also said,—
On all the vows which we have made,
   On all those charming scenes,
Which once, with glee, we pass'd away,
Pleased in each other, night and day,
   Nor envied kings and queens.

MESSAGE of MORDECAI to ESTHER.
FROM A MANUSCRIPT POEM.
BOOK II,——THE CONCLUSION.

BY TIMOTHY DWIGHT, D.D.

THOU know'ft, O Efther! from thy infant years,
   To rear thy form, to nurfe thy opening mind,
To teach thee every virtue, every truth,
To form thee finifh'd, lovely, great, and wife,
Was all my care fupreme. Friendlefs, alone,
An orphan fcarcely budded, well thou know'ft
I found thee; as a darling flower (the rofe,
That blooms in Sharon, or at Hermon's foot
The lilly of the vale) from midft the wild,
With every care remov'd thee to my field,
And faw thee rife, and bloom, and fend abroad
A fragrance, richer than the Arabian gale.
Why all adorn'd with beauty's living bloom,
In form as fome young Virtue of the fkies,
Of tincture died in health's immortal ftream,
Of eye refplendent, as the morning fun
Looks thro' the cloud's fair opening, and of grace,
Where heaven was pleas'd to move in mortal guife;
Why form'd with foul, fuperior to thy kind,
With thoughts expanding thro' the world's wide round,
And pinion'd to the fkies; with hardy mind,
Patient and daring, as the hero ftands
Upon the deadly and fierce flaming breach,
Serene while Death walks onward; yet more foft

Than the pleas'd infant smiles the favage dumb;
Why all accomplish'd, and why angel all,
I ponder'd long, and now from Heaven I learn.
This mighty hour the Eye Omniscient mark'd,
While fair, beneath his forming hand, uprose
Thy varied excellence.   For this Heaven gave
Thy virtue, gift supreme, that virtue crown'd
With wisdom's power; that wisdoms cloth'd divine
With beauty's angel form; that form around
Diffus'd the light of Heaven; and all adorn'd
With grace and sweetness, dignity and love.
On that proud day, when, from an hundred realms
Summon'd, came many a lord, and chief, and king,
Magnificent, to grace the monarch's feast,
And all the pomp of Persia round him spread;
When Vashti's insolence, beyond all thought,
Her presence to the illustrious train refus'd;
When, taught by Memucan he wisely bade
The haughty fair one wear the crown no more;
Even then a field I saw, by Heaven outspread,
To give thy virtue scope, and rich reward.
Pondering, I brought thee to the eunuchs' Prince;
Amaz'd, amid all Persia's beauteous maids,
Thee, thee alone he gaz'd.   Convinc'd, I knew
The crown reserv'd for thee.   With no surprise,
I saw thee lifted to the world's great throne:
'Twas thus the Skies decreed.   But, O bless'd fair!
Not for thyself the Heavens thy beauty gave,
Thy grace, thy wisdom; nor, for thee alone,
Did Mordecai uprear thy precious bloom.
Heaven's gifts are virtue's aids; for virtue us'd,
Are us d aright; or else are given in vain.

On thy great power to bless, all Israel builds
A solemn claim. A voice, as thunder loud,
Awful, majestic, from thy nation sounds,
And bids thee rise to save. Their cause thou know'st
The cause of heaven. In them religion lives;
From them Messiah springs, by whose bless'd hand
All nations good, and life, and glory gain.
The world's great happiness on them suspends.
Creation's end, and Providence' great scope.
Go then, thy nation save. Should every ill,
Even death, betide; yet what is life, or death,
When Israel calls, when God demands our life.
And know, O fair! if thou thy voice withhold,
Yet to the ruling Heavens, whose piercing eye
All mortal things surveys, ten thousand paths,
From danger's deepest caves, lead up to day:
Paths, tho' by man unseen, yet strait, and plain,
To God's all-piercing view. Thro Death's dark vale,
Such paths shall Israel guide to life and peace.
Then from the skies indignant, while thy race
To peace and joy ascend, thy fairest day
Of duty, glory, lost, thy soul shall feel
The piercing anguish of a wounded heart,
And waste with keen remorse, and sad despair.

Thus wrote the feeling Prince. Awhile, in deep
And solemn contemplation sat the fair,
Pondering the forceful message. Rouz'd at length
From off the sofa, all that softly sweet,
Angelic smile her face forsook; her eye,
Kindling with sacred fire, shot forth a ray
Of sunbright glory; high her bosom rose;

Her pulfe beat high, and loftily fhe walk'd
The fpacious room. Surpriz'd, her virgins ftood,
While thus her faithful Hatach fhe addrefs'd.
Go tell illuftrious Mordecai, my foul
Is warm'd to this great deed. His daughter's heart
Shuns not for Ifrael, or for Heaven, to die.
Undone by me, no duty fhall demand
Another's bofom ; loft by me, no hour
Of real glory fhall another crown
With fame, and life divine. Let Ifrael's race,
Thro' Shufhan's walls, with prayers, and tears, and fafts,
Implore the Skies ; and tho no bright'ning hope
Prefents the king complacent ; yet, to morrow,
My feet fhall tempt the court of gloomy danger,
And if my life's exacted, let me die.

END OF BOOK II.

ESTHER AND MORDECAI.

BOOK III.——(*The Beginning.*)

FROM midft a fhining cloud, whofe borders fair
   A golden light upturn'd, look'd forth the fun.
As clear, as bright, uprofe the Perfian Queen,
In all the pride of beauty. Rob'd in pomp
Of Afian fplendor, forth fhe flowly mov'd,
Attended by a royal train, that gave
New glory to the Fair. Strait to the throne

---

* L. 3. Up rofe the fun and up rofe Emily. CHAUCER.

Of sovereign majesty she bent her way.
Before her open'd wide the ivory gates,
On golden hinges turning; where, in purple
And gems, and gold, attir'd, with pomp supreme,
With port august, and aspect sternly dread,
She saw the Monarch thron'd.   Full on his eye
She dawn'd in all her beauty, rob'd in white
With silver intertwin'd, and flowers of gold.
Around her diadem, mid rows of pearls,
Twinkled unnumber'd stars.   Two cupids fair
Beside her walk'd in blooming innocence;
And two her train supported.   From their hands,
Flowers fell, and fragrance, that the palace wide
Breath'd living odours.   Soft and sweet the air.
The lovely Queen assum'd; her large, black eyes,
Mildly refulgent, shone, two morning stars;
While o'er her cheek, with lambent beauty, play'd
Colours, which neither flowers, nor gems, nor clouds,
Nor rainbows ever shed.   Full on the King
She cast a sweet, and soul-explaining smile
Of soft complacence; such as angels show,
To greet their fellows, when, from errand high
Return'd, they meet the sovereign euge bless'd.
The Monarch gaz'd; and, tho' his heart was fix'd
In all the sternness of Asiatic state;
Yet in the beams of beauty, soul inspir'd,
His softening bosom melted.   Fairer far
He view'd her, than when brought to bless his arms
With virgin innocence.   As in calm skies,
'Twixt two fair planets, walks in pride divine
The ascending Moon, o'er all the the immense of heaven

Reigning fole queen, and with enchantment fweet
Softening the world to filence. With mild eye,
She looks her empire round, and fees the ftars
With joy before her hide their little lamps,
And plains, and groves, and mountains in the beam,
Shadowy, afcend and brighten. Fair fhe fmiles,
And triumphs in her beauty ; while the bard
Eyes the bright queen, and wakes a thoufand dreams,
And thinks her emprefs of the realms above.
So rofe in all her bloom the wondrous Fair,
And fo the Monarch gaz'd. Spontaneous mov'd
His arm unbidden, and to greet the Queen,
Reach'd forth the golden fceptre. As the Fair,
Advancing, touch'd its ftarry point, he cried,
O Queen, what wifhes in thy bofom rife?
What prayer begins thy voice? Even to the half
Of Perfia's vaft domain, that prayer is giv'n.——

END OF VOL. I.

LIST OF SUBSCRIBERS.

THIS Lift is incomplete; feveral of the Subfcription Papers not being feafonably returned to the Editors. This they regret the more, as they are well affured of there being one Paper, in Philadelphia, which contains the names of more than Thirty Encouragers of this Undertaking.

N. B. Where the Editors have been unable to learn the addrefs of a Subfcriber, the Name is printed without any addition.

MR. Jofeph Adams, Litchfield.
Thomas Allen, Bookfeller, New-York, 6.
Richard Alfop, Middletown.
Mr. Gilbert Afpinwall, New-York.
Jonas Addoms, M. D. New-York.
John Allen, Efquire, Litchfield.
Thomas Amory, Bofton.
Jonathan Amory. jun. do.
Aaron Auftin, Efquire, New-Hartford.

B.

Rev. Azel Backus, Bethlem.
Gideon Ball, Catfkill.
Jofeph Barrel, Efquire, Bofton.
Auguftus Bates, Delaware.
Major Ezekiel P. Belden, Wethersfield, 2.
Samuel Bettle, jun. Philadelphia.
Uriel Blaau, Catfkill.
Jacobus Bogardus, do.
Jeremiah Boone, Philadelphia.
Walter Bowne, New-York.
Col. Aner Bradley, Watertown.
Mr. James Brace, Litchfield.
Elifha Bridgeman, Weft-Hampton.

LIST OF SUBSCRIBERS.

Mrs. Mary Bringhurst, Philadelphia.
Edward Bringhurst, do.
Joseph Bringhurst, jun. do. 6.
Charles B. Brown, Esquire, do.
Mrs. Broome, New-York.
William Brown, Esquire, Guilford.
Doctor William Buel, Sheffield.
James Burges, Washington.

C.

Aaron Case, Kent.
Doctor Jesse Carrington, Goshen.
Mrs. Betsey Chester, Wethersfield.
Thomas Chester, Esquire, do.
John Church, Hudson.
John Clark, New-York.
Doctor James Cogswell, do.
Doctor Mason F. Cogswell, Hartford.
Mr. James Cole, Catskill.
Mr. Norman Collins, Harwinton.
Arnold Colt, Esquire, Wilkes-barre, 6.
Miss H. Copperthwaite, Philadelphia.
Vicompte de Cornillon, Hartford.
Mr. Daniel Cotton, jun. New-York, 2.
Mr. Elias Cowles, Litchfield.
Doctor Thomas O'H. Croswell, Catskill.
Mr. Younglove Cutler, Watertown.

D.

David Daggett, Esquire, New-Haven.
Samuel W. Dana, Esquire, Middletown.
Hon. James Davenport, Stamford.
John Davenport, Esquire, do.
James Davidson, Kenebec, 2.
Jonathan Davis, do.
Hon. Thomas Dawes, jun. Boston.
Doctor William De Wese, Philadelphia.
John Doan, Catskill.
Elijah Doty, do.
Mr. William Dunlap, New-York.
Theodore Dwight, Esquire, Hartford.
Miss Sally Dwight, Northampton.
Mr. Nathaniel Dwight, Hartford.

E.

William Edmond, Efquire, Newtown.
Mr. William Edwards, Northampton.
William Ely, Efquire, Springfield.
Noah Evereft, Catfkill.

F.

Michael C. Fifher, New-Jerfey.
Rev. Ebenezer Fitch, Williamftown.
Rev. Abel Flint, Hartford.
J. A. Fonda, Manor of Livingfton.
Abraham Franklin, New-York.

G.

Rev. John S. Gardiner, Bofton, 3.
Hon. Ezekial Gilbert, Hudfon.
Angelica Gilbert,   do.
Afhley Gilbert, Catfkill.
Mr. Afa Gillet, Litchfield.
Mr. Judfon Gitteau, do.
Mr. Chauncey Gleafon, Simfbury.
Chauncey Goodrich, Efquire, Hartford, 3.
Elihu C. Goodrich, Efquire, Claverack.
Mr. Thomas C. Green, Bookfeller, New-London, 6.

H.

Hon. Nathan Hale, Efquire, Canaan.
Samuel Haight, Catfkill.
Jared Harrifon, Watertown.
Reuben Hart, Stockbridge.
Rev. Reuben Hitchcock, Sunbury, (Georgia.)
Mr. Roger Hitchcock, Litchfield.
Mr. Elnathan Holly, do.
Ph. L. Hoffman, Manor of Livingfton, 2.
Thomas H. Hooker, Catfkill.
Samuel M. Hopkins, Efquire, Gofhen.
Benjamin Horner, jun. Philadelphia.
Hez. L. Hofmer, Efquire, Hudfon, 2.
Titus Hotchkifs, Watertown.

J.

Ifaac Jackfon, Philadelphia, 2.
William Jackfon, Wetherffield.
Ammiel Jenkins, Hudfon.
William Johnfon, Efquire, New-York.

K.

Ephraim Kirby, Esquire, Litchfield.
William Kellogg, Cornwall.

L.

Benjamin Lane, Manor of Livingston.
Mr. Lyman Law, New-London.
David Lawrence, Hudson.
Mr. Samuel Lawrence, Hartford.
George R. Lawton, Philadelphia.
S. Lawton,   do.
Oliver Lazier, Catskill.
Doctor Michael Leib, Philadelphia, 12.
Mr. Elisha Lewis, Hartford.
John Livingston, Manor.
Abner Lord, Lyme.
John H. Lothrop, Esquire, Hartford.

M.

David Manwarring, jun. New-London.
Mr. Elisha Mason, Litchfield.
Nicholas S. Masters, Esquire, New-Milford.
Mr. Samuel M'Neil, Litchfield.
Mr. Donald G. Mitchell, do.
Simeon Mitchell, Washington.
John Montgomery, Harpersfie'd.
Benjamin Moore D. D. New-York.
William Moore,   do.
Benjamin J. Moore, do.
Anthony S. Morris, Philadelphia, 2.
James Morris, do.
Perez Morton, Esquire, Boston, 2.
Jon. Ogden Mosely, Esquire, East Haddam, 6.
M. Muller, Boston, 2.
Thomas Mumford, Esquire, New-York.

O.

Andrew Onderdonk, New-York.

P.

David Parmele, Esquire, Haddam.
Christopher Paterson, New-London.
Miss Lucy W. Payne, Philadelphia.
Miss Sarah Pemberton, do.

Mr. David Pierpont, Litchfield.
John Pinkerton, Jun. Philadelphia.
Timothy Pitkin, Jun. Efq Farmington.
M. Samuel W. Pomeroy, Bofton.
Cath. Powell,   do.

R.

Sampfon Rea, Philadelphia.
Tapping Reeve, Efquire, Litchfield, 3.
James Kivington, New-York.
Mr. Mofes Rogers, do.
Stephen P. Fois, Kent.
Mr. John Royfe, Hartford.

S.

Major Mofes Seymour, Litchfield.
Capt. Samuel Seymour, do.
Mr. Dudley Saltonftall, do.
Doctor Daniel Sheldon, do.
Mr. Samuel Sheldon,   do.
Reuben Smith, Efquire, do.
Mifs Mary S. Smith,   do.
Mr. James Stone,   do.
Mr. Samuel Shethar,   do
Mr. Ledyard Seymour, Hartford.
Mr. Jonathan Scott, Watertown.
Aaron Smith, Efquire, Watertown.
John C. Smith, Efquire, Sharon.
Mr. Thomas B. Saltonftall, New-london.
Capt Levi Stone, Kenderhook.
James S. Smith, Red-Hook.
Elnathan Smith, Jun. Efquire, Berlin.
William Pitt Smith, M. D. New-York.
Elijah Steele, Jun. Cornwall.
Elifha Stevens, Waterbury.
Mr. Afhbel Stoddard, Printer, Hudfon, 6.
Doctor Jofeph Strong, Middletown.
Zephaniah Swift, Efquire, Windham.

T.

Mifs Sally Talman, Philadelphia.
Peter Bodine Ten Broeck, Claverack.
John C. Ten Broeck, Hudfon.

Nathaniel Terry, Efquire, Enfield.
Peter Thompfon, jun. Philadelphia.
John Titus, New-York.
Mrs. Dolly P. Todd, Philadelphia.
Doctor Eli Todd, Farmington.
John Townfend, New-York.
Hon. Uriah Tracy, Litchfield.
John Trumbull, Efquire, Hartford.
Mr. Tudor, Bofton.

U.

Townfend Underhill, New-York.
Union Library Society, Wethersfield.

V.

Hezekiah Van Ordon, Catfkill.

W.

George Warren, Windflow.
Mr. Elijah Waterman, New-Haven.
General Samuel B. Webb, Claverack.
Mr. Jofeph Webb, Wethersfield.
Doctor James Wells, Berlin.
William W. Wetmore, Catfkill.
Levi Wheaton, on.
Roger Whittlefey, Efquire, Southington.
William W. Wilkins, Efquire, Philadelphia,
Rev. Jofhua Williams, Harwinton.
John Williams, Efquire, Wethersfield,
Ezekiel Williams, Efquire, do.
Mr. Ezekiel Williams, Jun. Hartford.
Mr. Solomon Williams, Lebanon.
Frederick Wolcott, Efquire, Litchfield.
Mr. William W. Woolley, New-York, 2.
Lieut. Samuel Woodruff, Litchfield.
Meffrs. Charles R. and George Webfter, Albany, 12.

Litchfield, June 1793.

ERRATA.
In the Selected Poetry.

Page 4th, *line* 5th, for *avails*, read " avail."

    25th,   3d, of the poem, dele the laft *f* in ' Patmos's.'

    28th,   17th, for *cheerful*, read " cheering."

    55th,   7th, from the bottom, for *and*, read " an."

    62nd,   1ft, for *Or*, read " On."

              8th, for *and child*, read " and *the* child."

    64th,   laft, for *plains*, read " plain "

    71ft,   4th, for *Mufes*, read " Nurfes."

    122nd,   21ft, read " I heard as *I* pafs'd, &c."

    123d,   9th, for *fquench'd*, read " quench'd."

    124th,   18th, for *and*, read " an."

    147th,   11th, for *venus*, read " venous."

    202nd,   25th, for *There*, read " Thefe."

    207th,   22nd. for *boody*, read " booby."

    230th,   2nd, for *She*, read " He."

    246th,   4th, for *clofed*, read " clafp'd."

In the Original Poetry.

Page 267th, *line* 5th, for *expire*, read " exfpire."

    275th,   9th, for *words*, read " word."

    292nd,   16th, for *top*, read " lop."

The Reader is requefted to correct the foregoing Errors, before reading the Poems.

NOTES

Though the text of the present facsimile is reproduced from a copy owned by the editor, the title pages, Preface, Postscript, and Contents pages are taken from copies in the Brown University Harris Collection of American Poetry and Plays, Roger E. Stoddard, Curator. Other copies of the original are held by American Antiquarian Society, Boston Public Library, Hartford Public Library, Harvard University, Library Company of Philadelphia, Library of Congress, Litchfield Historical Society, Newberry Library, New York Historical Society, New York Public Library, Princeton University, University of Michigan, University of Texas, and Yale University.

In all the copies collated in preparing the present edition, no evidence was found that the content of the poems was ever in any way changed during the single printing of *American Poems*. (Not even the Errata were ever corrected by the printer.) The copies examined were four in the Harris Collection, one held by the American Antiquarian Society, one held by the Boston Public Library, and the copy owned by the editor.

The examination revealed that three states within the single printing can be identified. These three states are apparently the result of the printer's twice unlocking certain chases in attempts to correct minor (not textual) errors or to alter the book's appearance. The three states are: (1) a version with a small design motif in the center of the title page (see the first facsimile title page), with two page foot letters "K" (binder's signal letters) and no "L," and two consecutive pages numbered "272," the first of which should be "271"; (2) a version with a large scroll "CB" (i. e., Collier and Buel) printer's mark in the center of the title page (see the second facsimile title page), and the same errors as above (two "K" foot letters, two pages "272"); (3) a version with the scroll "CB" mark on the title page as in (2) above, with the second "K" foot letter corrected to "L," with the first page "272" corrected to "271," but with the actual page "272" "erroneously corrected" to read "273," (hence two pages "273" appear). There is no way to demonstrate logically the order in which these states occurred. If the scroll "CB" mark was added to improve the book's appearance, the order of states suggested here may have been the actual sequence.

For further information about *American Poems*, Thomas Collier (1761-1842) and David Buel (Collier's partner from 1792-96), the establishment of the price of the book ($1.00), the date of publication, and its advertisement, see Samuel H. Fisher, *The Publications of Thomas Collier, Printer, 1784-1808* (Litchfield, Conn., 1933).

The only pre-1793 efforts in American literary history that rival *American Poems* for the claim to being the first anthology appeared in 1744 (or 1745), 1787, and 1791. The first is *A Collection of Poems by Several Hands*, Boston, B. Green and Co., a fifty-five page booklet. Most of the poems contained in it were written by Mather Byles (1706-1788), and the representative value of the brief effort is limited severly by this fact. It is discussed briefly by C. Lennart Carlson, ed., in *Poems on Several Occasions*, by Mather Byles (New York, 1940), p. vff. (Carlson offers evidence that *Poems by Several Hands*, though dated 1744, was actually published the following year.) The second is *Select Poems on Various Occasions. Chiefly American* (Philadelphia, Mathew Carey, 1787). The editor, Carey, failed to produce a book containing only works by American poets, as he did in his *The Beauties of Poetry, British and American*, 1791, the third volume in question (also published in Philadelphia). Carey planned an all-American volume prior to 1793, but it never materialized. See Fred L. Pattee, "Anthologies of American Literature Before 1861," *The Colophon; A Quarterly for Collectors and Lovers of Books* IV, iv (1934), no pagination. (Pattee also claims that Carey's magazine *The American Museum; or Repository of Ancient and Modern Fugitive Pieces &c. Prose and Poetical*, 1787-1789, should be called an anthology; but it is at least not purely a poetry anthology.) The first post-1793 American anthology is *The Columbian Muse. A Selection of American Poetry, from Various Authors of Established Reputation* (New York, J. Carey, 1794). It contains some thirty poems in common with *American Poems*, and many others as well, all by Americans. The next major American anthology is a three volume work by Samuel Kettell, ed., *Specimens of American Poetry, with Critical and Biographical Notices* (Boston, S. G. Goodrich, and Co., 1829).

The following notes do not include identification of allusions or references easily found in the *DAB, DNB, OED,* Bible, classical, historical, or literary dictionaries and encyclopedias; general encyclopedias; geographical sources. Such fuller notes appear in William K. Bottorff, "An Edition of *American Poems, Selected and Original, 1793*" (Ph.D. thesis, Brown Univ., 1964).

The first known printing of each poem is cited in the first note to each poem.

Page and line

1: *date.* The Massachusetts Spy; Or, Thomas's Boston Journal, IV, cxc (September 22, 1774), p. 4; IV, cxci (September 29, 1774), p. 4.

13: *title.* First published as a broadside, New Haven, 1771. St. John (1746-71) was a Yale tutor, Trumbull's close friend.

17: *title.* The American Museum; or Repository of Ancient and Modern Fugitive Pieces &c. Prose and Poetical, II, ii (August 1787), 206-07.

21: *title.* The American Museum, II, i (July 1787), 99-101.

25: *title.* The American Museum, II, i (July 1787), 97-99.

29: *title.* The American Museum, II, i (July 1787), 95-97.

33: *title.* The New-Haven Gazette, and the Connecticut Magazine, I, xxxii (September 21, 1786), 245-46.

39: *title.* The New-Haven Gazette, I, xxxv (October 12, 1786), 269-70.

46: *title.* The New-Haven Gazette, I, xxxvi (October 19, 1796), 277-78.

55: *title.* The American Museum, I, vi (June 1787), 563-66. Intended to influence deliberations at the Constitutional Convention.

62: *title.* The Boston Magazine, I, iii (December 1783), 71. Popular Revolutionary song, from c. 1778.

64: *title.* The American Musical Magazine, I, i (May 1786), 3-6, with music by Dwight.

66: *title.* The American Magazine, I (June 1788), 507-08.

68: *title.* The American Museum, V, iv (April 1789), 408-09.

70: *title.* Gazette of the United States, III, xxii (July 13, 1791), p. 2.

70: *title.* Gazette of the United States, III, xxii (July 13, 1791), p. 2.

75: *title.* The Miscellaneous Works of Colonel Humphreys (New York, 1790), pp. 102-10. Answer to Humphreys' poem-letter, p. 129.

76: *16.* Dwight married Mary Woolsey, 1777.

76: *22.* Dwight's father died in 1777.

78: *16.* Possibly Frederick the Great of Prussia, who aged prematurely (*keyser* is a variant of *kaiser*).

78: *17.* Charles Stanhope (1753-1816) or Lord Chesterfield (Philip Stanhope).

78: *20.* Fribble, Garrick's *Miss in Her Teens.*

79: *1.* Curl, Edmund Curll (1675-1747), printer of indecent literature.

85: *note.* The booklet dates from 1778, not 1788.

86: 12. Cf. *Paradise Lost,* II, 561. See Susanna E. Matteson, "The Influence of Milton on Early American Poetry up to 1800," unpubl. M. A. thesis (Brown Univ., 1931), p. 76.

86: 15. Possibly Andrew Lewis (c. 1720-81), frontier Indian fighter.

94: note. First published separately, Hartford, 1781. From this and the preceding poem grew Barlow's *The Vision of Columbus* (1787) and *The Columbiad* (1807).

97: 10. Hosmer, see the succeding poem.

108: title. First published separately, Hartford, 1782. Hosmer (1737-1780), a Connecticut Lawyer, was Barlow's patron, encouraging him to write *The Vision of Columbus.*

110: 13. See Ben Jonson's *Cynthia's Revels,* V, vi, 3.

117: title. Connecticut Courant and Weekly Intelligencer, June 19, 1786, p. 4.

120: title. The American Museum, III, iii (March 1788), 273-74.

123: title. Connecticut Courant, October 9, 1786, p. 3.

126: title. The American Museum, III, iii (March 1788), 274-75.

127: title. The New-Haven Gazette, I, xlix (January 25, 1787), 373, a part of *The Anarchiad,* V.

129: title. The Miscellaneous Works of Colonel Humphreys, pp. 97-102. Humphreys was secretary to the Congressional committee for "forming commercial treaties in Europe" (Adams, Franklin, Jefferson).

132: 4. I have been unable to identify the German agent.

132: 9. I have been unable to identify Quebec's "son."

132: 10. I have been unable to identify the "naval chief" alluded to.

132: note. "He sits, holds the cithara, and sings for a reward, and with his song soothes the waters of the sea." *Fasti,* II, 115-16.

134: title. The New-Haven Gazette, II, xxxi (September 20, 1787), 243-44.

137: title. Connecticut Courant, November 7, 1785, p. 3.

139: title. First known periodical printing, *The New-York Magazine; Or, Literary Repository,* IV, vii (July 1793), 445, almost simultaneous with the July, 1793 printing of *American Poems.* Smith must have known of Hopkins' intention to publish it in New York, got a copy, printed it as a "Selected" poem.

142: title. American Mercury, III, cvii (July 24, 1786), p. 3.

143: title. First published separately, Philadelphia, 1789.

143: 3, 4. F, Dr. John Foulke; Dr. William Shippen, both of Philadelphia. See George E. Hastings, *The Life and Works of Francis Hopkinson* (Chicago, 1926), p. 425.

151: note. Gaspar Tagliacozzi, pioneer plastic surgeon.

154: title. First published separately, New York, 1747.

156: 32. Possibly Thomas Secker (1693-1768), spokesman in the 1740's and 50's for establishment of an Anglican episcopacy in America, which Livingston opposed.

157: 7. W, Noah Welles (1718-76), Livingston's classmate at Yale, named in the Trenton edition of the poem, 1782.

157: 21. A, probably Thomas Arthur (1724-50/51), Yale, 1743. The name Arthur appears in the 1782 edition.

158: 5. S, William Peartree Smith (1723-1801), another Yale classmate of the poet. See Theodore Sedgwick, Jr., *A Memoir of the Life of William Livingston* . . . (New York, 1833), p. 62. Smith and Welles wrote essays lauding Livingston for the first edition of the poem.

158: 11. Cf. *Paradise Lost,* IV, 257-58. Matteson, p. 78.

159: 21. Cf. *Paradise Lost,* V, 306. Matteson, p. 78.

161: 5-7. Cf. Genesis i; *Paradise Lost,* III, 9-12; VII, 232-42.

162: 5. Cf. *Paradise Lost,* VII, 41. Matteson, p. 33.

163: 11. Cf. *Paradise Lost,* VII, 243. Matteson, p. 78. Also cf. Genesis i. 3.

163: 17. Cf. *Paradise Lost,* II, 11. Matteson, p. 78.

164: 11. Dives, Luke xvi. 19-31.

168: 22. Cf. *Paradise Lost,* VI, 750. Matteson, p. 78.

169: 5-16. Cf. Pope, *An Essay on Criticism,* II, 364-73.

171: 15. William Derham (1657-1735), British naturalist, philosopher.

171: 26. Livingston married Susanna French, 1745.

172: 29ff. Cf. Nathaniel Ward's *The Simple Cobbler of Aggawam* and Pope's *Moral Essays,* II, on women's dress.

175: 27. Cf. *Paradise Lost,* IV, 506. Matteson, p. 78.

176: title. Columbian Centinel, XIV, xxiv (December 4, 1790), p. 3, in a considerably different version. The poem was expanded into *Beacon Hill* (Boston, 1797). Philenia was Sarah Wentworth Morton (1759-1846).

177: 11. Emporium, John Smibert's Faneuil Hall (1742).

177: 25. I have been unable to identify any "Fort William" then at Boston.

179: 26. Probably John Winthrop (1714-79), Harvard professor.

180: title. The Massachusetts Magazine: or, Monthly Museum of Knowledge and Rational Entertainment, I, x (October 1789), 660-61, with music by Hans Gram.

182: title. The Massachusetts Magazine, I, vii (July 1789), 449, signed Constantia, Morton's first pen-name.

183: *title. Columbian Centinel,* XVI, xxiii (November 30, 1791), p. 4.

184: *title.* First appeared in Morton's *Ouâbi: or the Virtues of Nature, an Indian Tale* (Boston, 1790), p. 52. Della Crusca was Robert Merry (1755-98).

186: *note.* The first of the four Alfred-Philenia poems appeared in the *Columbian Centinel,* XIV, lii (March 12, 1791), p. 3. The poetic correspondence imitated that of Robert Merry and Hannah Cowley in the *London World,* which series itself was reprinted in part in the *Centinel.* Alfred may have been Robert Paine, Jr. (1773-1811), Joseph Dennie (1768-1812), or William Hill Brown (1765-93).

187: *title. Columbian Centinel,* XV, x (April 16, 1791), p. 4, but first somehow pirated for *The Massachusetts Magazine,* III, iii (March 1791), 183.

188: *title. Columbian Centinel,* XV, xviii (May 14, 1791), p. 3.

190: *title. Columbian Centinel,* XV, xxii (May 28, 1791), p. 4.

193: *title.* First published separately as *The Poem which the Committee of the Town of Boston Had Voted Unanimously to Be Published with the Late Oration; with Observations Relating Thereto; Together with Some Very Pertinent Extracts from an Ingenious Composition Never Yet Published* (Boston, 1772). It later appeared at the end of the book *Orations Delivered at the Request of the Inhabitants of the Town of Boston, to Commemorate the Evening of the Fifth of March, 1770 . . .* (Boston, 1785), and in *The American Museum,* IV, iv (October 1788), 380-82. Each successive printing was more patriotic or nationalistic than the last (the poem was originally suppressed as a Tory tract). James Allen (1739-1808) was an eccentric dilettante poet.

198: *19.* Cf. Pope's *An Essay on Man,* II, 1.

199: *title.* Though Smith places it with the "Selected" poetry, no previous printing of the poem has been established.

199: *22.* Lord Hugh Percy (1742-1817).

201: *title. The Boston Magazine,* III, ix (September-October 1786), 393-96. Richards (?-1814) was, like Greene, a Rhode Islander.

202: *12.* Cf. *Macbeth,* I, v, 14; Charles Churchill's *Epistle to William Hogarth,* 57.

206: *note. New Hampshire Spy,* I, xxx (February 2, 1787), p. 3. The poet remains anonymous. Jennette Tandy, *Crackerbox Philosophers in American Humor and Satire* (New York, 1925), p. 20 (cited by Walter Blair, *Native American Humor* [San Francisco, 1960], p. 24) confuses the poem with "Occupations of a Schoolmaster," *The Eagle or Dartmouth Centinel,* II, xxxvi (March 30, 1795), p. 4, and *Federal Orrery,* II, lxxv (July 9, 1795), p. 298, by William Biglow (Charles Chatterbox, 1773-1844). Biglow probably was inspired by the earlier poem, but undoubtedly did not write "The Country School."

206: 6. Cf. Job xx. 16.

206: 12. Cf. Job xx. 28.

208: 28. Z, then pronounced separately Izzard.

209: note. *The New-Haven Gazette,* II, xiv (May 24, 1787), 105-06. *The Anarchiad* was a series of Federalist tracts intended to influence the Constitutional Convention. A full account of it, with copious notes, appears in Luther G. Riggs, *The Anarchiad: A New England Poem. Written in Concert by David Humphreys, Joel Barlow, John Trumbull, and Dr. Lemuel Hopkins. Now First Published in Book Form* (New Haven, 1861). Leon Howard, *The Connecticut Wits* (Chicago, 1943), p. 194, calls "The Speech of Hesper" the series' climax. No source convincingly identifies an individual author; Annie R. Marble, *Heralds of American Literature* (Chicago, 1907), p. 159 assigns it to Hopkins, but Marcia E. Bailey, *A Lesser Hartford Wit, Dr. Elihu Hubbard Smith, 1771-1798* (Orono, 1928), p. 69, refutes this. Hesper (Hesperus, evening star of Greek myth) personifies the United States.

217: note. *New-Haven Gazette,* III, vii (February 21, 1788), last p. It is signed Theodore Dwight (1765-1846) in *The American Magazine,* I (August 1788), 675.

219: note. *Gazette of the United States,* I, lxxx (January 16, 1790), p. 2. Biographical evidence and stylistic points indicate the poet may have been E. H. Smith himself (the same is true of the succeeding "Cake Heart" poem; more tenative is his authorship of "Utrum Horum Mavis, Elige"). Bailey, p. 69.

221: title. *The American Magazine,* I (April 1788), 345-46. Bailey, p. 32.

222: title. "Choose Whichever One You Prefer." *The American Magazine,* I (May 1788), 427-28.

226: title. *The New-York Magazine,* II, iv (April 1791), 235-38. This "Norwegian" story is apparently imaginary.

231: title. *The American Museum,* VII (January 1790), 1-2 of Appendix I. The poet was Samuel Joseph Smith (1771-1835); *The Miscellaneous Writings of the Late Samuel Joseph Smith, of Burlington, N. J., Collected and Arranged by One of the Family. With a Notice of His Lfe and Character* (Philadelphia, 1836).

234: 10. Cf. Ben Jonson's *Cynthia's Revels,* V, vi, 1-4.

234: title. The American Museum, I, i (January 1787), 79-82. The poet was Thomas Chalkley James (1766-1835), a Quaker poet.

235: 6. Cf. *Paradise Lost,* I, 16.

239: title. Freeman's Journal, IV, ccviii (April 13, 1785), p. 2.

240: title. Gazette of the United States, III, v (May 14, 1791), p. 1. The poet may have been Joseph Bringhurst, Jr. (1767-1834). Though other names have been advanced, a strong argument for Bringhurst's authorship of all the "Birtha" pieces in *American Poems* appears in Bailey, pp. 41-47. Ella was a pen-name of E. H. Smith in a poetic periodical correspondence with "Birtha" and "Henry," whose identity is uncertain.

242: title. Gazette of the United States, III, xi (June 4, 1791), p. 2.

245: title. Gazette of the United States, III, xix (July 2, 1791), p. 1.

247: 16. Cf. *Paradise Lost,* IV, 602-03. Matteson, p. 76.

249: sonnet. Gazette of the United States, III, viii (May 25, 1791), p. 2.

251: Alsop. Like Freneau, Alsop (1761-1815) was a precursor of Romanticism in subject matter, image, and theme, though his prosody is neo-classical.

253: 14. I have been unable to identify Amyntor, as has Alsop's biographer, Karl P. Harrington, *Richard Alsop, "A Hartford Wit"* (Middletown, Conn., 1939), p. 105.

255: 1. I have been unable to identify the cryptic *Jer--.*

255: title. MacPherson's Ossian hoax was undiscovered at the time of the poem's composition.

265: title. Alsop apparently translated "Ragnarök" from the *Elder* or *Poetic Edda.*

269: note 3. Alsop's identification "the Mother of Odin" is invalid.

272 [271]: title. The poem is a highly embellished adaptation of Snorri Sturluson's *Heimskringla,* "Ynglinga Saga."

272 [271]: 1. Cf. *Paradise Lost,* IV, 609. Matteson, p. 76.

276: 2. Cf. Hosea viii. 7.

277: 25. Herb, Marihuana.

277: 30. Antonio, Anthony Wayne.

292: note. A version of the poem appeared in the *Gazette of the United States,* III, xx (July 6, 1791), p. 2.

294: 17. The rainbow at Niagara Falls.

297: title. I have been unable to identify the woman addressed by Howe (1746/47-75).

297: 21. Cf. Horace, *Odes,* III, 27.

302: note. The Canterbury Tales, "The Knight's Tale," 2273.

303: 30ff. Cf. *Paradise Lost,* IV, 605-09. Matteson, pp. 31-32.

SELECTIVE INDEX

321